The Humanistic Psychology of Carl Rogers

The Humanistic Psychology of Carl Rogers

Understanding the Person-Centered Approach

STEPHEN A. JOSEPH

OXFORD
UNIVERSITY PRESS

OXFORD
UNIVERSITY PRESS

Oxford University Press is a department of the University of Oxford. It furthers the University's objective of excellence in research, scholarship, and education by publishing worldwide. Oxford is a registered trade mark of Oxford University Press in the UK and in certain other countries.

Published in the United States of America by Oxford University Press
198 Madison Avenue, New York, NY 10016, United States of America.

CIP data is on file at the Library of Congress

ISBN 9780197790601

DOI: 10.1093/9780197790632.001.0001

Printed by Integrated Books International, United States of America

The manufacturer's authorized representative in the EU for product safety is Oxford University Press España S.A., Parque Empresarial San Fernando de Henares, Avenida de Castilla, 2 – 28830 Madrid (www.oup.es/en).

FSC MIX Paper FSC® C183721

Contents

List of Figures

List of Boxes

Foreword

It is truly an honor to be asked to write the foreword for this timely, erudite, and scholarly text by Professor Stephen Joseph. I first met Stephen around 2007 when he was giving a talk shortly after joining the University of Nottingham. At that time, I was a part-time lecturer at the University of Nottingham, School of Education. I was teaching part time on a counselor education program alongside working as a psychologist and person-centered psychotherapist. Professor Joseph talked about the phenomenon of posttraumatic growth and how Carl Rogers's theory of personality could quite satisfactorily provide an explanation for both experiences of posttraumatic stress *and* how people often experience growth through their search for meaning following adversity. Back then, I was still learning about the person-centered theory and how it applied in my work doing trauma therapy. This talk turned the way of thinking about trauma upside down for me, in the very way that Professor Joseph shows in this book that Carl Rogers's theoretical developments had done. Like many of Professor Joseph's works, the ability to link contemporary phenomena in the field of mental health with person-centered theory is a real gift within this book. The same day of his lecture, I managed to get to speak to Professor Joseph, and within a year and within a year I was appointed to work alongside Professor Joseph in the Centre for Trauma, Resilience and Growth, a research and clinical group that he had established within the University of Nottingham in partnership with the Nottinghamshire Healthcare National Health Service Foundation Trust. This was the beginning of a long-standing relationship, and I am now thankful to say he is not only a colleague and a mentor, but also a friend.

In the years that I have known Professor Joseph, we have engaged in countless discussions amounting to hundreds of hours about many of the topics covered in this book. Each of those discussions was a rich learning opportunity for me, and in reading this book you will also be able to get much of the learning that I feel fortunate to have benefited from. Many of our discussions resulted in writing journal articles together. We wrote in psychotherapy and counselling journals, social work journals, and education journals. We also authored a book together titled *Trauma and the Therapeutic Relationship* and contributed chapters for edited books we have both completed as personal projects. All this writing together felt like an apprenticeship for me, learning from Professor Joseph how to become an academic. But importantly, he also helped me to understand the person-centered approach in a much deeper, practical, and experiential way.

Reading this text in preparation for writing this foreword reminded me of this journey from aspiring academic to now being a professor of psychology and education—a journey made possible, I believe, only because of my relationship with Professor Joseph. By reading this book, I am sure you, too, will learn a great deal from his deep knowledge of the person-centered approach and its applications.

In this book, Professor Joseph takes readers on a reflective personal journey in which he shares the meaning that the person-centered theory holds for him and the world. This is not an easy theory to grasp; as Professor Joseph explains so well, the parsimony that Rogers generated in explaining ideas belies an intricate, nuanced, and subtle complexity for understanding human experience. For example, this book sets out the way that person-centered theory reconfigured the concept of psychopathology from a medical/illness model to a growth model. This transformative thinking is brought to life in terms of how Professor Joseph's personal journey of transformation occurred from aspiring clinical psychologist to academic scholar and person-centered psychotherapist, then coach, supervisor, and educational facilitator.

As anyone familiar with Professor Joseph's previous writing will know, his academic contributions span the fields of social, clinical, health, counseling, coaching, organizational, and educational psychology. Within this contribution to knowledge, there is a profoundly consistent message, the same one running throughout this book. That message is best understood as a call to anyone who thinks and believes that human nature is constructive to stand firmly in this belief. It is a call to commit to whatever profession or aspect of life one finds oneself in and do what is right. To have such an eminent psychologist as Professor Joseph acknowledge the place of ontological standpoints underpinning all theories of psychotherapy and research is surely a message to all of us. It calls us all to examine our own perspectives and views and to acknowledge that our work and relationships are all underpinned by a particular ideological foundation. In this book, Professor Joseph is unapologetic and calls those who have hidden from acknowledging their own assumptions and ideological views to be more transparent. This book is a challenge to the whole field of psychology.

And finally, this book covers applications of the person-centered approach to not only psychotherapy but also education. I have had the privilege of being in a classroom with Professor Joseph for the last decade or more. We have co-facilitated thousands of hours of counselor education groups together. One of our observations has been, as noted in this book, how deeply embedded in people's personality a highly conditioned approach to learning is. A key message in this book is that people have both the right and capacity for self-direction in their lives. Yet because of the conditioning of learning traditional education requires, releasing a learner's potential is not an easy task. As Professor

Joseph notes, people will often look for alternate explanations that allow them to relinquish their own responsibility for their learning. But as someone with a commitment to freedom such as required from the person-centered approach, Professor Joseph shows how learners are to be trusted and supported to find their own directions. Herein lies the challenge of this book, its uncompromising quest for a better world through a humanistic approach to human relations. Professor Joseph states at the beginning of this book that he was not sure whether he should author the book and add yet another text to the list of person-centered literature. I have to say that I am extremely grateful that he did, as I am sure everyone who reads this book will be.

David Murphy PhD, AFBPsS, MA, BSc
Professor of Psychology and Education
University of Nottingham

To Vanessa, with love

Acknowledgments

My thanks to Volker Wedekind, who, as Head of School, authorized my study leave, during which I was able to begin this book. My gratitude also to friends and colleagues at the University of Nottingham, especially those teaching on the MA in person-centered psychotherapy and counselling–Shun Chen, Richard Doyle, Jen Holland, David Murphy, Awa Ottiger, Urszula Plust, Sue Price, and Emma Tickle, from whom I have learned so much from our writing and teaching together, and to all my students over the past decade, from whom I have learned so much. At Oxford University Press, my thanks to Sarah Harrington, my editor, for commissioning the book, and Andrea Smith, my project editor for her help and guidance throughout. My thanks also to Fathima Nisana, project manager at Integra, and to Cindy Angelini for her copyediting and helpful notes. My thanks to Jef Cornelius-White and the anonymous reviewers for their helpful comments and suggestions on an earlier version of this manuscript. To James Kingsland, my thanks for his skillful editorial help and advice on an early draft of the manuscript. Finally, thank you to Vanessa Markey for her help and feedback on earlier drafts and for her support during the writing of the book.

Author note

What is said in the therapy room is confidential, so it is important to say that any illustrations of client work in this book are a mixture of different people's experiences, with all personal details changed so that no one person is identifiable. In doing so, I have opted for an approach known as *faction*, where one essentially tells a fictional story that incorporates fragments of experience from real people and events. This provides what I think is the only ethical way to tell a fact-based story involving psychotherapy clients.

Introduction

An idea ahead of its time

A few years ago during a house move, I came across notes I had taken in a lecture as part of my undergraduate psychology course in the mid-1980s. There in front of me, in my own handwriting, were my notes on humanistic psychology and Carl Rogers's theory of personality development and therapy. I was taken aback because I had no recollection of the lecture or that I had even heard about Rogers at that point in my life. How could ideas that were to become so influential and important for me later in life have been so easily forgotten?

As I thought about why I had forgotten, I remembered one of the most significant insights I have taken from Rogers's approach, which is that we can only truly learn something when we are ready for it. At that age I was not ready for his ideas. It was obvious from my notes that I had understood the theory in the sense that I could have repeated it later in the exam, but not in the sense that I had taken on-board its deeper meaning, relevance, and significance for me as a person. I could see from the notes that it had been a comprehensive lecture that covered Rogers's theory of personality development and his theory of therapy. But like so many other things that we are taught when we are younger, because we cannot yet relate them to our own experience, we retain the information only for as long as we need—in this case for an exam—and then we forget. We haven't truly learned.

Rogers's ideas were ahead of time for me personally at that age, but I don't think I am alone in that. Rogers remains one of the most mentioned psychologists in introductory psychology textbooks, recognized as one of the greatest psychologists of all time, but what comes across is often only a superficial understanding of what he was all about, which is soon forgotten. For learning to take place, the material must be personally meaningful.

Traditional teaching is like pouring water into a cup: the teacher delivers the information to fill the student. The student is mostly passive in the learning process. There is often little meaning or significance in it for the student. As it was for me, the lecture notes are taken, but without engagement with experience there is no real learning happening. But it does not have to be this way. Rogers turned traditional education on its head when he discussed student-centered learning. This assumes the student can engage in self-direction and take responsibility

The Humanistic Psychology of Carl Rogers. Stephen A. Joseph, Oxford University Press. © Oxford University Press (2025). DOI: 10.1093/9780197790632.003.0001

for what is to be learned and what will happen in the classroom. The student is active in the learning process. They can create for themselves the necessary experiences from which to learn. It is not an easy process: students may not recognize their own ability to self-direct if, until that point, they have relied on others for direction. But in regaining it they are learning how to learn, equipping themselves with this most valuable skill for living: the ability to self-direct.

Rogers's development of student-centered education was a natural extension of his earlier therapeutic work, in which he had turned the world of therapy on its head when he introduced client-centered therapy. Therapy was no longer something that the therapist did to a patient; it was about creating a relationship that freed the client to be an active agent for their own change. This was a truly innovative approach that went against the grain of previous psychoanalytic or behavioral therapies, and to this day it is an idea that permeates the helping professions.

In the chapters that follow, I will discuss student-centered education and client-centered therapy in detail, but my point for now is that Rogers's person-centered approach—whether applied in the classroom, the therapy room, or anywhere else—is so different from traditional methods that it is hard to truly appreciate as an observer looking in from the outside, from the pages of a book, or from the words of a teacher. Rogers's ideas are challenging when first encountered in practice. His writing may seem dated and full of obscure terminology, such as *organismic valuing*, *actualization*, *self-concept*, *congruence*, *unconditional positive regard*, and *conditions of worth*. It can seem like learning a new language, one that can take many years to become fluent in. For these reasons, readers can be turned off, and contemporary psychology textbooks often fail to convey the richness and depth of Rogers's ideas.

Rogers is well known among psychologists for his development of client-centered therapy, which involves therapists being empathic, genuine, and unconditional in their regard and trusting in the client to know what's best. This is the essence of Rogers's approach, but what this looks like in practice, how subversive and challenging it turns out to be, and what it means to live it are often beyond the grasp of someone reading about the approach in a textbook. So, in this book I want to bring a more personal style of writing in the hope that I might be able to convey something of the challenges of learning about the person-centered approach.

Much of what I have to say is informed by the past 10 years of my career, which have been spent as a course tutor for therapists training in Rogers's approach. My colleagues and I adopt student-centered principles so that students can learn more deeply the meaning and significance of the approach. If our students can embrace self-direction in their learning and in their own lives, then they will be better equipped to help their clients find self-direction too. Student-centered education, just like client-centered therapy, is about helping a person look deeply within themselves to discover who they are, find out what their best directions in life are, and begin to move forward toward their unique potential. Such learning requires courage to face ourselves openly and honestly and to take responsibility for ourselves. Whether in a classroom, a clinic, or anywhere else, the application of Rogers's theory is essentially the same: it is a theory that leads to a new way to approach human relations of all kinds—the person-centered approach.

I find Rogers's view that learning takes place when people are intrinsically motivated and driven by their own curiosity valid and helpful.[1] But if all a person has ever known is traditional education, which seems to be based more on external incentives and fear than on intrinsic motivation and curiosity, it is likely that their ability to explore for themselves will have been stifled. So the transition to a person-centered form of education is daunting. Every year, incoming students say how much they like the ideas of Rogers, but when actually confronted in the classroom by the challenges of learning *about* his person-centered approach *through* a person-centered approach, they clamor for the familiarity of traditional teaching. They may become impatient and frustrated when no one stands up to lead the class from the front or opens a PowerPoint presentation and begins to lecture. We continue sitting in a circle of chairs, and the conversation unfolds in whatever direction the group takes it that day. Perhaps the impatience and frustration is felt so intensely that the expression of those feelings becomes a direction. Feelings are acknowledged and met with acceptance. There follows a conversation about previous experiences of educational settings, comparisons are made, and expectations shared. Discussion turns to the role of authority, the purpose of education, and what it means to learn. Already we are grappling with fundamentally important concepts, not only talking about student-centered learning but living it.

There can be comfort in thinking that we are not responsible for ourselves and the choices we make. But ultimately we are. Experiencing the discomfort of taking responsibility for our own lives can become the most significant of learnings.

In a person-centered approach to learning, experience must be central. The learning comes from relating one's own experience to theory. Working with students over these past 10 years and seeing them make this transition—which is often a painful one—from passive learners to active learners has given me insight into the stumbling blocks that are often encountered when learning. In this book I have tried to capture the many classroom conversations I have had with students and the common misunderstandings these have revealed.

I also wanted to move beyond traditional texts and offer a more contemporary insight into the significance of the person-centered approach. Over the past two decades, interest in human flourishing has blossomed across the social sciences and the helping professions. But interest in human flourishing is not new. It has a long history, most recently in the humanistic scholarship of the mid-20th century. One scholar within this movement was Rogers, who challenged the then-prevalent notion that successful outcomes in therapy or elsewhere entailed moving people from a psychiatric diagnostic category to one considered normal. In 1969, Rogers wrote about this:

> Change in diagnosis is not a description of therapeutic outcome that is satisfying to me. . . If I turn to another type of concept, I find that the person whose psychological growth is optimal is said to have achieved a positive mental health.[2]

Although Rogers died in 1987, he remains one of the most influential psychologists of all time. But as noted by his biographer, Howard Kirschenbaum, much of Rogers's thinking has been so deeply incorporated into theory and practice that his ideas now seem like common sense, such that many scholars and practitioners are likely unaware that they are treading in his footsteps and do not recognize quite how radical his theory was. Rogers's influence cannot be overstated, but it is so "in the water" that people do not recognize it. Likewise, they often have a misguided understanding with regards to his ideas.

Time and again, his ideas are reinvented by others. An example of this was the emergence of the contemporary positive psychology movement at the turn of the century[3] and the wider interest in human flourishing that followed. Positive psychology seemed initially oblivious to the fact that the study of the good life was something already pioneered by Rogers and his colleagues decades earlier. John Shlien, a Harvard psychologist and one of the early pioneers of person-centered psychology, wrote the following in 1956:

> In the past, mental health has been a "residual" concept—the absence of disease. We need to do more than describe improvement in terms of say "anxiety reduction." We need to say what the person can *do* as health is achieved. As the emphasis on pathology lessens, there have been a few recent efforts toward positive conceptualizations of mental health. Notable among these are Carl Rogers' "Fully Functioning Person."[4]

And writing in 1984—still well before positive psychology emerged—another of the foremost representatives of humanistic-experiential psychotherapy practice and research, Julius Seeman, said that Rogers "perhaps more than any other clinical theorist, has paid attention to the development of a theory of optimal human functioning."[5] I include these quotes to emphasize just how prescient his approach was in foreshadowing positive psychology almost 40 years later and to demonstrate that this was not an obscure aspect of Rogers's work, but one of its defining characteristics. In this way, his ideas were ahead of their time within the social and behavioral sciences.

An aim of mine has been to explore topics in human flourishing from the person-centered perspective. Indeed, the subtitle of this book at one point was to be *The Person-Centered Approach to Human Flourishing.* I wanted to write a book that would be of interest to positive psychologists and others interested in human flourishing who would otherwise not know that this was a book that might interest them. But I was advised that those interested in learning about the person-centered approach—the main audience for the book—but who don't yet realize that it is about human flourishing might be turned off. Until one understands that Rogers's approach is actually all about what we now call human flourishing, and also inevitably its absence, such a title would mislead people to think that this was a book about a much narrower topic, one that was not relevant to them. Those new to the field often think of therapy only in terms of medicalized ideas of treatment and cure and not in terms of the ideas of growth and development that are central to the person-centered approach.

One of the most important turning points for many in understanding the person-centered approach is to replace their medicalized view with one of growth and development. Thus, my reason for wanting to contextualize the person-centered approach within the newer field of positive psychology is to show that what we do sits comfortably among those who are interested in human flourishing. A secondary reason is to help bring Rogers's work to wider contemporaneous attention. I want to show that his theory is not just a footnote in the history of psychology. The principles of the person-centered approach are increasingly recognized, and its lessons are of importance within contemporary scholarship and practice, which they still challenge to this day, as much as they did when they were first introduced.

Eugene Gendlin started working with Rogers in the early 1950s, and decades later reflected on Rogers's influence, writing that he "faced down the hatred of most of the profession because in the workplace, classroom, therapist's office and all around him, he turned the social system upside down."[6] Similarly, Pete Sanders said of the person-centered approach that in its heyday it "was *the* radical, vibrant, anti-establishment, system-threatening, research-based psychotherapy practice—and at its heart was humane and just."[7]

Sadly, many of these pioneering scholars and others I will mention throughout this book—who dedicated their careers to developing and promoting the person-centered approach—are no longer with us, but their words remain true. I think that is why Rogers's ideas are so hard for people to fully grasp: they are just too far outside their experience, not only in education, but in their everyday lives and in how we understand our institutions and systems. Rogers is asking us to completely transform our existing worldviews. As I will discuss, the person-centered approach rests on an image of what it means to be human. It is ultimately a philosophical viewpoint, one that says that people can be trusted to move in constructive directions, given the right circumstances. Looking back at the work of Rogers is not simply a matter of historical curiosity; it still promises a more humane and just vision for the future. Rogers's approach, and humanistic psychology more generally, offered progressive ideas about human nature. Positive psychologists may now have caught up with part of what Rogers had to say, but the rest of his message has yet to follow. It is a message that seems ever more important in today's world with all its social and political turmoil.

Textbooks often present an image of a field as if it were already fixed, but here I want to convey that the person-centered approach is fluid and still developing, and I want to encourage students who are new to the approach to see this as an invitation to be part of its future. I would like them to see how Rogers's ideas, which are still ahead of their time, can be used to inform new policy, practice, and research. For that reason I have also included chapters which I hope will encourage research into the person-centered approach and its applications to human flourishing.

Despite its prescience, Rogers's work has become a backwater off the mainstream flow of scholarship and practice. The person-centered approach has fallen into relative obscurity over the last few decades. Since Rogers's death, it has been kept alive by a relatively small body of scholars and practitioners who are dedicated to this humane and just approach. The name Carl Rogers occurs frequently in the psychological literature, and his ideas are often mentioned, but this is usually only superficially. While Rogers is now widely recognized, his ideas are often diluted, misrepresented, and misunderstood. Criticisms that arise from such misunderstandings abound, such as that the approach is too individualistic, that it promotes selfish behavior by encouraging people to do just as they like, and that it is naïve and too trusting, ignoring the destructive side of humanity. As I aim to show in this book, these are all unfounded criticisms.

Also, Rogers's ideas are sometimes dismissed as simplistic. There is indeed a parsimony to his theory, which is one of its great strengths as a scientific approach, but in practice it is endlessly complex and requires more thoughtfulness, personal development, and integrity than any other branch of applied psychology I have ever seen.

...

I have been studying, researching, and writing about Rogers's person-centered approach now for over a quarter of a century. Discovering the work of Rogers shifted the direction of my career.[8] But at the beginning, as a lecturer in psychology in the early 1990s, I too would have been one of those who diluted, misrepresented, and misunderstood his ideas. Like many others, I gave my lectures on psychology as if Rogers was just a historical footnote on the way to a more developed science of psychology. That is what I understood at the time. In hindsight, I was ignorant of his work, its depth, and its richness. Even so, my inclination toward the person-centered approach had already begun, although I wasn't aware that this was the direction in which I was going.

Early in my career, I felt discomfort with what I was reading and studying as a psychologist. It seemed to miss what I felt were the obvious effects on people of the social and political world in which they live, in favor of biological and genetic explanations and treatments that seemed to ignore the existential and very human experiences of distress and dysfunction. It seemed so obvious to me that the stresses and strains of life for many people were overwhelming. They were always under threat with, for example, the fear of homelessness and unemployment, but felt powerless to make a change and devoid of meaning in life and a sense of purpose. It seemed incredible that textbooks of the time appeared to downplay such factors. But on reading Rogers again I could see a different way. Throughout the 1990s, I immersed myself in Rogers's books and other writings about the person-centered approach. I came to see that what he and his colleagues achieved from the 1950s onward offered a new paradigm for the psychological sciences.

My own research at this time was into the effects of trauma and its treatment. I discovered that the leading theories I had been reading about and using in my own studies were almost identical in their essence to what Rogers had described several decades earlier. Of course, Rogers was writing well before the modern age of trauma psychology, so his ideas had gone unnoticed. But in applying his theory, I began to develop new ideas about how reactions to trauma are a natural and normal process of adjustment.[9] For me this was the lightbulb revelation that his ideas were so transformational that they could be applied in ways that had not yet been explored. An idea ahead of its time, Rogers's approach was always about trauma-informed practice.

I have researched and written about traumatic stress, posttraumatic growth, authenticity, therapy, coaching, social work, mindfulness, positive psychology, and education. But most of my teaching and research has been informed by one single thread, Rogers's person-centered theory. It has been a journey in which each step along the way has been a deepening of my understanding of the person-centered approach. Thus, some of the themes I will discuss I have written about before in other books and articles, but what I hope to convey here that is different is a more nuanced and sophisticated understanding that speaks more directly to the challenges of learning about the approach. There are themes in the book that I will return to time and again, going deeper with each iteration.

I have done a lot of reading and rereading during the writing of this book. At times, as I immersed myself in the vast, rich literature on the person-centered approach, I questioned whether the world needs another book on the topic. There is so much already to read. To truly understand the approach, there is no alternative but to take the time to read Rogers's books and papers widely and in depth to reflect on the ideas and learn for oneself what they mean. But as I reflected on the struggles of my students to pull it all together and make sense of the approach and its language, I felt strongly that something new was needed. Rogers's writings about the person-centered approach, and those of many other authors, span more than 80 years, so there is too much for any one book to do the work full justice, but what I can do is provide a map of how to prepare oneself for the journey ahead.

My aim is to present Rogers's humanistic approach in a more holistic way than other textbooks, to convey more of the sense of what makes it different, and to show it clearly within contemporary psychology. There are many great books on the person-centered approach, but they tend to be written for counselors and psychotherapists, for whom a background in psychology and research is not always a requirement. For that reason, they do not tend to contextualize Rogers's work within the wider field. I want the reader to see Rogers's work from this perspective and to understand how it is applied to downstream activities such as therapy and coaching, but also to more upstream activities such as education and organizational scholarship, and indeed how it can be applied to all human relationships. His is a theory that recognizes that who we become and how we behave are products of our social world and that we can design a different world if we choose, whether it is simply in our own lives or at an international level.

I have tried to present some of the more familiar ideas in a novel way that I hope will convey the approach's well-defined system of interrelated concepts and offer newer ideas that might challenge preconceptions. I aim to convey some of the complexity in such a way that the book will be valuable to scholars and practitioners who want to link theory to practice and understand how research underpins this link and what the issues and challenges are. It is my hope that this book will reach a wider audience and introduce new readers to Rogers's work as well as being of interest to my colleagues and friends in the person-centered community and to students new to the approach.

While I am writing with graduate psychologists in mind, I also hope this book will challenge all its readers to think about their practice in a new light and inspire new directions for research. It is ultimately about human flourishing, a term that is not specific to any one scholarly profession but is an umbrella that now also extends to counselors, educational theorists, leaders, managers, psychotherapists, sociologists, and anyone interested in topics related to well-being and how to live a good life. They may be people who have only touched gently on the work of Rogers and now want to find out more as they choose their careers or who are perhaps more established in their careers but now feel drawn toward the person-centered approach to achieve a more humane and just way of working. You might want to reflect on what has brought you to this point in your life where you choose to learn about the person-centered approach (see Box 1).

Box 1 Reflection: What interests you?

If you are at the beginning of your own journey into the person-centered approach, take the opportunity to reflect on why you have come to be interested in it. There are many different approaches in psychology—what is it about this approach that attracts you? What are the events and experiences in your life that have led you to this point? What are your expectations for yourself and for your learning?

Throughout the book there will be reflective questions such as those in Box 1. These are important because the aim of this book is not only for you to gain knowledge about the person-centered approach, but also for you to relate this to yourself and your experience of life. That is what makes the difference between knowledge and understanding. Understanding brings a deeper level of insight and the ability to apply one's knowledge. People will differ in how they respond to the questions in Box 1, and for some it may feel that there is little to say. They might not have thought about why this interests them, or indeed, it might not interest them. It may be that they are reading this book simply because it is on a list that they are expected to read and they have no expectations, except maybe to pass a course. The questions themselves might seem unusual if you have gone through an education system that offers little chance for learning to be intrinsically motivating. If that is your experience of the questions, take a moment to reflect on the significance of experiencing them in that way and what it means for you.

Many of the most important turning points in my own life where when I felt I had to go in directions that were not of my own choosing. I think it is my own acute awareness of what it feels like not to have agency in one's own life that allows me to appreciate the person-centered approach. Over many years, I have observed that those of us attracted to Rogers's approach seem to have a deep appreciation of freedom and responsibility, often from having had little of either in our early lives, and a distaste for authoritarian and hierarchical structures of control.

This book is about my own discovery of Rogers's work, but I use the term *discovery* in the same way that Columbus "discovered" America—it was already there and full of people. The scholarship in the tradition of the person-centered approach is rich. I mention many of the scholars who have most influenced me, but I haven't tried to be comprehensive in my coverage of all the academics, research, and ideas in the wider person-centered approach over the past 80 years. After eight decades of discussion and debate, inevitably there will be gaps. Many scholars and practitioners who studied with Rogers, or who were his colleagues, or who were in other ways influenced by him went on to develop their own approach to therapy. This book is not about those subsequent developments. The contributions of Robert Elliott, Eugene Gendlin, Leslie Greenberg, William Miller, Garry Prouty, Natalie Rogers, or Dion Van Werde, for example, are all important, but they are not the focus of this book, nor are other recent offshoots such as the experiential approach, process work, relational depth, or pluralism, as developed by scholars such as David Rennie, Richard Worsley and Mick Cooper.

Rogers's influence on the development of psychotherapy was wide-ranging.[10] But as I said, this book is not intended to be about this wider world of therapies associated with the person-centered approach, only an introduction to the work of Rogers and the person-centered, non-directive approach that he developed and those scholars and practitioners whose work remained more or less consistent with it. In this way, I will discuss some of my own work, in which my aim is simply to understand Rogers's ideas in relation to conceptions of psychopathology and contemporary psychology. Many critics schooled in psychiatric ideas see Rogers's approach as not having an adequate theory of psychopathology. It is valuable, therefore, to be able to articulate how his theory applies to understanding conceptions of psychopathology, not to condone the illness ideology but to offer an alternative humanistic perspective. The motivation for such work is to create space for the person-centered approach within traditional systems. But what we really need are different systems. As I've already mentioned, Rogers's approach seen in its contemporary context is also a form of positive psychology. Viewing Rogers's work in the context of positive psychology does not change or adapt his theory, but hopefully helps us to better understand its relevance in the modern world and what those new systems might look like.

Rogers said many times in different ways that he did not want his approach to be reified in such a way that it became stuck or rigid. For some, that might seem to be what I have done here. But what I think Rogers meant was that we should continue to test his theory using scientific methods and that, through the results of this empirical research, changes could come. In this way, his is not a theory that is stuck, but one that has stood the test of time, and as such, it should remain as it was until there is new evidence pointing in another direction. That is not being stuck; it is following the evidence. That is not the same as taking the notion of a theory in development as a license for an "anything goes" approach or adding new ideas on top despite a lack of empirical evidence that they're needed.

The main challenge, as I see it, in learning about the approach is to begin to look at the world differently. People tend to look at new ideas through the lens of their old ideas. Instead of transforming their old ideas into something new, they assimilate the new ideas into their old ones. This often happens when people are first introduced to the person-centered approach. Initially we can only understand it through the lens of what we already know, and this prevents us from seeing just how radical and revolutionary an approach to human relations it is.

This book is about the non-directive approach, or to put it another way, it is about the self-direction of the person, be they the client or the student. Self-direction is the defining principle of the approach. To minimize or bypass this principle is, in my view, to merge with the mainstream traffic in psychology and lose its revolutionary zest. Self-direction implies the non-directivity of the practitioner. To deviate from the principle of self-direction is not person-centered; it is practitioner-centered. That makes the focus of this book closer to what has been called the "classical person-centered approach." Some might see this as limited and constricted, preferring to add practitioner-centered ideas and techniques, but I don't see it this way. Indeed, I've often heard it said that there are around 400 types of psychotherapy. I've never tried to count them, but whether this is true or not, they are all essentially variations on the same theme. In my view there are only two forms of therapy: client-centered and therapist-centered. All of the 400 types of therapy are one or the other. This book is about my understanding of being a client-centered therapist and all the other applications of the non-directive attitude toward human relationships. Only a non-directive approach offers something different. It is what makes the approach genuinely client-centered, student-centered, or person-centered and a contrast to all other approaches, which are in their own distinct ways practitioner-centered.[11]

What is distinctive about the person-centered approach is its respect for the self-determination of the person, which implies that to varying extents all of these other ways of working don't respect the self-determination of the person. They are all in their own ways violations of the person's autonomy. Not many therapists, coaches, or other helping professionals see their practice in this way, but that is the challenge to their understanding of what they do that is presented by the person-centered approach.

Later in his career, Rogers went on to discuss his ideas beyond the therapy room, offering a perspective on interpersonal relations, whatever the context. He became more interested in the wider applications of his approach, for example, its upstream applications in education and social policy that could help create a better and more civil society. I hope to offer a broader overview of Rogers's work and its contemporary applications in the wider field of human flourishing. Rogers developed a new approach for the social sciences and helping professions more broadly. Thus, this is not a book about person-centered therapy per se, but about the person-centered approach—a way of thinking and a set of theoretical hypotheses about human relationships. In other words, I am interested in how the approach can be applied "upstream," as well as downstream after problems have arisen in people's lives and they are in need of help.

I have been a therapist at many points in my career, and I have spent many years working in the education of therapists, but what I'm really interested in is not therapy per se; it is the approach itself: its philosophy and all the different ways it can be applied. I am continually fascinated by the history of Rogers's work, how it came to be, its influence on what came after, its role today, and most of all, its vision for how to create a good life and a good society. The person-centered approach isn't only about therapy; it is a way of *approaching* any situation or person in life. It is a mindset, a way of being.

As a therapist and educator, immersing myself in the philosophy and practice of Rogers's approach and writing about his work and its applications has occupied me for over a quarter of a century and has enriched my life in many ways. It has been important for my own personal development, has provided intellectual stimulation, and has led to new and exciting challenges in my job as a university educator. I will share much of this here, specifically my appreciation of how Rogers's approach to human flourishing was based in his theory of human nature, such that people flourish when the social environment is right. It is a subtle but profoundly unique way of applying psychology. I hope that my engagement with Rogers's worldview has, in turn, also been helpful to others. Now, as I approach the end of my career, I wanted to distill my learnings, and this book is the result. I will draw together in this book my experiences as both a practitioner of therapy and an educator in the approach, coupled with my research over two decades.

Book overview

In Chapter 1, I will introduce the field of humanistic psychology, Rogers's contributions and achievements, the change from non-directive therapy to the person-centered approach, how he challenged us to see the world in a new way, and, finally, how his approach is relevant to positive psychology. Rogers is now recognized as an early pioneer in positive psychology. Despite this, the radical and revolutionary nature of his ideas and how they upturn traditional thinking remains less well understood, which is the topic of the subsequent chapters. In Chapter 2, I will discuss the meta-theoretical foundation of Rogers's theory that human beings have a basic propensity and potential for self-organization, self-regulation, and growth toward the realization of their full potential. The term Rogers used for this was *the actualizing tendency*. A helpful analogy for this tendency is how gravity affects a falling apple. The apple will simply move in the direction of the ground unless intercepted by other forces. People likewise will move toward the development of autonomous determination, expansion, and constructive social behavior and flourishing unless intercepted by a damaging social environment. I will discuss how this remains a revolutionary idea that challenges the individualized and medicalized nature of most applied psychology because it suggests that applications are no longer about targeting the person but, rather, their social environment.

In Chapter 3, I will describe the three ways in which Rogers's theory challenges the illness ideology through its emphasis on the influence of the social environment, its respect for the self-determination of the person, and its focus on the movement toward optimal functioning. In Chapter 4, I will discuss how his theory is used to understand the various problems in living that people have, such as depression, anxiety, and trauma. I will explore how such problems in living can be understood in a non-medical way as a thwarted tendency toward actualization: a form of alienation. In Chapter 5, continuing this theme, I will discuss the application of the approach, that there is ever only one treatment for all cases, that it is flexible and pluralistic, and that it is always non-directive—which is one of the most misunderstood of all Rogers's concepts. In Chapter 6, I will move away from the more abstract discussion of the approach and discuss what it means in practice to be person-centered, beginning with some discussion of general principles, specifically around the idea that this is a way of being.

In Chapter 7, I will discuss the synergy of the person-centered approach and positive psychology. In particular, I will explore the offshoots of this synergy in positive organizational scholarship and positive education and the things we can do to create better policy and practice to improve people's lives to prevent distress and dysfunction from occurring in the first place. In Chapter 8, I will offer a series of reflections on research and practice. Specifically, I will argue that all applied psychological research is carried out from an ideological position, but that this is rarely acknowledged. In Chapter 9, I will discuss in more detail the results of research, not only as they relate to the person-centered approach, but also in the wider field of positive psychology, and how these combine as a strong evidential base for the approach.

Finally, in Chapter 10, I will draw together some of the threads in the book, especially as they relate to the future of the person-centered approach and the study of human flourishing. I conclude that while the power of relationships to promote human flourishing is now well beyond dispute in the social sciences among scholars and academics of all persuasions, Rogers's approach is about a specific type of relationship. It is about creating the right climate in which people's natural tendency toward development and growth is promoted and in all the contexts in which we can do this—whether in our professional roles as therapists, coaches, educators, teachers, consultants and leaders; in our personal lives as parents, friends, and family members; or in how we engage with the wider social and political world through our everyday activities.

Chapter 1
The quiet revolution of Carl Rogers
From non-directive therapy to the person-centered approach

Carl Rogers was a clinical psychologist and researcher. He developed the first ever research programs to investigate the effectiveness of psychotherapy. Out of his research and clinical observations he developed what became known as the client-centered approach. It was the first evidence-based psychotherapy. Indeed, Rogers can be credited with developing psychotherapy as a subject for research. Until that point, psychotherapy had been a mysterious undertaking that took place behind closed doors in secrecy, but Rogers wanted to understand how it worked. In this way, he revolutionized the profession of psychology and the wider helping professions by insisting that his practice be led by evidence.

The evidence suggested that people flourished in life when the social environment was right. This was, and remains, a radically different idea from the more popular and traditional methods of psychology, which all involve nudging, coaxing, and manipulating other people to behave in ways that are deemed to be more appropriate for them. In contrast, in Rogers's approach, by changing ourselves, we provide the right social environment in which others can find their *own* solutions. Put crudely, the idea is not to try to change the fish, but to change the water in its bowl. Today, several decades after his death in 1987, the detail and depth of his work are often overlooked. Typically, textbooks of psychology present Rogers, along with other 20th-century pioneers of psychotherapy, as mere historical context.

Even in the latter years of his life, Rogers was no longer seen as the influential figure that he once had been. This was certainly the case when I was a student. Back then, in my undergraduate days, behavioral and cognitive psychology were the exciting new ideas that were beginning to transform clinical psychology. The message was that the ideas of people like Rogers were not to be ignored altogether, but having built on these foundations, the field had now moved on to better things. That is my experience of how most therapists understand Rogers and the person-centered approach: they believe it offers something important to build on, but by itself it is not enough. I don't agree with that, of course, or I wouldn't be writing this book, but in my undergraduate days that is probably

The Humanistic Psychology of Carl Rogers. Stephen A. Joseph, Oxford University Press. © Oxford University Press (2025). DOI: 10.1093/9780197790632.003.0002

what I was taught and what I thought. I imagine that my experience is typical of many. We get a bit of an introduction to Rogers and the person-centered approach, and then we move on.

But I came back to it a few years later. I had become a university lecturer in psychology, teaching very mainstream topics in what was then referred to as abnormal psychology. I decided to train as a therapist, and the person-centered approach seemed like a good starting point. I had no intention of abandoning what I was already doing as a psychologist in my teaching and research; I just thought that adding some therapeutic practice to my CV would be a good idea. I did not realize that I was about to encounter a different theoretical view that would overturn my assumptions as a psychologist.

Learning about the person-centered approach, immersing myself in its philosophy, and practicing it as a therapist and educator has occupied me for over a quarter of a century. It seems such a simple and straightforward thing to say that people are their own best experts, but looking back to when I first became interested, I can see that while I knew what this was intended to mean, it has taken me many years to truly understand it in a way that permeates my relationships, whether in the classroom, the clinic, or elsewhere. It is hard to overcome the more prevalent thinking—which seeps into all our relationships—that people need external direction. What I have come to realize is that the depth and detail of Rogers's ideas and how he revolutionized the helping professions are often not well understood. And this is true for even the most experienced psychologist or psychiatrist unless they have deliberately dedicated a portion of their career to understanding themselves and exploring what it truly means to trust others to find their own direction—to be their own best expert.

Rogers's approach is an alternative to the medicalization of human distress, offering instead a more social psychological view. He talked about fully functioning decades before positive psychology was developed, and he hypothesized that human relationships, rather than techniques, are necessary and sufficient in therapy for constructive personality change to take place. That much might be widely known, but what it actually involves in practice and feels like to those who are fortunate enough to experience such relationships is not easily understood.

In one of his later books, *Carl Rogers on Personal Power*, Rogers reflected on a moment when someone asked him about the politics of his approach. When he replied that there was no politics of the client-centered approach, this was greeted with a laugh. Puzzled, Rogers asked what was so funny. The person explained how, as a graduate in clinical psychology, everything they had been taught had been upturned on learning his approach: "You completely reversed the relationship of power and control which has been built up in me over three years. And then you say there is no politics in the client-centered approach!"

This was a turning point for Rogers. From that moment his work took on new significance. He called it a "quiet revolution," realizing that what he had developed was a way of being in the world and with other people that challenged hierarchical structures of power and control. It meant trusting in people to move in constructive directions for themselves and others, given the right social environment.[1]

In this chapter I will introduce the field of humanistic psychology as the context for Rogers's work, going on to list some of his contributions and achievements before describing what I think is unique about the person-centered approach and how it challenges us to think differently, to see the world in a new way, and to be part of that quiet revolution.

Humanistic psychology

Initiated in the 1950s, humanistic psychology represented a scholarly alternative to the then-dominant approaches in psychology, namely the psychoanalytic and behavioral schools of thought.

Psychoanalysis had originated in Europe in the late 19th century with the work of Sigmund Freud and his colleagues and became popular among American psychologists in the 1920s. Psychoanalytic thought viewed human beings' behavior as resulting from the interplay of subconscious processes, which competed to manage the demands of primitive impulses. Behaviorism arose in the 1930s with figures such as John Watson proposing that psychology should only concern itself with the study of observable and measurable behavior. Psychoanalysis and behaviorism were the two dominant forces in psychology before humanistic psychology came on the scene. Dissatisfied by both, humanistic psychologists challenged the status quo. They believed that psychoanalysis painted an overly pessimistic image of humans as driven by destructive impulses outside their conscious awareness, whereas behaviorism was reductive and lacked any understanding of humans' ability to make choices and take responsibility. Theirs was a more optimistic view of humanity that emphasized people's freedom to shape their own lives.

Another critical difference was that both the psychoanalytical and the behaviorist approaches focused on what went wrong with people, whereas humanistic psychologists were interested in studying people at their best, at the height of their potential. Thus, humanistic psychology was also known as "height psychology." As Anthony Sutich and Miles Vich, editors of the 1969 book *Readings in Humanistic Psychology*, wrote,

> Two main branches of psychology—behaviorism and psychoanalysis—appear to have made great contributions to human knowledge, but neither singly nor together have they covered the almost limitless scope of human behavior, relationships, and possibilities. Perhaps their greatest limitation has been the

> inadequacy of their approach to positive human potentialities and the maximal realization of those potentialities.[2]

Such short caricatures do not do justice to the disciplines of psychoanalysis and behaviorism, each of which has its own distinguished lines of scholarship and practice, but in essence it was along these lines that humanistic psychology offered a different view: a more optimistic image of humanity and an emphasis on people's agency and what they can achieve. Humanistic psychology came to be known as the third force, following the first two forces of psychoanalysis and behaviorism. It can also be said to be the precursor of today's positive psychology movement and the worldwide interest in human flourishing, a topic I will return to later.

Only a decade on from the horrors of the Second World War, the 1950s saw the emergence of the civil rights movement and protests, such as the Montgomery bus boycott, and the birth of popular music, with figures such as Fats Domino and Bill Haley. It was the peak of the American Dream of equality and the prospect of prosperity. Against this background, Abraham Maslow founded the American Association for Humanistic Psychology in 1961 (renamed the Association for Humanistic Psychology in 1963).

In 1964, James Bugental put forward five basic principles of humanistic psychology, which were later adapted by Tom Greening to define the parameters of humanistic psychology:[3]

> 1. Human beings, as human, supersede the sum of their parts. They cannot be reduced to components. 2. Human beings have their existence in a uniquely human context, as well as in a cosmic ecology. 3. Human beings are aware and aware of being aware—i.e., they are conscious. Human consciousness always includes an awareness of oneself in the context of other people. 4. Human beings have some choice and, with that, responsibility. 5. Human beings are intentional, aim at goals, are aware that they cause future events, and seek meaning, value, and creativity.

Guided by these principles, humanistic psychologists developed research into what makes life worth living and how to promote a good life, focused attention on the importance of our relationships with each other, and the ecology we are part of. They sought to understand the nature of humanity and the problems faced in the quest to live harmoniously and peacefully together and within nature. Humanistic psychology was an approach to psychology that promised to change the world, and for the first decade of its existence it went from strength to strength.[4]

Humanistic psychologists located the causes of psychological suffering in people's interpersonal and social world rather than in their biology or brain chemistry. This is not to say that biology is not important—all psychological suffering has biological correlates[5]—but they questioned the emphasis on medication as the solution to what might otherwise be considered existential issues rooted in the social world and the relationships that exist between people.[6] While such views, which challenge the medicalization of distress, are now more mainstream and shared by many clinical psychologists, for decades it was humanistic psychologists alone who were calling for alternative approaches to mental health. As Donna Rockwell, a contemporary humanistic psychologist and past president of the American Psychological Association's Society for Humanistic Psychology, wrote,

> It is our job, through the [therapeutic] relationship, to help clients face the existential stuff of their lives directly, and discern ways to reenter the path to personal growth and development. Therapists act as guides in the therapeutic encounter, becoming, as it is, the relational metaphor for our clients' waltz with life itself. It is not Pollyanna to talk about therapy in this way; it is existential truth.[7]

Such talk might not seem so novel today, but at the dawn of humanistic psychology it was revolutionary. Rogers was one of the pioneers of the original humanistic psychology movement, and it was in that context of scholarly work and practice that he originated client-centered therapy and what later came to be called the person-centered approach. In the previous quote, Rockwell is referring to humanistic therapies more generally, rather than client-centered therapy in particular, but she neatly sums up client-centered therapy: it is relational, existential, and growthful. As we will see, client-centered therapists questioned the illness ideology and offered a new way to think about people's psychological suffering. Instead of seeing suffering as illness or disease, they saw it as a form of alienation with roots in social oppression and systems of coercion.

Carl Rogers, client-centered therapy and beyond

Rogers was born in Illinois in 1902. He was the fourth of six children. Rogers wrote that his parents cared greatly for them but that it was a controlling environment. He recalled his childhood as "marked by close family ties, a very strict and uncompromising religious and ethical atmosphere, and what amounted to a worship of the virtue of hard work."[8] When he was 12, his parents bought a farm, and it was here that Rogers developed his feeling for scientific ideas, as they were being applied to agriculture at the time.

As a young man he briefly studied agriculture at college in Wisconsin, changing to study history with the aim of joining the ministry. In 1922, he was one of a dozen students from America to go to China for an international World Student Christian Federation conference. Away from home for over five months, traveling, and meeting different people, he had a transformational experience. "I was forced to stretch my thinking, to realize that sincere and honest people could believe in very divergent religious doctrines. In major ways I for the first time emancipated myself from the religious thinking of my parents."[9] In 1924 he joined the Union Theological Seminary to study theology. This was also the year that he was married to Helen Elliott, whom he had known since childhood. The marriage lasted for 55 years, until Helen's death.

It was during his time at the seminary that Rogers became increasingly interested in psychology and registered to take courses at Teachers College, Columbia University, eventually transferring full time to Teachers College in 1926 to train as a psychologist. In 1928 Rogers took up a position as a clinical psychologist at the Rochester Society for the Prevention of Cruelty to Children in New York City. He spent the next 12 years of his professional life in the society's Child Study Department, delivering therapy and providing assessments in the traditional form of clinical psychology that he had been taught. During his time at Rochester, however, he began to question some of these traditional activities, becoming frustrated with the directive and diagnostic approaches that were practiced in psychoanalysis. He started to develop his own methods, which put more emphasis on the client's inner resources and knowledge about what they needed. In early 1939 he was appointed as the first director of the newly formed Rochester Child Guidance Clinic.

Before his appointment, Rogers was challenged on the grounds that as a non-medically trained practitioner he lacked the qualifications to be its director. As he later wrote,

> A vigorous campaign, partly above-board and partly behind the scenes, was made to discontinue my services as director and to substitute a psychiatrist. There seemed to be no question about the quality of my work. The argument was simply based on the view that a psychologist could not head up a mental health operation—it was simply "not done."[10]

Rogers won out in the end, through support from the board of directors, and his victory helped to change the face of psychology. Nonetheless, the use of the term *psychotherapy* was controversial. At the time, psychotherapy was seen as an activity reserved for those from a medical and psychoanalytical background. To get around this, Rogers chose to use the term *counseling*, but he didn't view his approach as any less psychotherapeutic. Rogers was by now becoming well known, and it was also during 1939 that he was offered the post of full professor at Ohio State University, where he worked from 1940 to 1944, a time when he completed some of the most important work of his career.

On December 11, 1940, Rogers gave a talk to the Psi Chi honor society in psychology at the University of Minnesota, Minneapolis, entitled *Some Newer Concepts of Psychotherapy*. Rogers later wrote that, looking back, he felt that was the day client-centered therapy was born.[11] His central arguments were that therapy is about removing obstacles to normal growth and development; that the emphasis should be on using emotions in the present as a guide rather than examining the past; and that the frame of reference of the client and not the appraisal of the therapist is important. In essence, he argued that therapy should be about the facilitation of personality development, emphasizing the non-directive approach of the therapist as a way to support the self-direction of the client. This was a radical departure from the traditional forms of psychotherapy, involving interpretations by the therapist. Given Rogers's subsequent influence, it might be imagined that he was greeted with rapturous applause, but accounts suggest otherwise. Instead, the reception for what he had to say was cool and not at all enthusiastic.[12]

While 1940 might be considered the year client-centered therapy was born, the ideas had been fermenting for several years. Rogers said in a later interview that traces of his ideas could be seen in his 1939 book *The Clinical Treatment of the Problem Child*. In that book he emphasized the importance of the environmental conditions under which a child lived and how, through manipulating those conditions, a difference could be made.[13] For example, Rogers discussed the importance of the attitudes and behavior of the parents toward the child and the emotional tone created at home.

Rogers's move to Ohio State University allowed him to pursue his ideas in more depth, resulting in his 1942 book *Counseling and Psychotherapy: Newer Concepts in Practice*. This is considered to be Rogers's first major work in which he developed his ideas around non-directive therapy. In this book he presented a revised and expanded version of his 1940 lecture. It was the beginning of what became the client-centered approach, although that term had yet to be introduced. In *Counseling and Psychotherapy*, Rogers instead used the term *non-directive therapy* to describe how it was the therapist's task to follow the client's lead. This allowed him to contrast his new approach with the "older" approaches, in which the client was expected to follow the therapist's lead. In these early writings, however, Rogers was still approaching therapy as the application of techniques rather than as the relationship-based approach it would develop into.

A few years later, in 1945, Rogers moved to the University of Chicago. As before, there were criticisms that he and his colleagues were practicing medicine without a license, but it was here that the newer form of therapy really began to unfold with the development of new psychotherapy research projects and the emergence of a community of scholars and students who subscribed to the new ideas. It is also noteworthy that during this time Rogers was continuing his clinical practice and had become experienced in working with Second World War veterans and was aware of the psychological impact of trauma.[14] In 1947 he served as president of the American Psychological Association. He had become a leading figure in the psychological community.

This intense period of activity resulted in one of Rogers best-known books, *Client-Centered Therapy*, which was published in 1951 and helped to spark a revolution in practice. The book built on his previous writings but moved forward in the understanding of the importance of the *attitudes* of the therapist, as opposed to their techniques. The general principle of non-directivity remained, but he now chose to refer to it as client-centered therapy as opposed to non-directive therapy. This was intended to bring clarity, as the term *non-directive* had led to confusion, with critics thinking it implied no direction.[15] The name change made it clearer that while the therapist was non-directive, this did not mean there was no direction; rather, it meant that the direction of the client could be trusted. This was the central hypothesis of the approach. Rogers wrote the following in *Client-Centered Therapy*:

> *If* the individual or group is faced with a problem, *If* a catalyst-leader provides a permissive atmosphere, *If* responsibility is genuinely placed with the individual or group, *If* there is a basic respect for the capacity of the individual or group, *Then*, responsible and adequate analysis of the problem is made, responsible self-direction occurs.[16]

This quote captures three things that I will return to throughout the book. First, it introduces the way in which Rogers was thinking in 1951 about how self-direction can be facilitated by what he calls a permissive atmosphere, an idea that he had yet to fully develop into what he later described as the "six necessary and sufficient conditions." Second, it is interesting to note how Rogers used the language of *If* and *Then* deliberately, carefully crafting his sentences to ensure he was providing scientifically testable hypotheses. This remains one of the great strengths of the approach. Third, he now began to see his ideas as applicable beyond one-to-one therapy, deliberately using language that was appropriate to a range of contexts.

Furthermore, as its title made clear, *Client-Centered Therapy* helped to consolidate the notion that this was as much a psychotherapeutic activity as it was counseling. To this day the terms *counseling* and *psychotherapy* remain interchangeable among those practicing within the approach.

In the late 1950s, Rogers published his two major theoretical works, in which he developed these ideas further. The first, entitled "The Necessary and Sufficient Conditions of Therapeutic Personality Change," was published in 1957 in the American Psychological Association's *Journal of Consulting Psychology*.[17] The second was a book chapter, "A Theory of Therapy, Personality and Interpersonal Relationships, as Developed in the Client-Centered Framework," which was published in 1959 in a volume edited by Sigmund Koch entitled *Psychology: A Study of Science, Volume 3: Formulations of the Person and the Social Context*.[18] In these two works his *If* and *Then* style of writing was again used, such that his theories of therapy and personality development were clearly articulated as a series of testable scientific propositions.

In the 1957 article, Rogers proposed his six necessary and sufficient conditions for constructive therapeutic change, which I will describe in more detail in Chapter 3. This included the three therapist attitudes for which Rogers is probably best known: congruence, empathy, and unconditional positive regard (see Box 1.1). Rogers wrote that this was a theoretical statement hypothesizing why therapy, of any persuasion, is helpful.[19]

Box 1.1 The three therapist attitudes

Congruence. This refers to self-knowledge; self-awareness and understanding of one's bodily sensations, thoughts, and feelings; emotional literacy; and the ability to relate to others in a genuine, transparent, and real way.

Empathic understanding. This involves sensing the meaning and emotions in another's experience and communicating that to them. Sometimes this is meaning at the edge of the other's awareness, but it is always communicated in a tentative and exploratory way.

Unconditional positive regard. This refers to an unchanging and consistent warmth and prizing of the other person as a unique individual.

In his 1959 chapter, he outlined a vision for how the approach could be applied beyond one-to-one therapy. While he had already begun this process in his 1951 book, he now went further in offering a broad paradigmatic vision for the social sciences and the study of human relations and their applications.

I will go on to discuss in more detail these two major works in the next chapter, but for now I continue with the broad overview of the historical development of the approach and the emergence of the term *person-centered.*

Rogers left Chicago to move to the University of Wisconsin in 1957 to take up a position as joint professor of psychology and psychiatry. He remained at Wisconsin until 1963, when he left academia. It was in 1961, 10 years after the publication of *Client-Centered Therapy*, that he published what is perhaps his best-known book, *On Becoming a Person: A Therapist's View of Psychotherapy.* In this, he discussed how his ideas could be used to understand any human relationship and the potential of congruent, empathic, and unconditionally regarding relationships in contexts outside therapy.

. . .

Wisconsin marked a shift in direction for Rogers. During his time there, he embarked on a study to investigate client-centered therapy for people with a diagnosis of schizophrenia. The Wisconsin study, as it became known, promised the advance of client-centered therapy into psychiatric settings, but by the end there were tensions among the investigation team working with Rogers. As well as this, data were incomplete and the findings were inconclusive. Many subsequently interpreted the results as showing that client-centered therapy was ineffective in this context. However, there were a number of methodological issues, such as a high rate of patient withdrawal and the quality of the therapy actually offered to patients, that raise questions about the rigor of the research and whether what was being tested was actually client-centered.[20] The study clearly lent little support to the approach as a treatment for schizophrenia, but it did not actually refute Rogers's theory.

Thus, although the study began with promise that it would herald a new age for client-centered therapy, it turned out to be more of a death knell. In the aftermath of the Wisconsin study, and perhaps because of its results and the personal tensions that arose, Rogers turned his attention toward other applications. He left Wisconsin, moving to La Jolla, a small coastal town in the northern outskirts of San Diego, and spent the remainder of his career, from 1963 onward, working in independent institutions based in California, namely the Western Behavioral Sciences Institute and the Center for Studies of the Person.[21] He was a leading figure during the sixties in these more progressive, liberal, and countercultural organizations, which were interested in exploring human relations and human potential.

Throughout his career Rogers was a prolific scholar, publishing numerous academic papers about the person-centered approach he had developed. Beyond the sixties, he began to apply his ideas in other contexts, such as education, conflict resolution, and encounter groups (see Box 1.2).

Box 1.2 Encounter groups

An "encounter group," sometimes known as a T group (training group) or sensitivity training group, involves a number of people meeting to learn and grow through sharing thoughts and feelings in the present moment and in relation to each other. It can be an intensive emotional experience. Smaller groups range in size between 8 and 15, and larger groups may have around 20–30 participants. But there can also be groups of more than 100 people. Groups can last from several hours to days or weeks. Depending on the experience of the group members, there may be one or more facilitators. Rogers described how he facilitated such groups, saying that he trusted in the group to move toward its potential, given the right facilitative climate was in place, and that he would have no preprepared goal for the group, only that he would try to create the facilitative climate.[22] Such groups were popular in the 1970s as part of the humanistic and countercultural movement, and they remain an important core part of training and learning in the person-centered approach.[23]

Over time, the term *person-centered* came to be used more frequently, particularly from 1977 when Rogers and Thomas Holdstock used it in the title of their chapter, "Person-Centered Personality Theory," in Raymond Corsini's book *Current Personality Theories*.[24] Rogers presented his wider vision in various books, such as *Freedom to Learn* (1969), *Carl Rogers on Personal Power* (1977), and *A Way of Being* (1980).[25] One of Rogers's achievements was that he continued to develop the person-centered approach and apply his ideas everywhere human relations were important. In 1987 he was nominated for a Nobel Peace Prize for his work in South Africa and Northern Ireland. Rogers recognized that there was a much bigger picture to his work: to facilitate people's ability to truly understand each other and find ways to engage in seeking answers to collective problems. Looking far beyond therapy, he envisaged a society in which relationships mattered. As one of his former students and colleagues, Maureen O'Hara, wrote in 2007:

> By the end of his life Rogers had lost interest in counselling and therapy almost entirely: He felt the field—even the person-centered community—had come to see itself too much from within an instrumentalist medical industry framework. He questioned the individual focus, and felt the practice was becoming too de-contextualized and alienated from the looming cultural issues. He felt increasingly that the problems facing humanity were on a scale far beyond what

> could be helped through individual counselling . . . He and his colleagues had come to see the strength of the [person-centered] process not merely as an effective therapeutic approach but as a powerful pedagogy for transformational learning in which people with the skills, attitudes and levels of critical consciousness characteristic of the persons of tomorrow, and adapted to life in the never-before-experienced conditions of globalized modernity, could develop.[26]

For Rogers, the person of tomorrow—shaped by the new climate that would follow if human relations were governed more by the philosophy of his theory—would have a desire for authenticity, an indifference toward materialism as a way of life, a compassionate and caring approach to others, and a wish to be close to others, have shared purpose, be more in tune with nature, and be more trusting of themselves.[27]

Rogers's work from his later years communicates his optimism that the generation reaching adulthood in the 1960s and 1970s had the potential to shape a better future, to transcend the values and rigidity of his generation, to create a better society. As O'Hara notes, his interests during his years in California had expanded to include world peace and organizing conferences and workshops on this important theme around the world. He had become more of a thought leader, activist, and political figure. But it is hard to see, from the perspective of today, that his optimism was borne out; it certainly was not in terms of the change in conscious awareness and interpersonal and intergroup relations that he might have hoped for. Does that mean he ultimately failed, or was his quiet revolution simply ahead of its time, one that we can still hope for?

Rehumanizing an inhumane world

Rogers is often mentioned as one of the most important and influential psychologists of all time and cited frequently in textbooks, but despite this, mentions of his work are often piecemeal. While he is remembered as having made significant contributions, the actual contributions are largely forgotten. What Rogers offered was a broad paradigmatic framework for psychological practice in which all the parts were interconnected and only truly made sense when seen as a whole. For example, unconditional regard is an important aspect of practice, but it only makes sense in relation to his theory of actualization (the idea that people are intrinsically motivated toward growth and development unless thwarted by social environmental influences). Empathy is important, but only in the context of unconditional regard. I will go on to discuss this interconnectedness in more depth later, but for now, my point is that by the end of Rogers's life, and in the years that followed, the person-centered tradition in psychology had begun to dwindle to a flame kept alive by relatively few, and interest in the potentialities of being human—which had always been a feature of humanistic psychology—was often greeted with some skepticism.

By the 1980s, the cognitive revolution in psychology was taking hold. Humanistic psychology was increasingly seen as something from the past. Had the counterculture of the 1960s lost it credibility? Rogers himself seems to have thought so, saying in a 1975 interview that the more extremist offshoots of the encounter group and progressive education movements could damage them in the public's eyes.[28] It seems likely that humanistic psychology lost its power and influence, not only for these reasons, but also because it was, as David Elkins wrote in the *Journal of Humanistic Psychology*, "inherently incompatible with the basic assumptions and values of contemporary mainstream psychology and with the conservative ideologies that have increasingly gained power in American culture since the 1960s."[29]

By the late 1990s, mainstream scholars mostly viewed humanistic psychology as obsolete, irrelevant, and lacking in scientific rigor.[30] Martin Seligman, the founder of the positive psychology movement whose work I will introduce later, initially criticized humanistic psychology for neglecting conventional empirical research. In this way he was able to position positive psychology as something new and distinct from its predecessor. It is true that many humanistic psychologists challenged conventional scientific methodologies, introducing new ideas around phenomenological ways of knowing. To their credit, they pioneered qualitative techniques that are now widely established and used.[31] Nonetheless, despite the innovations, conventional empirical research interest in humanistic psychology had dwindled, and in this respect the critics were right. But although they were right when thinking about some of the activities within the wider field of humanistic psychology, it was not a criticism that was equally deserved of all humanistic psychologists and certainly seemed unjustified if applied to Rogers himself. This is a topic we will return to in Chapter 7.

But now, more than 20 years on from the emergence of positive psychology, I would argue that positive psychology simply picked up the baton from an exhausted humanistic psychology. It did so with the arrogance of youth, but today positive psychology is itself a young adult and has matured such that it is sometimes hard to tell the difference between the two. The approach to methodology by positive psychologists has softened, and they, too, now recognize the value in a range of methodologies that include qualitative ways of knowing.[32] The issues and concerns raised by the humanistic psychologists more than 60 years ago seem at least as relevant today as they were then. A concern for how to achieve more harmonious living between different people and with the environment is the prime example.

One could argue that we have now firmly moved into globalized modernity but failed to develop as persons of tomorrow, as envisaged by Rogers. O'Hara is one of the person-centered scholars who continue to promote this way of thinking about how the approach can transform global society. She writes that it would be helpful for those in the person-centered community to move away from thinking of ourselves as psychologists or therapists—professions focused on one-to-one work—and instead see ourselves as social innovators. She quotes a former president of the American Psychological Association, Frank Farley, as proposing that the true calling of psychology should be "rehumanizing an inhumane world."[33]

In this respect, I would agree that we need to find another way to position the work we do and also to see the bigger picture of the work we could be doing. The term *person-centered approach* is used to recognize the broader applicability of Rogers's theory to human relations, such that it has become commonplace to talk about person-centered education, person-centered management, person-centered facilitation, person-centered therapy, and so on. "Person-centered" as such does not denote a change in the practice; it is simply a recognition that the approach is no longer only about therapy. When it comes to therapy, Rogers did not intend *person-centered* to replace *client-centered*, and many therapists still refer to themselves as client-centered, using the terms interchangeably. For those new to the approach, however, this can seem confusing until its history is understood.

Perhaps more confusing, the popularity of Rogers's work led many others to extend his ideas to other settings and adopt the same terminology, but over time, those building on this work in these other settings lost touch with the original theory and its meaning.[34] Today, for example, the term *person-centered* is also widely used in healthcare settings, but not in a way that we would recognize as strongly connected to the approach as developed by Rogers. In the Rogerian tradition, person-centered means something very specific and well defined that is based in his theory. While writing this book, I was alerted to a recently published paper that used the term, but on reading it I could see that it was not person-centered in the Rogerian tradition, and I posted a comment about this on social media. One of the authors disagreed, pointing to the fact that Rogers emphasized the importance of attending to the subjectivity of the client's perceptions. That is true, but it is just one element of his theory. All of the elements must be present simultaneously. If not, the approach simply is not person-centered in the Rogerian sense. Many different theories and approaches emphasize the subjectivity of the client's perceptions, but this by itself does not make an approach person-centered. I will discuss this in more depth in the next two chapters, where I will describe Rogers's theory and set out what I think are the characteristics of the approach in practice, which must be tightly interwoven.

Similarly, other terms used by Rogers, such as *student-centered*, which he used when writing about the applications of his theory to education, are now widely used, but in ways that are disconnected from his theory and sometimes in ways that are actually contradictory to the person-centered approach, or misunderstand it.[35] In writing this book, I even wondered if it might be possible to do so without using the term *person-centered*, given the confusion, but that seemed an impossible task. On reflection, I felt that a more hopeful objective would be to clarify what it means in its original use to refer to ideas and practice developed by Rogers and his colleagues and to restore a term that has become worn by misuse.

However, even those authors and practitioners who do trace their ideas clearly back to Rogers use the term *person-centered* to mean slightly different things. But like the branches of a tree, they all grow from the same trunk and share some of the same characteristics, albeit with disagreement on some aspects. This book will not be so concerned with the different branches—other books explore some of them in more detail[36]—but with the trunk itself, the principle of non-directivity. This is what sets the person-centered approach apart from all other forms of practice.

One central inherent principle of the approach

Jerold Bozarth, who was one of the leading proponents of the approach, identified non-directivity as its central inherent principle.[37] I would agree that the non-directive attitude of the practitioner remains the central defining feature, but, interestingly, it is not included as one of the terms in the set of definitions that Rogers provided in the introduction of his 1959 chapter, his most comprehensive and finalized statement of theory and therapy. Some might suggest that this omission implies that non-directivity is actually not an essential part of the person-centered approach. In response I would argue that by the time Rogers wrote the 1959 chapter, it had become clear to him that *non-directivity* was a confusing and therefore unhelpful term. It was better to describe the approach for what it was, client-centered, rather than what it was not. Germain Lietaer provided this definition:

> *Non-directivity*—a dimension more accurately termed "client-centeredness"—refers mainly to an attitude of respect: to approach the client as a unique and independent person, with the right to live according to his own viewpoint. In contrast to this stands a more paternalistic attitude in which one treats the client from one's own frame of reference. Some aspects of the contrasting paternalistic

> attitude are: lack of respect for the privacy and the pace of the client, and the intention to mold the client toward one's own patterns of feeling, thinking, and behaving.[38]

The non-directive approach is understood not as what the therapist does, but as their attitude in their attempt to help the client. Raskin wrote that it was not a "matter of acquiring technique, but of gradually gaining the conviction that people do not have to be guided into adjustment, but can do it for themselves when accepted."[39] Non-directivity is the characteristic of the approach that can be most challenging (see Box 1.3).

Box 1.3 Reflection: Who has the right to self-determination?

What are your initial reactions to reading the quote that people have the right to live according to their own viewpoint? Does it immediately feel correct, or is there something that jars with you as you read it? Are there people who should be excluded from this right? If so, why?

Can you think of times in your own life when you felt your right to live according to your viewpoint was curtailed and other times when it was respected?

Think about the people in your life at that time. Why do you think they made the choices they did for you?

Despite Rogers's intention to avoid the confusion surrounding the term *non-directive* by instead referring to the approach as "client-centered," the confusion persists to this day. He may even have inadvertently added to it by changing the terminology. I've heard some critics say that client-centered therapy is no longer non-directive, thinking that because Rogers was no longer using the term to describe his approach, he had abandoned the idea of non-directivity. It is true that there were other later developments in therapy that were based on or inspired by Rogers's work that introduced more therapist-directed activities, and these approaches are often included under a wider umbrella of related humanistic therapies, but that is a subject for a different book. For now I am only writing about the humanistic psychology of Rogers.[40]

In my view, the two terms, *non-directivity* and *person-centered*, are synonymous, and Rogers did not abandon the idea of non-directivity. Writing in 1977, a quarter of a century after the publication of *Client-Centered Therapy*, and the change in terminology, he was clear about what the approach was:

> A conscious renunciation and avoidance by the therapist of all control over, or decision making for, the client. It is the facilitation of self-ownership by the client and the strategies by which this can be achieved; the placing of the locus of decision making and the responsibility for the effects of these decisions. It is politically centered in the client.[41]

Other characteristics were also distinct to Rogers's humanistic thinking, and one of these was the focus on positive human potentialities. This is, of course, no longer a distinct feature, because there have subsequently been others who, seemingly unaware that this was already well-trodden theoretical ground, claimed the focus on human potentialities as their own. As I will discuss in Chapter 7, over the past 20 years there has been a surge of interest, sparked by the positive psychology movement in the early 2000s, in what makes for a good life. Interest in positive psychology has since spread to many other scholars and professionals, all concerned with how to promote human flourishing. But because of the central principle of non-directivity, how human flourishing is thought to be best promoted is different in the Rogerian tradition. Specifically, this is Rogers's focus on the social environment as the means to promote change.

Rogers's theories were developed in the context of his work as a clinical psychologist and personality theorist, and for that reason he is often seen as offering an individualistic understanding. In fact, his ideas were social psychological, even sociological in their application. Rogers understood personality processes and the development of the self to arise out of social interaction. Therefore, he also saw the role of the therapist, and later applications of his approach, to be ultimately social ones.

All the different applications of person-centered psychology—whether downstream in the domains of clinical psychology, coaching, counseling, conflict resolution, and psychotherapy or upstream in business, education, encounter groups, leadership, management, parenting, and policy—are about changing the social environment. This is because they are grounded in a vision of humanity in which people are always striving toward becoming fully functioning, a tendency that will automatically be released when the social environment is optimal. The notion of non-directivity that underpins this thinking is based on the *radical ontology* that humans can be trusted: people know what hurts and what is best for them.

In subsequent chapters, I will go into the detail of the theory, but for now, I will share the metaphor most often used to convey the theoretical principle: an acorn has the potential to develop into an oak tree, and, given the right nutrients from the soil and the right balance of sunlight and shade, it will grow to its fullest potential as an oak tree. In the same way that each tree is striving to be the fullest version of what it can be, hindered only by the environment, people are striving to be their most human in their own way. We know that we can't make the tree grow, but we can water it and ensure it has sufficient light. This is what makes the person-centered approach distinctive: the fact that its interventions are always about changing the social environment and not about changing the person. In changing the social environment, people will change in such a way that they become more fully functioning. This remains one of the most radical ideas in psychology that challenges us to look at the world through a new window.

Seeing the world through a new window

I hope I have given a flavor of Rogers's life and work in this chapter, but over many years of teaching about him and his work, I've come to understand how challenging it is to truly see what Rogers offered because it is so different from typical expectations. My aim in this section is to shake up any preconceptions about the person-centered approach. When people first come to the approach, they see it in an old light. That is to say, they can only understand it through whatever worldview they already have; they fail to understand it fully for what it is. The learning journey is for them to be able to turn that around to instead look at their existing worldview through the window of person-centered theory.

I will give an example from my own experience. For over a decade at the University of Nottingham in the School of Education, we have offered a successful Masters level program in person-centered counseling and psychotherapy, from which many students have now graduated as professional therapists. We have had students from all corners of the world, many of whom have taken their learnings back to their home countries, where they now continue to develop and promote the person-centered approach. There are not many such university-level programs specializing in the person-centered approach, so my colleagues and I feel privileged to have this opportunity to introduce new students to it. One of the questions we get asked every year by at least one of the new students is, why are we based in the School of Education and not in the School of Mental Health?

It is not just new students who ask this. Even our colleagues in other parts of the university ask. It is a reasonable question. Answering it is often the first step in forming a new worldview. What are the assumptions packed within such a seemingly straightforward question? The question arises because it is more usual to see therapy training programs in schools of nursing, medicine, health, or psychiatry. Most people think of counseling and psychotherapy as forms of healthcare, or even as part of medicine. But the person-centered approach is not about curing or treating someone for an illness or a disorder. It is about helping the person to become themselves, to free themselves from their social conditioning, to develop and grow as a person, and to become more fully functioning as a human being. Therapy from the person-centered approach is about helping people to become themselves. Seen in this light, therapy is a form of education, not healthcare.

Person-centered therapists are educators. One way of thinking about this is that in the medical model, the process begins with the experience of an illness or maladjustment, leading to diagnosis and the prescription of a treatment, which then leads to a return to normal, at which point the patient is said to be cured. The educational model begins with the experience of a need or dissatisfaction, leading to the clarification of aims and goals, the selection of a teaching or training program, and then to a satisfaction of the need, in which the learner is said to have developed or grown.[42] Different metaphors can be used to describe what therapy is. David Orlinsky, one of the world's most renowned psychotherapists wrote in the journal *Clinical Psychology Review* that there were "four basic images, which represent psychotherapy alternatively (a) as mental health treatment, (b) as personal education, (c) as a reform or correctional process, and (d) as moral or spiritual redemption."[43]

Which metaphor we choose influences what therapy becomes, what patients expect of their therapists, and what therapists do. Thinking about the role of therapy as education rather than a form of healthcare challenges a lot of the assumptions that society makes about the nature and purpose of therapy. It might therefore surprise some readers to think of therapy as education rather than as healthcare. It might seem to some that this is just playing with words and it doesn't really matter, but I would argue that it does. Through our use of language, we shape the world around us and how we make sense of our interactions with each other.

There is an ongoing tension between therapists and the professional bodies about these different images of therapy. There is no one correct vision. Different forms of therapy exist, each with its own image, and they jostle together competing for resources.[44] My point here is that when we consider the work of Rogers, it immediately takes us into the middle of this debate. It also opens up another discussion about what education is. There is much debate over the meaning and application of the term *education*. Some might see it simply as a way to instill certain facts and figures into the minds of young people, to prepare them for a life of work. Others see it as a way to nurture their growth as fully rounded human beings and create the citizens of the future. Under the former, more restrictive definitions of education, it is hard to see what counseling and psychotherapy have to do with education. But with wider definitions of education, which see it as a way of promoting flourishing at intellectual, emotional, and social levels of development and something that takes place across the lifespan, then yes, anything that is about helping a person to become more fully functioning as a human being is a form of education.

But with a wider perspective on the concept of education, it also becomes clear that a lot of what passes for education is not educational. Curricula that must be followed regardless of a child's abilities or talents and overlook the child's own motivations, interests, and directions are likely restrictive of the child's development and impede their flourishing. So it is not just that person-centered therapy is a form of education; it is also that education must be person-centered to be truly educational. In his career, Rogers moved from writing about therapy to the topic of education itself, and in his book *Freedom to Learn*, he develops these ideas.

Scholars in education are always in the midst of debates and discussions over what education is and are passionate in their vision for what it could be. When I look around at what passes for education in our schools and colleges, I am saddened and disheartened at how limited these institutions are in what they are able to provide for our children and young people, and also when I see how education is lacking for people as they enter adulthood. It is as if we think that the need for education stops at a certain age, rather than understanding that learning and growing as human beings is a lifelong and continuous process. That is what the person-centered approach is all about—helping people flourish—whether it is being applied in the classroom, therapy room, management meeting, conflict resolution session, or any other context that involves human relationships.

I wanted to introduce these thoughts around the nature of what therapy is, and what education is, early on, as these are important themes throughout the book. The aim is to loosen our preconceptions around these concepts before we dive any deeper. It is also an opportunity to ask, what is person-centered therapy actually for? What role does it serve? The answer that it exists to help people feel better is simply too glib. Certainly that is why many people seek therapy—to deal with difficult and tangled emotions—but all the theories of therapy contextualize people's feelings in a way that makes therapy always a political act. This is most explicit in the person-centered approach. In person-centered therapy, the purpose is simply to help people be more true to themselves, more authentic, or, to use Rogers's term, more congruent. But in helping people become themselves, person-centered therapy is about freeing them from their social conditioning. It is a theory that locates the problems in living that people experience as arising not from within them, but from the social world and its pressures to conform. From that perspective, other therapies that don't take that view can begin to look as though they condone or ignore the impact of the social world. For the general public, the world of therapy is not generally seen as anything to do with politics, but within the profession of therapy itself it is well understood that therapy is ultimately a political action of sorts and that the type of therapy one practices is an expression of an ideology. For many students who just want to learn to be therapists, this can be a shock and an unwelcome message, one that can take some time to digest and understand.

All of this opens a conversation about whether therapy, generally speaking, ought to be a vehicle for producing conformity and adjustment to the norms of society or a means to promote insubordination, activism, and protest. Insubordination, activism, and protest are not the inevitable outcomes of person-centered therapy, but insofar as the expected outcome is greater authenticity then, yes, these will be the likely outcomes in a society that is experienced as coercive and controlling. Authenticity is the expected outcome of the person-centered approach, but can the same be said for the helping professions as a whole? I believe that much of what passes for therapy and psychological intervention in today's world is, in fact, a form of control and coercion to social norms. This is a subtle process, but that is what it is nonetheless, if your goals are already decided in advance by your therapist or psychologist. Only the person-centered approach has the unique selling point that the client is their own best expert and genuinely tries to live up to this sales pitch of being a quiet revolution.

The legacy of Rogers and beyond

In its heyday, the 1960s and 1970s, Rogers's approach became widely known and practiced throughout the world. But following his death in 1987, interest dwindled. Among humanistic psychologists, client-centered therapy remains one of the main forms of psychotherapy practiced today, alongside emotion-focused therapy, focusing-oriented experientialpsychotherapy, gestalt therapy, and existential psychotherapies,[45] but humanistic psychology itself is a reduced field, with fewer proponents and specialist journals. Looking to the wider psychological professions, Rogers's influence has also lessened. He is not completely forgotten—far from it. Many scholars and practitioners across the disciplines of education and learning, business and management, and psychology and psychotherapy acknowledge the importance of empathic, genuine, unconditional relationships to provide healthy social environments. Many would say that such ideas are now baked into the applied psychology professions. But in response, I would say that this exists only in a piecemeal fashion, not in the theoretically coherent and holistic way that Rogers conceptualized. He has certainly not been forgotten, but the full significance of his work for the wider psychological profession has.

There are various reasons for this, one of which, I believe, is that Rogers's success in taking the approach to wider audiences came at the expense of its hold in the academic departments of psychology, which by then were becoming increasingly research-focused and staffed by a new generation who were unfamiliar with his work and the ideas of humanistic psychology. I was one of those people and in my early career was dismissive of the person-centered approach as I then understood it. Looking back, I realize that although I knew the general ideas, I didn't really understand the approach. I thought that psychology had progressed, having built on this earlier tradition. Now I question this.

It might seem perplexing why anyone would fixate on a theory from the 1950s to an extent that they would devote their career to what, for others, is a historical footnote. I don't see it that way because I think the full significance of Rogers's work was truly revolutionary. I see Rogers as a figure who could have done for psychology what Charles Darwin did for biology. Darwin recognized the process of natural selection, which remains the organizing principle of modern biology. Rogers saw the importance of the growth model and how that could be an organizing principle for the psychological sciences. Rogers was a person of his time; he synthesized ideas that were in the zeitgeist, and he had the ability to draw them together in a meaningful way to offer a new paradigm for the social sciences. He set the parameters of this new discipline with the theoretical foundation of the actualizing tendency, his theory of personality development, and his theory of the relationship conditions that lead to constructive personality change.

As I have already noted, scholars and practitioners acknowledge Rogers's work, but often in a piecemeal way akin to birds swooping down to pick at a piece of food left on the ground. They take a bit and fly off again, dropping some of it as they go. Many contemporary psychologists would say that Rogers's contribution was just one building block in the edifice of knowledge that they have built around, or on, but what I see is a flock of birds picking away, taking little bits and carrying them off to their own nests. In this way, the holistic and integrated nature of Rogers's theory gets lost. All of modern biology is based on Darwin's theory of evolution, but psychology as a discipline lacks such a foundation. We continue to seek such a foundation, failing to realize that that is exactly what Rogers provided.

The focus of much of my own work has been on how the person-centered approach can underpin a range of contemporary applications, notably positive psychology, trauma psychology, organizational scholarship, coaching, and education. I have developed lines of empirical research into these topics informed by person-centered theory. I believe that the approach has much to contribute to contemporary thinking around human flourishing, offering something unique and much needed in the modern world. It is a way of helping people, but much more than this, it is also a vision for the future of humanity.

Much of modern psychology has no single fundamental philosophical assumption about human nature explicitly underpinning its activities. As a result, research and practice are grounded implicitly, most often in the medical model, but sometimes in psychoanalytical and behaviorist models or the actualizing tendency of Rogerian theory. That this is the case usually goes unspoken and unnoticed. To the person-centered observer, therefore, mainstream psychology seems like a rudderless ship. It offers the semblance of a cohesive and developing body of knowledge, but all professional helping relationships that involve human interactions are ultimately governed by one's deep-seated philosophical assumptions about human nature. Essentially, the objective of all practitioners in psychology or education is either to control and restrict, mold and shape, or empower and free people. These are the implications of the biologically based drives in Freudian theory, the blank slate of behaviorism, and the actualizing tendency of Rogerian theory, respectively. These are fundamental but conflicting theoretical orientations. Many psychologists and others might think of themselves as atheoretical, simply following the evidence where it takes them, but this is a naive position that fails to recognize their implicit assumptions, which, generally speaking, involve the need to do things to other people. But when we dig down into the "whys" of what we do as helpers, we will always find inescapable assumptions about human nature at the core.[46]

. . .

As revolutionary as Rogers's approach was, this is not to paint an unrealistic portrait of the man himself. As mentioned above, Rogers synthesized ideas and brought them together. Early on, he was clearly influenced by his experiences at Teachers College, Columbia University, where he encountered the thinking of the philosopher, psychologist, and educator John Dewey through William Heard Kilpatrick.[47] Kilpatrick was an instructor in the history of education and an influential figure in the progressive education movement of the 20th century. For Kilpatrick, and Dewey, the teacher should not be an authoritarian figure but instead a guide to help children direct their own learning through experience.

Rogers was writing at an interesting time in the history of psychology, and one of his central themes was that of congruence. But such ideas seem to have been in the zeitgeist, with, for example, Leon Festinger writing in social psychology about cognitive dissonance, a similar idea about the importance of seeking consistency. And it was Rogers's student Stanley Standal who developed the ideas around unconditional regard as part of his doctorate work at the University of Chicago,[48] not Rogers himself. The most important concept in Rogers's framework was the tendency toward actualization, but once again, similar ideas were being discussed by others, not least Abraham Maslow, and it is clear that both Maslow and Rogers were themselves influenced by the work of Kurt Goldstein, a major intellectual figure of the time, whom I will say more about shortly.

Rogers was also influenced by the psychoanalyst Otto Rank and the psychologist Jessie Taft, who in the 1930s were at the University of Pennsylvania and the Philadelphia Child Guidance Clinic, respectively. Taft had been a student of Rank. In terms of Rogers's approach to therapy, his biographer, Howard Kirschenbaum, writes that Taft was the person who influenced him the most, with her similar emphasis on self-organization processes and the role of the relationship. Ivan Ellingham, who has written in depth about this, goes so far as to say that the similarity between Rogers's initial descriptions of non-directive therapy and Rankian relationship therapy was such that the former was essentially "a re-espousal of Rankian relationship therapy," and the therapeutic casework carried out by Taft and Rogers's original form of the non-directive therapeutic approach were essentially one and the same.[49]

This is not a criticism—Rogers himself clearly acknowledged the influences.[50] Scholars will always be influenced by each other, and everyone works within a zeitgeist. But it is clear that he wasn't the lone genius who developed his approach out of nothing; rather, he was able to synthesize ideas in new, creative, and meaningful ways. That was his strength, his genius. As Robert Kramer wrote,

> By teasing out Rogers's close affinity with Rank, however, I do not intend to diminish in the slightest the genius of Carl Rogers, whose contribution to psychology is extraordinary. For me and countless others in the helping professions, Rogers remains, without exaggeration, "the most influential psychologist in American history."[51]

Rogers began to lift what he was doing out of the discipline of psychology and make it an approach that was available to everyone—social workers, educationalists, business and management people, the general public. Although Rogers began a process of lifting his approach out of, and differentiating it from, the mainstream psychological and medicalized approaches of the day, it was not a task he ever accomplished fully. His approach is still too much associated only with the therapy profession and the language of psychiatry, hindering people from seeing its true transformational potential.

Certainly, Rogers was truly revolutionary in ensuring that therapy did not become the sole province of medicine, and he opened the door to a broader audience, but in disseminating the approach so widely and so early in its history, I wonder if it became too diluted. Out of all his accomplishments, bringing the person-centered approach to a wider audience might have been Rogers's biggest mistake in terms of the longevity and credibility of his work. Eugene Gendlin wrote the following:

> To learn this method of therapy requires some years of practice, supervision, and consultation, but academic education does not help. That led (and Rogers followed where it led) to the conclusion that one does not need degrees to be a therapist . . . Why not train church workers, nurses, mothers, teachers—anyone—to be a therapist? There was no inherent reason not to, and irrelevancies did not stop him.
>
> Although millions were trained, Rogers did not win this war. Rather than really sensing each point, the method was simplified. It became verbal repetition . . . The method ended up discredited. This listening is hard to learn.[52]

To this day, the approach appeals to those who value its practice—the openness to others' experiences and its non-judgmental attitude to whatever a person brings. But for those who only see that side of it, it can all seem just too woolly-minded. And for those who practice it, the truth is that if it slips free from its intellectual rails, it can indeed become too woolly-minded. What needs to be understood is that this is a form of practice predicated on a very clear theory and that the wheels of practice must be kept in contact with its intellectual rails.

Concluding comments

If this book is a map of the person-centered approach, this chapter would be the point at which we slide the map out of its folder and open it up to get our first overview of the terrain. As I have shown, Rogers evolved his ideas and approach over time, most notably his use of the term *non-directivity*, which became *client-centered* and then *person-centered*. This represented a shift from initially describing what his approach was in terms of what it did not do to describing what it did and then recognizing its broader applicability. But despite the change in terminology, the essence of the approach did not change. It remains non-directive and based on the idea that people are their own best experts. By the end of his life, Rogers was most interested in the wider applications of his ideas, the potential of which remains relatively unexplored. Having sight of the terrain ahead, the next chapter will provide the detail of Rogers's theory of personality development, the foundation of the approach.

Chapter 2

There is nothing so practical as a good theory

A theory of therapy, personality, and interpersonal relationships

One of the original founders of social psychology, Kurt Lewin, famously said, "There is nothing so practical as a good theory."[1] I would argue that Rogers's theory provides a brilliant illustration of Lewin's quote because once a person understands the theory, and if they accept its validity, then practice follows naturally. In this chapter I will discuss Rogers's theory of personality development and begin to explain how it underpins the practice of the person-centered approach. In the previous chapter I gave an overview of Rogers's career and the history of the approach, describing how dipping into any article or book of his could be confusing until one can see the whole of the theory and understand each piece in its historical context. Over several decades, Rogers was a prolific author of academic papers and books. For students new to his writings who may be wondering where to start, at the beginning of his writings or at the end, the answer is somewhere in the middle.

Introducing Rogers's theory

Rogers first began to introduce his ideas in the 1940s, but client-centered therapy only really became firmly established in the 1950s with the publication of *Client-Centered Therapy* in 1951.[2] This book might seem like the perfect starting point. Certainly it conveys the spirit of the approach and why the person-centered therapist holds that the client is the best expert on themselves. In it, Rogers outlines his theoretical views at that time.

Importantly, the book positions client-centered therapy as a perceptual theory and a phenomenological approach. It is thought of as a "perceptual" theory because Rogers declared that reality as experienced by an organism is determined by its perceptual field: "We live by a perceptual 'map' which is never reality itself."[3] In therapy, when the perception changes, the behavior of the

The Humanistic Psychology of Carl Rogers. Stephen A. Joseph, Oxford University Press. © Oxford University Press (2025). DOI: 10.1093/9780197790632.003.0003

individual changes. Therefore, all behavior will make sense once we begin to understand it from the point of view of the individual themselves. This is a very important takeaway message from his book, and if there is a first steppingstone into the approach, this is probably it.

But in 1951 Rogers's ideas were still in development. In my view, the best starting point to understand Rogers is not actually *Client-Centered Therapy* but a chapter he wrote in 1959 for a book edited by Sigmund Koch, *Psychology: A Study of a Science.* The chapter, titled "A Theory of Therapy, Personality, and Interpersonal Relationships, as Developed in the Client-Centered Framework," is Rogers's defining theoretical work. Certainly, he went on to write much more in the coming decades, but this was largely to unpack and explore the significance and applications of the ideas that had by then already been developed. Previous writings can be seen in the context of a theory in the process of development, and subsequent writings as the further unpacking and unfolding of all its applications, not only in therapy, but also beyond the therapy room. When I refer to Rogers's theory in these pages, it is this 1959 work that I am pointing toward.

An earlier version of his theory was published in 1951, in his book *Client-Centered Therapy*, in a chapter entitled "A Theory of Personality and Behavior" in which he described the 19 Propositions.[4] This is where he sets out the perceptual nature of his theory, and it is certainly worth reading, but I am skipping over this here because, in my view, the 1959 chapter is the place to start for anyone wanting to get to know Rogers's theory. It is the more developed and definitive version of Rogers's theory. In my experience, students new to Rogers can find it confusing to dip in and out of his various writings unless they understand them in their historical context as a work in the process of development.

In those early years of the 1950s, Rogers was still largely occupied with therapy. His approach was radical and still is to this day, for one simple reason. In most therapies, the therapist's aim is to do something to provoke change in the person sitting in front of them. That is not the case for the person-centered therapist. The person-centered therapist's only aim is for themselves, namely that they are genuine, accepting, and empathic. They should have no other objectives for the person in front of them. That must surely be one of the most radical ideas ever: to help someone change, you must get out of their way. You get out of their way so that they are free to change in whatever direction they choose. But if that sounds passive—as if the therapist is doing nothing—take a few moments to imagine what a genuine, accepting, and empathic relationship feels like if you are in it. By being genuine, accepting, and empathic, the therapist gets out of the way while being deeply present and in relationship with the client, creating the freedom for them to move in a new direction. Think how rare it is in life to find ourselves in a relationship where we feel free to move in any direction we choose or to have the freedom to find our own direction—to live our lives in a way that feels true to ourselves, to be congruent.

More often, we find ourselves in relationships that feel false, with people who have expectations about how we should be and take no time to understand us. Whether at work or with family or friends, such relationships are common in everyday life. And often, because of our roles in life, we ourselves create such false relationships for others. Maybe we are aware of this but feel we have no choice, or perhaps we no longer recognize the inauthenticity in ourselves (see Box 2.1).

Box 2.1 Reflection: Are you free to be yourself?

Think about the relationships in your life, the people you consider close friends, work colleagues, and family members. To what extent do you feel you have to put on an act, a facade, with the people in your life to fit in? Are there some people with whom you feel you can never be yourself? Who in your life do you feel completely free to be yourself with? What would your life look like if you could be completely free to be yourself? What would you do differently?

What does it mean to be true to ourselves? Rogers discusses this idea at great length because it is ultimately what his theory of therapy is about. His approach is a way of helping people come to understand themselves better, to live more harmoniously within themselves and with others. As I said in the previous chapter, the wheels of practice need to be kept in contact with the intellectual rails of the theory, the foundation of which is that human beings possess an inherent tendency toward actualization.

Actualizing Tendency

Rogers's theory is built on the meta-theoretical foundation that human beings have a basic propensity and potential for self-organization, self-regulation, and growth toward the realization of their full potential.[5] According to Rogers, we are striving to become all that we can be. He referred to this directional force of becoming as the actualizing tendency, which he described as follows in his 1959 chapter:

> the inherent tendency of the organism to develop all its capacities in ways which serve to maintain or enhance the organism. It involves not only the tendency to meet what Maslow terms "deficiency needs" for air, food, water, and the like, but also more generalized activities. It involves development toward the differentiation of organs and of functions, expansion in terms of growth, expansion of effectiveness through the use of tools, expansion and enhancement through reproduction. It is development toward autonomy and away from heteronomy, or control by external forces.[6]

A helpful analogy for the actualizing tendency is the way gravity affects a falling apple. The apple will simply move in the direction of the ground unless intercepted by other forces. People likewise will move toward the development of autonomous determination, expansion and effectiveness, and constructive social behavior unless something impedes them. This involves meeting needs for hunger, thirst, and so on, as well as seeking mastery over the environment around them. Think of an infant in her crib crying out for sustenance and reaching out to touch bright objects: these behaviors are the expression of the actualizing tendency. Rogers argued that this tendency was the one natural motivational force of human beings and that it was always directed toward constructive growth.

The growth model, as it is sometimes referred to, is a familiar theme across a range of humanistic psychologies,[7] but Rogers's theory best encapsulates it. It is important to clarify what the idea of growth means. When humanistic psychologists are talking about growth, they mean it as a biological process in which living creatures strive to develop to their best potential. This is different from the other way that *growth* is often used, which is in an economic sense, meaning that something is getting larger. We can talk about the economy growing or the statistical growth in the national prevalence of an illness over time, for example. When humanistic psychologists are talking about growth, they mean it as a way of understanding human experience, not simply as an increase in a state, but in the sense of development, maturation, increasing complexity, and a natural propensity toward the fulfillment of their potential.

In humanistic psychology the idea of growth as a biological process is a familiar idea with a long and distinguished heritage throughout the 20th century, going back to the writings of Goldstein, whom I mentioned briefly in Chapter 1 and who deserves to be singled out as a major influence, notably through his book *The Organism*, published in 1939.[8] Goldstein worked with soldiers with brain injuries during the First World War, and his observations of these men led to his conclusion that the organism always behaves as a unified whole, not as a series of differentiated parts, and that organization is the natural state of the organism. With the soldiers, his observation was that the men were not simply the same as they had been minus the brain damage, but that the organism reorganized itself to incorporate the damage. For Goldstein, self-actualization was the master motive behind the self-organizing processes of an organism. Many times, Rogers cites Goldstein's work and notes his influence.[9]

For Rogers, the tendency toward actualization was the one motivation for change and the foundation of his person-centered approach. In 1961, in his book *On Becoming a Person*, he put it this way:

> It is the mainspring of life, and is, in the last analysis, the tendency upon which all psychotherapy depends. It is the urge which is evident in all organic and human life—to expand, extend, become autonomous, develop, mature—the tendency to express and activate all the capacities of the organism, to the extent that such activation enhances the organism or the self. This tendency may become deeply buried under layer after layer of encrusted psychological defenses; it may be hidden behind elaborate facades which deny its existence; but it is my belief that it exists in every individual and awaits only the proper conditions to be released and expressed.[10]

A few years later, in 1963, in a chapter entitled "The Actualizing Tendency in Relation to Motives and Consciousness," Rogers wrote again about how he viewed the actualizing tendency as the basic and sole motivation of people and how since he had first written about these ideas, he had discovered that they were supported by biological research. He also notes how his theory includes responses to the needs in Maslow's hierarchy, such that the tendency toward actualization may lead to the seeking of food or sexual satisfaction. In this way, all behavior is motivated by the actualization tendency. It encompasses other concepts such as drive reduction, tension reduction, and need reduction. This is important because the concept of actualization is often misunderstood as something that happens only after these other more basic needs have been satisfied, but that was not what Rogers meant. For Rogers, as he wrote in this 1963 chapter, it is only ever about the tendency toward actualization:

> We are, in short, dealing with an organism which is always motivated, is always "up to something," always seeking. So I would reaffirm, perhaps even more strongly after the passage of a decade, my belief that there is one central source of energy in the human organism; that it is a function of the whole organism rather than some portion of it; and that it is best conceptualized as a tendency toward fulfilment, toward actualization, toward the maintenance and enhancement of the organism.[11]

So the actualization tendency is the core theoretical construct in Rogers's theory—no other drives or motives need to be introduced, and this one concept of the actualizing tendency can be seen in all behavior. For Rogers, the person-centered approach was based on an image of the person who can be trusted to find their own direction not only as an individual, but also socially. As he said at a conference in his famous dialogue with Martin Buber, the Jewish theologian, in 1957,

> One of the things I have come to believe and feel and experience is that what I think of as human nature . . . is something that is really to be *trusted* . . . I'll try to put it in another way. It seems to me that orthodox psychoanalysis at least has held that when the individual is revealed, when you really get down to what is within the person, he consists mostly of instincts and attitudes and so on which must be *controlled*. That runs diametrically contrary to my own experience, which is that when you get to what is deepest in the individual, that is the very aspect that can most be trusted to be constructive or to tend toward socialization or toward the development of better interpersonal relationships.[12]

The last line of the above quote points to an example of Rogers's clarity in his writings that the actualizing tendency was directed toward socially constructive behavior. It is important to emphasize this because it is an aspect of his theory that is often misunderstood by critics who claim his theory encourages selfishness in people. Person-centered theorists do not accept that people have an inbuilt selfishness. Indeed, some person-centered theorists, such as Renate Motschnig-Pitrik and Godfrey Barrett-Lennard, have developed the idea of "co-actualization" to extend the actualizing principle to the level of relationship systems, based on a belief that people have a natural tendency toward forming constructive relationships and that these have their own self-developing qualities.[13] Another oft-cited but incorrect criticism of the actualizing tendency is that it implies that people are born good. But that puts some moral value on the theory that was not intended. The actualizing tendency is a biological tendency, not a moral imperative. It is important, therefore, not to be idealistic about what the approach can achieve. As John Shlien and Ronald Levant wrote in 1984 of the growth motive,

> Growth is a "positive" force, but it is neither good nor evil in a moral sense. Client-centered therapy is *hospitable* to the idea of goodness; client-centered therapy has witnessed goodness produced at choice points in successful outcomes; but neither the theory *nor* the therapy can be held to prove the essential goodness of human nature.[14]

A related criticism is that Rogers's approach suggested a more "Pollyanna" view of life than was realistic. Again this is a misunderstanding. Central to Rogers's theory is that the actualizing tendency often becomes thwarted and usurped, such that people self-actualize in more destructive and dysfunctional directions. Below I will discuss this in more detail.

How the actualizing tendency becomes thwarted and usurped

As we have seen, the idea of the actualizing tendency is that people strive for autonomy and self-direction in which they are free to be themselves in a way consistent with a view of human nature in which people are inclined toward being socially constructive rather than destructive. In reality, however, it is a tendency that can be easily thwarted. Famously, in his 1977 book *Carl Rogers on Personal Power*, Rogers told a story from his childhood about a potato bin in the basement of the family farm where he grew up. It was here that the family stored its winter supply of potatoes. The bin was several feet below a small window. Rogers noticed how, unlike the healthy green shoots that potatoes sprout when planted in the soil, the potatoes stored in the basement produced pale, white, unhealthy-looking sprouts:

> These sad, spindly sprouts would grow 2 or 3 feet in length as they reached toward the distant light of the window. They were, in their bizarre, futile growth, a sort of desperate expression of the directional tendency . . . They would never become a plant, never mature, never fulfil their real potentiality.[15]

Thus, his is as much a theory of how people become distressed and dysfunctional as it is a theory of how people reach the heights of their potential. He goes on to compare these spindly sprouts with patients he had seen on the wards of psychiatric hospitals:

> So unfavorable have been the conditions in which these people have developed that their lives often seem abnormal, twisted, scarcely human. Yet the directional tendency in them is to be trusted. The clue to understanding their behavior is that they are striving, in the only ways available to them, to move toward growth, toward becoming.[16]

In this example, Rogers illustrates how the concept of the actualization tendency applies to understanding human distress and dysfunction. While the direction might be toward maintenance and enhancement, in the realities of day-to-day living, that direction is more often thwarted, even resulting in psychiatric hospitalization. These might be the more extreme examples, but the actualizing tendency can be thwarted and usurped in everyone to a greater or lesser extent. Our *self-actualization* invariably conflicts to some degree with the realization of our full potential (see Box 2.2).

Box 2.2 Reflection: Using the metaphor of the tree

In this exercise you will draw a tree to represent yourself. Take a blank sheet of paper and some colored pens, and at the very bottom of the page, start by drawing a tiny acorn. Then think of yourself when you were a child around the age of seven and begin to draw a small tree, taking up no more than half of the page, that represents you at that age. When you have done this, think of yourself now and draw yourself as a fully grown tree. Don't worry about drawing over what you have already drawn. Use the rest of the page to draw yourself as that tree. Don't think too much about the task or how tall, full, leafy, or upright the tree is; just let the tree take whatever shape it has. Once you have finished, take some time to reflect on how what you have drawn represents you and your life experiences.

The actualization conundrum

In Rogers's theory, *self-actualization* means something very different from the term as used by Maslow and how people generally understand it. Maslow used it to refer to a state in which a person is optimally adjusted. But in Rogers's theory, self-actualization simply refers to the realization of the person's *self-structure*, which he defined as

> an organized configuration of perceptions of self which are admissible to awareness. It is composed of such elements as the perceptions of one's characteristics and abilities; the precepts and concepts of the self in relation to others and to the environment; the value qualities which are perceived as associated with experiences and objects; and the goals and ideals which are perceived as having positive or negative valence.[17]

This confusion about the meaning of the term *self-actualization* is one of the most common stumbling blocks people encounter in learning about Rogers's theory. It's understandable given that Maslow's theory is so widely known, but some of the confusion originates in Rogers's own works. He initially used the term *self-actualization* in his 1951 book in a similar way to Maslow to suggest movement toward optimally functioning behavior, but when he finalized his theory, he was no longer using it in this way.

"The Actualisation Conundrum" is a paper by Tony Merry in which he further discusses this shift in Rogers's use of the term. As I've said, it is best to look at everything up to the 1959 chapter as a work in progress and to consider the chapter as providing the definitive version of his theory, in which he defined self-actualization as how the tendency toward actualization expresses itself as a sense of self, taking into account the ways in which it has been thwarted.[18] Thinking about the reflective exercise in Box 2.2, the tree that you have drawn represents how you have self-actualized.

The psychiatric patients in the above example would be said to have self-actualized in a way that seemed twisted and scarcely human. The term *self-actualization* simply refers to the phenotypical expression: the characteristics of the person resulting from the interaction of their genotype with the environment. In the next section I will unpack Rogers's description of the kind of social environment that thwarts the actualizing tendency and, conversely, the sort of social environment that is supportive. This is a developmental process that primarily occurs in our early years of life. Rogers's theory is therefore a theory of child development, both "healthy" and "dysfunctional."[19] Right from the moment we are born, we respond in ways to seek love and affection from parents, caregivers, and significant others in our lives.

Need for positive regard

The person-centered approach is a developmental theory that proposes that we have a basic *need for positive regard*. Rogers's argument was that the need for positive regard is universal, pervasive, and persistent. Contemporary evolutionary psychologists would concur with this notion because, if we are to survive, it makes sense that we need to build bonds and a sense of belonging with those around us. The need for positive regard is a much stronger motivator in early life because the young and developing person needs safety and security that can only be provided by the older members of the community. As in Rogers's potato metaphor, they will reach out in whatever way is necessary for survival.

However, because love and affection from others can be communicated either conditionally or unconditionally, the child learns to regard themselves in one of two ways. *Unconditional positive self-regard* refers to a person's acceptance of all of their subjective experiences—without reference to the perceived attitudes, rules, or values of others—in such a way that they relate to themselves with warmth, compassion, and non-judgmental understanding. Unconditional positive self-regard therefore allows the self-actualization of the person and the actualizing tendency to be coordinated so that there is a "unitary actualizing tendency."[20]

Only through the experience of unconditional regard can a person's need for regard be satisfied such that their intrinsic drive for personal growth and socially constructive behavior is released. As Rogers wrote,

> If an individual should *experience* only *unconditional positive regard*, then no *conditions of worth* would develop, *self-regard* would be unconditional, the needs for *positive regard* and *self-regard* would never be at variance with *organismic evaluation*, and the individual would continue to be *psychologically adjusted*, and would be fully functioning. This chain of events is hypothetically possible, and hence important theoretically, though it does not appear to occur in actuality.[21]

Whereas unconditional positive regard allows the universal motivational force toward growth and development free rein, this directional developmental force is thwarted by *conditional positive regard*. All of us grow up with some degree of *conditional* regard from the world around us—that we are lovable and worthy of affection only if we behave in certain ways that meet the expectations of others. In this way, we learn to look to others for approval rather than inwardly to what Rogers described as the *organismic valuing process* (OVP). This is a person's ability to listen to their own inner bodily wisdom, their intuitive sense of what is right or wrong for them. The OVP guides us to seek out environments that are conducive to our development. Rogers's past student and collaborator Eugene Gendlin went on to develop this idea using the term *felt sense*, which he described as follows:

> A bodily awareness of a situation or person or event. An internal aura that encompasses everything you feel and know about the given subject at a given time—encompasses it and communicates it to you all at once rather than detail by detail. Think of it as a taste, if you like, or a great musical chord that makes you feel a powerful impact, a big round unclear feeling.[22]

It cannot be emphasized enough that it is this notion of the actualizing tendency that underpins the approach and its central inherent principle of non-directivity in therapy and other applications. People connect to this tendency through the OVP. The tendency toward actualization is the theoretical foundation of the person-centered approach. The implication is that the client knows best. This is not to say that when people come to therapy, they are not feeling confused, lost, or disoriented. It is a more complex notion that as organisms we know what is right for us, as expressed in this idea of the OVP, or felt sense, or more colloquially in the idea of "knowing in one's gut." Most of us have some awareness that important personal things can be felt physically in the body; sometimes it might be a discomfort in the stomach when we are frightened, a lump in the throat when we are challenged, a pounding heart when we are excited, or the sense of being in a fog when anxious (see Box 2.3). Because of this, in the person-centered approach, there is the assumption that people have it within them to know what their own best directions in life are. But it must be emphasized that this is not thought to be an easy process for most people as they become alienated from their OVP. It is something that needs to be learned anew, that comes for people when they are in relationships that are unconditionally regarding.

Box 2.3 Reflection: The felt sense

To what extent would you agree with the following statements?

- I can trust what I sense inside myself.
- I make sure to find time in my day-to-day life to check my inner sense of just how I am.
- When talking to someone, I check with my bodily sense to know the right things to say.
- When I face a problem, I listen inwardly to get a sense of what I need to do.
- When worrying about things, I pause and step back to listen to my feelings.

The more you agree with the above statements,[23] the more likely you are to be aware of your "felt sense" and be comfortable with it and able to act on it.

Conditions of worth

Imagine that a smiling infant reaches out to her parent but, in doing so, knocks over a hot drink that the parent has. Luckily, the child is not hurt, but the parent is scalded and reacts in shock, pushing the infant away, toward safety. The infant is confused and interprets this experience in her limited, age-related way—perhaps that she should not seek attention—one more minor event in a series of hundreds of thousands yet to come that will all be part of the developmental experiences that shape how she understands herself in the world. Think of the ways in which parents and other caregivers talk to their children and how they give conditional messages, implicit or explicit, about what is expected from them if they are to be valued. These are referred to as the *conditions of worth* that we receive from our parents or other carers, teachers and religious educators, the media and television, and so on.

Conditions of worth—these expectations that originate with others—come to be introjected within our own personalities. The term *introjected* refers to how these conditions begin as external to us, but over time we internalize them as our own. This leads us to become estranged from our OVP, which is now in conflict with our conditions of worth as our guide for seeking environments that are conducive to our health. There is a loss of trust in the evidence of our own senses to determine the value of an experience. What this means is that individuals who, over time, have introjected many conditions of worth become alienated from the actualization tendency and will instead often defer to the judgment of others to determine the value of an experience.

Through this developmental process personality is shaped, and in such a way that by the time most people reach adolescence, they have become alienated from themselves to varying degrees, in the sense of being out of touch with their OVP. So whereas Rogers proposed that the tendency toward actualization was positive and prosocial, self-actualization is not. It simply refers to how the self is realized through the tension that exists between the OVP and conditions of worth. This is not a controversial idea. If love is withheld from a child when he cries, he gets the message "In order to be loved, I mustn't cry." A child who is in pain but pleases her parents by smiling gets the message "To be valued, I must always smile and be happy for others, no matter how much I am hurting" (see Box 2.4).

Box 2.4 Reflection: Conditions of worth

Without thinking too much about it, but just saying whatever comes immediately to mind, how you would complete the following sentences?

To be lovable, I must ...
To be of worth, I should ...
To be valued, I always ...

Think about what your answers might tell you about your conditions of worth. What memories come to mind? Is there a time or place that this prompts you to remember? Can you picture a parent or a relative and what they said or did?

Growing up, if all that is on offer from our caregivers is conditional regard, then that is what we reach out for. All of these messages tell us about what is important in life and what we must do to be valued. Over time, such messages shape a young person and become the defining feature of their personality. All of us introject conditions of worth and, to varying extents, self-actualize in the direction of our conditions of worth rather than how we would have self-actualized if we had received only unconditional positive regard. There are few psychologists who would challenge the idea that this process plays an important role in developmental psychology. But for the Rogerian psychologist, this process is set center stage as the explanatory framework for personality development (see Figure 2.1).

But can such a simple-sounding process really account for the wide range of individual differences in personality? Above, I used the example of a child spilling a hot drink. Typically, such examples are used to illustrate the mechanism that the theory describes, and although helpful, such an example on its own caricatures what is actually a complex process. One has to imagine how this process operates moment by moment, day after day, year after year, to visualize how a person's self-structure is built up from conditions of worth, like layers of an onion as it grows. It can be a relentless process throughout the child's life, continuing into their adolescence and beyond. The deeper layers of the onion are not in the person's awareness or easily accessible to them.

Conditions of worth, such as to please, to be invisible, or to be helpful, can be established within a family, but the family and other caregivers also transmit the values of the culture—both the immediate local culture and the wider culture—such that prejudices and other social norms become introjected. The concept of conditions of worth is a social psychological one because it describes the mechanisms through which society's values are transmitted. In this way, one might talk about gendered conditions of worth or racial conditions of worth, for example. The process of how social values become introjected that Rogers was describing is one that is well established in sociological theory, for which such ideas are central. As Berger wrote,

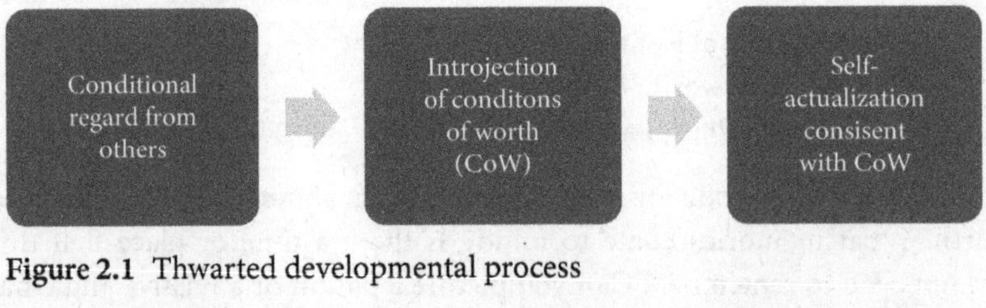

Figure 2.1 Thwarted developmental process

> What happens in socialization is that the social world is internalized within the child . . . Society, then, is not only something "out there," . . . but it is also "in here," part of our innermost being. Only an understanding of internalization makes sense of the incredible fact that most external controls work most of the time for most of the people in a society. Society not only controls our movements, but shapes our identity, our thought and our emotions. The structures of society become the structures of our own consciousness. Society does not stop at the surface of our skins. Society penetrates us as much as it envelops us.[24]

I would argue that it is helpful to understand the sociological nature of Rogers's theory as well as its psychological aspects. Such an understanding of the sociological aspects just makes the usefulness of the theory more explicit.

We can also think about congruence as a personality disposition or a moment-to-moment state. Imagine that there are 100 layers to an onion and that you have managed to peel back the first 10; that is the depth of your self-understanding. It might be said that this is the ceiling of your congruence as a person. But on a day-to-day basis, you may fluctuate in the degree of your congruence up that ceiling. There will always be ever more layers to uncover as our conditioning in society runs so deep.

A universal meta-theory

Rogers's theory describes developmental processes; the role of the social environment in shaping personality; how problems in living, as well as more fully functioning behavior, emerges; and the means through which interventions can be applied at various levels, from the individual to the group, and in different contexts, such as parenting, education, therapy, and management. As a theory, it must be predictive, allowing researchers to design experimental studies. Such a broad theory is unusual in the field of psychology, which is typically characterized by more specific models that only focus on their discrete areas of study. Most psychology textbooks offer collections of unconnected findings and topics. Findings on developmental psychology, social psychology, and clinical psychology, for example, are not joined in meaningful ways. There is a failure to develop a genuinely progressive and incremental science. Person-centered psychology is different.

I will return to this theme of evidence later, in Chapter 8, but for now I want to turn our attention to how this thinking relates to the cross-cultural applicability of Rogers's theory. Recent years have seen the theory criticized on the basis that it comes from a white Western male, with the implication that while what Rogers said might be true for some people, it may be limited in its applicability elsewhere in the world. Certainly one of the difficulties of social science research is that its theories do reflect basic assumptions about reality, which are largely a product of culture and upbringing. So it is valid to ask whether Rogers was able to escape those influences on him. The onus is on all of us to reflect on this question, but I would add that just because Rogers was from a particular time and culture doesn't necessarily mean that the theory lacks cross-cultural applicability.

It may be true that in their writings, Rogers and other scholars did not pay enough attention to cross-cultural considerations. Does that mean the theory needs to be adapted in some way? I can understand how this question might apply to some other theories in psychology, but it misunderstands the nature of Rogers's theory in one respect. The theory is a meta-theory in the sense that it is based on an image of the person and an understanding of human nature, and therefore can be applied to a wide range of topics in psychological science that involve human social interaction.[25] As a meta-theory, the person-centered approach is not bound to any one discipline or culture. It is concerned with all of humanity. If the theory doesn't apply to any one group of people anywhere in the world, it is not that the theory should be adapted; it must be thrown away entirely. The idea that the actualizing tendency is at the heart of human development is either true or it isn't. It can't be that there are cultures in which this theory of human nature applies, but other cultures in which it doesn't. If this were so, it would demolish the notion that this is a universal theory of human nature.

This is not to deny that there are differences across cultures. Each culture creates its own conditions of worth, so although the process of actualization is a universal one, self-actualization is not uniform. It inevitably reflects the individual's family and immediate circumstances as well as their wider social and economic context, for example, the extent to which a culture emphasizes individualism or collectivism. Rogers saw human nature as having both of these aspects. He wrote about how the actualizing tendency is toward autonomous and socially constructive functioning and that it is in our nature to strive toward both. Conditions of worth are social products: in one society we may develop positive regard for ourselves around our ability to be more autonomous; in another society we may develop it around our ability to be more collectively minded. American culture is very individualist, for example, whereas Asian cultures are traditionally more collectivist. We will self-actualize in ways suited to our societal conditions of worth. In this way, the theory doesn't need to be adapted to different cultural contexts, but it does challenge cultures. Where cultures offer extreme views of the person and clash with the theory, it is not the theory that should be adapted, but the culture. This is a countercultural theory in the sense that it values the person and their tendency toward actualization over and above their conditions of worth.

An overly individualist culture that operates at the expense of the collective thwarts a person's development in respect of their need for collective functioning. Conversely, an overly collectivist culture that operates at the expense of the individual thwarts a person's development in respect of their need to become autonomous. The tendency is for the organism to develop itself in all its capacities, but development will be mediated by the social context, such that in one society self-actualization will veer toward collectivism but in another, individualism. Jookyoung Kim, in an article in the journal *Person Centered & Experiential Psychotherapies* also argues for the applicability of Rogers's theory to culturally varying clients, suggesting "...that organismic potentialities of individuals involve the tendencies toward both independence and interdependence that may be manifested by the actualizing tendency in different ways, influenced by different cultures."[26] There is nothing in Rogers's theory that makes it only ever individualist, as some critics seem to think. He is quite clear in his writings that the tendency is toward both autonomy and socially constructive behavior. Self-actualization is always only understood in relation to the social context of the person.

It was not by accident that Rogers's theory and humanistic psychology were part of the counterculture movement of the 1960s. They didn't fit within the Western worldview, either then or now, so it is a mistake to see Rogers's theory as an expression of Western culture. It originated in the West, but it was itself an attack on the prevailing culture. It is also worth noting that while Rogers was an American, those who influenced him, such as Goldstein, were often European.

Rogers's theory is intended as a universal statement of the human condition, and as such we would not expect there to be differences in the general processes as described from one group of people to the next. But I believe it is a mistake to think that the approach is not relevant to other cultures. The fact that it was seen as countercultural at the time of its development opens up a discussion about what it means to criticize the approach for being a reflection of Western culture. And it remains countercultural today, standing against the medicalization of distress and the oppression of people through conditions of worth, and in that way is equally countercultural in many societies across the world. In that respect, as a form of therapy it does not sit easily within many cultures. In saying this I am not denying therapists' responsibility to be aware of the issues and challenges that come with working with people from different backgrounds. After all, that is exactly what is demanded in an empathic relationship.

Thus, the person-centered approach is an expression of counterculture, and it remains so to any culture that operates from a different view of human nature and condones conditions of worth as part of a rigid socialization process. But it is also true that Rogers's writings, which are now several decades old, did not address these issues head-on, but left them implicit. Nonetheless, his theory is a universal one that has cross-cultural applicability because the process of self-actualization is not only unique to the person but a reflection of their culture.

Rogers posited that a tendency toward actualization was inherent in all people, who, as a consequence, are continually motivated toward reconciling the incongruence between self and experience in such a way as to develop, maintain, and enhance the organism. The concept of the actualizing tendency provides the theoretical cornerstone for the person-centered approach. To understand how radical such ideas were at the time of Rogers's writing, and remain today, consider how radically different this approach can be from the ways in which other people, systems, and organizations typically respond to us. As David Brazier wrote in 1993 in his book *Zen Therapy*,

> The bedrock of Rogers' philosophy was the notion that the person is a living experiencing organism whose basic tendencies are trustworthy. It is still difficult for most people in the modern age to appreciate how revolutionary this simple idea is. It is not until we start to consider how much of our energy in modern society is spent on building and maintaining structures, the primary purpose of which is to eliminate the (dangerous) human element from human interactions, that we begin to get a glimpse of how radical Rogers' vision was and still is.[27]

Continuing with my argument that it is misleading to caricature Rogers's theory as a product of Western culture that fails to account for cultural diversity, I would also point to how the theory offers a worldview that is similar in many ways to Eastern worldviews such as Buddhism.

Imagine what it would mean if a person's experience and self-structure, as Rogers describes them, were perfectly aligned, such that there was no incongruence whatsoever. This to me implies a state in which there is only experience and the awareness of it, without any distortions in perception. Seen like this, the person-centered approach is based on a theory of non-self, consistent with much Buddhist thought, although this aspect of Rogers's theory is often misunderstood. There is no definite self in Rogers's theory except for that which arises through the introjection of conditions of worth. The sense of self is therefore always a social construction, and therapy is a process through which it is dismantled and rebuilt. In a 1991 article entitled "Characteristics of the Self-Actualized Person: Visions from the East and West," published in the journal *Counseling and Values*, Raylene Chang and Richard Page wrote the following:

> Zen Buddhism, like Taoism, emphasises that all people possess an inner perfection, a Buddha-nature. The intent of Zen Buddhism is to help people attain *satori*, an inner state of perfection or tranquility. When one becomes enlightened (or attains satori), one's entire personality merges with nature, or reality, and a state of perfect harmony is experienced . . . To become free from negative feelings such as fear, anxiety, insecurity, and frustration or from inhibiting ideas or imaginations, it is necessary for people to experience themselves without division.[28]

To me that sounds similar to what would be expected in Rogers's theory if self and experience were ever to be in perfect alignment, that is to say, full congruence. In the book *On Becoming a Person*, Rogers mentioned Lao-Tzu and the Eastern philosophy of the *Tao Te Ching*. Rogers returned to this theme in 1973 in an essay entitled "My Philosophy of Interpersonal Relationships and How It Grew." The word *tao* means "way" or "path." This refers to the natural order of things, the creative processes present in nature, and is achieved through *wu-wei*, described as actionless activity. Many writers have since discussed the similarities between the non-directivity of the person-centered approach and the philosophical concept of doing nothing and being natural in Taoism.[29] In their discussion, Chang and Page wrote how Taoism, Buddhism, and the theories of Maslow and Rogers

> have congruent elements because these theories reflect something universal about human experience . . . It may be that there exists an inherent tendency toward self-actualization that can be expressed in a number of different ways, always within the context of a particular culture.[30]

We are used to seeing the world using certain categories, thinking from the point of view of the medical model. Think about how psychological interventions are typically about trying to change the person, making decisions about what is best for them, and finding ways to cure them in line with expectations of how they should be. The challenge in learning about the person-centered approach is to trigger a perceptual shift in how one sees the social world. It's like the famous perceptual illusion where you are presented with a picture of a duck, but as you stare it, suddenly you see it as a rabbit. The duck is all the assumptions, beliefs, and values that are packed into our pre-existing way of seeing human experience, whereas the rabbit is all the assumptions, beliefs, and values packed into the person-centered approach that we come to see. In teaching about the approach over many years, I have found that it takes time to see the rabbit.

The person-centered approach is deceptively simple, so much so that it is easy to read chapters in textbooks and think you understand what it is all about—but this can be misleading. It is a parsimonious theory but one that unfolds into practice in complex ways. The thing that is hard to grasp is that the person-centered approach is an alternative lens through which to look at the world. The word *paradigm* is often overused to refer to new ideas and practices, but its real meaning is that of a worldview underlying the theories and methodology of a particular scientific subject. Within the history of psychology, the growth model of person-centered psychology represented a genuine paradigm shift from the first and second forces in psychology: the behaviorist image of the human being as a blank slate on which anything could be written and the psychoanalytical view of the human being as driven by destructive impulses.

This is one of the reasons why the approach is often described by its proponents as radical and revolutionary. This description stems from the fact that the person-centered approach runs counter to much of contemporary culture and social conditioning about, for example, what education is, what therapy is, and what to expect when seeking help. Twenty-five years ago I thought I understood the approach, but as my learning deepened, I realized I had only been standing in the shallows. Each year as I read, write, and practice, my learning deepens, such that I feel that I could go on for another 25 years still growing and developing my appreciation of the nuances of the approach and how it overturns so much of what I thought. Our social conditioning goes so deep within us that it cannot be easily overturned. To unpack all the assumptions, values, and beliefs that we have previously learned in order to see the world anew can be a lifelong journey.

I mentioned earlier that there is often confusion over the term *self-actualization* and that this confusion came about through the reading of Rogers's earlier works, where he uses the term differently from how he came to use it by the time he wrote his 1959 chapter. As a result, it is understandable that many scholars and critics continue to misunderstand Rogers's theory because while his 1951 book continues to be widely read, his 1959 chapter is much less so. In 1980, Rogers himself famously wrote in his book *A Way of Being* that his 1959 chapter was "the most thoroughly ignored of anything I have written."[31]

Later in the same paragraph, he added that it did not concern him that the 1959 chapter was not as widely read because he was wary of how theories can become dogma. This was a point that he made several times in different ways throughout his career: that he saw his theory as something that should be given the opportunity to develop and evolve. I would agree that this should be the case, but it is important to understand what that means.

The 1940s and the early years of the 1950s were an exciting time for the development of the theory as it was constantly being updated and modified as new evidence and experience accumulated. But by the late 1950s the theory had been consolidated into what we are still familiar with today. So the theory is a set of scientific hypotheses about human development and human relationships, and it is only through testing those hypotheses and finding them wanting that new hypotheses are introduced and tested. When new evidence presents itself, the theory can be amended. It is a rigorous process, and to this day, Rogers's 1959 theory remains to be refuted. It is a parsimonious theory, able to offer a depth of analysis on human development, various problems in living, and how people can be helped to live better lives. I don't take Rogers's statement about dogma as an invitation to ignore the scientific method but to engage in it, openly and honestly.

In his 1959 chapter, he described the actualizing tendency, the fully functioning person, and how authenticity emerges by being freed from conditions of worth. This is a growth model about human potential, the process of awakening to our emotional and psychological maturity as human beings. We become more attuned to ourselves, more open to experience, existential in our living, and creative in navigating the world and fulfilling our needs, and as we develop inwardly, we expand outwardly, becoming more empathic and accepting of others and harmonious with the world. These are observable and measurable characteristics of people. Rogers's theory is firmly grounded in a scientific 'if-then' style of writing, in which he describes the process of human development driven by the actualizing tendency as a biological imperative, and how it can be thwarted and promoted.

As already noted, Rogers' described his theories of personality and helping clearly in his 1959 chapter, and it is this work that is considered his most comprehensive, but there was one further notable development that came almost two decades later. In a 1978 article in the *Journal of Humanistic Psychology*,[32] Rogers described the tendency toward actualization as part of a wider formative tendency, which refers to a wider force in the universe towards development, order, differentiation, complexity, and interrelatedness. As Rogers wrote of the formative tendency:

> In humankind it extends from a single cell origin to complex organic functioning, to an awareness and sensing below the level of consciousness, to a conscious awareness of the organism and the external world, to a transcendent awareness of the unity of the cosmic system, including people.[33]

This notion of the formative tendency, which Rogers introduced toward the end of his career, is sometimes overlooked as relatively unimportant. But it was the one theoretical idea that he introduced after 1959 that substantially modified his theory. It is an intriguing and controversial part of his work. For some it takes his theory too far, but for others it is a recognition that Rogers wanted to put his work into a wider context. Jeffrey Cornelius-White, a leading authority on

Rogers's work and the person-centered approach, wrote about how critics often misrepresent Rogers's views on the actualizing tendency as having an individualist bias, whereas understanding it as part of the formative tendency further helps to highlight how it is relational and ecological.[34] Cornelius White wrote this about the implications of the formative tendency"

> ...then the responsibility of person-centered practitioners shifts to releasing the natural tendency of not just individuals, but groups, other organisms, and perhaps most importantly the ecology...the formative tendency helps us realize that 'everythingisconnectedtoeverythingelse' in such a way that our ethical obligation must be greater than to the individual.[35]

The formative tendency also takes Rogers's work into the realm of transpersonal psychology, that branch of psychological scholarship that is concerned with the spiritual and transcendental aspects of human experience. Indeed, it is likely that Rogers introduced the notion of the formative tendency, at least in part, to take it in this direction, because that seems to be what he felt was missing from his earlier writings. In 1980, Rogers described transcendence experiences as "concomitants of the person-centered approach."[36] He wrote, "Our experiences in therapy and in groups, it is clear, involve the transcendent, the indescribable, the spiritual. I am compelled to believe that I, like many others, have underestimated the importance of this mystical, spiritual dimension."[37]

As such, for some the formative tendency extends the application of Rogers's theory in new and exciting ways that are yet to be fully developed, but for others it is seen as a step too far, a sign that Rogers had taken his work in mystical directions, something that increasingly interested him in his later years.

There are those who argue that ideas about the actualizing tendency and a formative tendency are irrelevant to person-centered practice, which they justify by what they see as the ethical rightness in viewing each person as entitled to self-determination. While I can agree that each person has a right to self-determination, I disagree that when it comes to a deliberate helping relationship that such ideas are irrelevant. For me, the notion of the actualizing tendency is the first premise justification for practice. It provides an explanatory mechanism for why non-directive relationships are expected to lead to more fully functioning behavior. But as a scientific theory, we can more easily test whether the experiences of our senses is consistent or not with the notion of an actualizing tendency,[38] much less so with that of the formative tendency. Ultimately, these are constructs developed to make sense of the world and of being human and should be subject to critical interrogation, with the intention of developing ever more realistic understandings of ourselves and the world we live in, a topic I will return to in chapter 8.

Concluding comments

The heart of Rogers's approach is his meta-theoretical view of human nature, which led him to focus on the inner resources of the person—be they psychotherapy clients, students in education, or persons in other contexts—and how, under the right social conditions, they will be intrinsically motivated to self-organize, seek out knowledge to satisfy their curiosity, and pursue goals that are meaningful to them. Rogers's theory makes a very clear hypothesis about the direction and nature of change that unfolds in people when they experience the right social environment. This sometimes leads critics to call him naive, as if he was proposing that people will always behave in good and trustworthy ways. But that is to misunderstand his theory, which is about how personality development gets thwarted. This will be a theme of the following chapters, in which I will begin to unpack in more detail how person-centered practice reflects this view of human nature.

Chapter 3
Three characteristics of the person-centered approach
Social environment, self-determination, and fully functioning

The first clinical psychology practitioners worked under the direction of psychiatrists. The main role of these early clinical psychologists was to administer tests rather than to conduct therapy, which was done by the psychiatrists themselves, who were trained in medicine and, at that time, influenced by psychoanalysis. This led clinical psychologists to adopt the methods and assumptions of their psychiatric counterparts. At the outset of his career as a clinical psychologist, Rogers would have been subject to these expectations, and when he was appointed as the director of the Child Guidance Clinic in 1939, there was criticism from the psychiatric establishment, which did not think a clinical psychologist was fit to be in such a role. Rogers challenged this with the development of his new form of therapy. In hindsight, we can see that clinical psychology was at a crossroads.[1] Rogers and many others in the humanistic psychology movement took one road, but as a wider profession, clinical psychology took the other. Clinical psychology did not so much challenge the influence of medicine as fall under its spell. To the present day, the illness ideology has been a pervasive influence on the professions of psychology and psychotherapy.[2] To truly appreciate the person-centered approach as a countercultural force, one has to understand the prevailing cultural context of the illness ideology and how the person-centered approach took a different road that challenges it in three ways.

Rogers initially described his approach by saying what it was against, namely the directivity of traditional therapy. To recognize something, we need to look at the object against its context, the figure–ground phenomenon, and in this case we need to be able to see Rogers's approach against the background of the illness ideology.

To explain this ideology, it is helpful to imagine our own experiences when, for example, we go to see a medical practitioner with an ailment such as stomach pains. We are likely to be uncertain what the cause of our pain is and be anxious

The Humanistic Psychology of Carl Rogers. Stephen A. Joseph, Oxford University Press. © Oxford University Press (2025). DOI: 10.1093/9780197790632.003.0004

for our practitioner to accurately identify the problem and quickly provide the correct solution. To do this, the practitioner needs to be an expert diagnostician. They need to examine us to identify our specific symptoms in order to diagnose the most likely cause, so they need to have knowledge of the likely conditions we may be suffering from and the symptoms of each. They will ask us questions about the nature of our pain, its location and duration, and physically examine us for bruises, swelling, and so on. Having reached a diagnosis, they will be in a position to prescribe the correct treatment, which will depend on what condition they think we are suffering from. The diagnostician is a scientist-practitioner in the sense that their diagnosis is a hypothesis. Only the right treatment will make a difference. Thus, our practitioner will need to monitor us for a period of time to see if our symptoms abate. If they do, this would seem to confirm their initial hypothesis. If our symptoms do not abate, then the practitioner will develop a new hypothesis to explain our continued symptoms and provide a new prescription. This process continues until we are symptom-free. An incorrect diagnosis could be the difference between life and death for us, so the more skilled the practitioner is as a diagnostician, the better they are at their job.

By adopting the medical ideology within psychology, the assumption is that psychological problems are like medical problems: they, too, require expert diagnosis in order for the right treatment to be prescribed. Such a way of thinking is illustrated when one looks through many of the standard textbooks in clinical and abnormal psychology. Typically, the chapters of such books are structured by disorder. Each introduces the reader to the research on, for example, anxiety disorders, somatoform and dissociative disorders, mood disorders, schizophrenia, substance-related disorders, sexual disorders, personality disorders, and so on. The purpose is to show the novice that these are the various conditions a person can suffer from and what the appropriate treatments are for each.

The professional clinician is trained in the use of the American Psychiatric Association's *Diagnostic and Statistical Manual of Mental Disorders*, which is now in its fifth edition and which describes the range of psychiatric disorders and the detailed procedure for the diagnosis of each. For each diagnostic category there are various psychometric tests that are available to aid in diagnosis and to facilitate research. Diagnostic categories provide a common language for researchers as they examine the causes, correlates, and most effective treatments for each disorder. As a result, the most influential research strategy in clinical psychology is driven by the diagnostic process as information is sought to understand each disorder and to determine which treatments are most effective. The implication of the diagnostic system is that each client is treated as representative of the category to which they are assigned by diagnosis. There are three defining characteristics of the medical model in practice.

First, medical ideology locates the source of people's problems within them. In psychiatry, for example, biological causes are often sought. Because clinical psychology was initially developed in the context of being a servant to psychiatry, it is not surprising that it inculcated these ideas of looking within the person for the origin of their difficulties. Clinical psychologists may not emphasize biological factors to the same degree as psychiatrists, but they do focus on cognitive processes that are internal to the person.

Second, in adopting the diagnostic system, each client is treated as representative of the category to which they are assigned by diagnosis. This is entirely appropriate from the perspective of the medical ideology when dealing with physical complaints. But what it means is that the role of the practitioner is to be an expert on the diagnostic categories, to be able to use them and thus determine what the patient needs. In this way, it is the practitioner who knows what is best for the patient.

Third, the medical model defines a successful outcome as the absence of negative symptoms. In the medical model the clinician is interested in curing what is weak and defective about people and alleviating the suffering caused by the illness. Seen this way, the therapist is the expert on what the patient needs, and rightly so. But also, taking the medical analogy further, their focus is inevitably on what is not working properly or is broken within the patient and how to cure it.

Generations of psychology graduates have now been inculcated in this medicalized way of thinking to such an extent that it has become deeply ingrained among today's psychologists. This was my own experience as a new graduate. But are psychological problems really the same as medical problems?

Psychology as a discipline is over 100 years old, and during its existence hundreds of thousands of scientific articles and books have accumulated. But has it made real progress? I am not sure it has. In my view it took a wrong turn about 60 years ago when clinical psychology—still largely in its infancy—chose the medical model over the growth model of humanistic psychology.[3] Rogers and the other humanistic psychologists challenged the traditionally accepted parameters in psychology, including the model of a practitioner, taken from medicine.[4]

One of the misunderstandings about the person-centered approach is that it is positioned against the medical model. But what it is against is simply the misapplication of the medical model. If a person has a medical condition, then they do need expert help from someone who can diagnose and provide the right treatment. You can be sure that if I have a physical illness, I will not be railing against the medical model but rather seeking help from an appropriate medical consultant. But if I am confused about the direction of my life, anxious about the decisions I am making, struggling to find meaning and purpose and to work out who I am, I don't want to be treated as if I am ill. I'm sure many of those who are prescribed medication by their doctor for how they are feeling are facing challenges of this sort in their careers and relationships. This is not to say that how they are feeling as a result is not real. They may be very distressed indeed and having trouble managing their lives, but it is not an illness in the medical sense that they are suffering from.

What the person-centered approach challenges us to do, especially in the context of Western culture, is ask the question of whether the ways people suffer psychologically are actually valid as medical conditions. It says that if we look deeper behind the various labels that are used to describe psychological suffering, often what we will see are not illnesses but actually more existential concerns and struggles to find meaning and purpose and to be true to oneself.

The person-centered approach focuses on the client as expert on what is best for them. It is interested in the constructive and healthy potential of people, and it is concerned with social systems and how external forces act on the person. Because of this, it is in direct opposition to the medical model in three ways.

First, Rogers described how normal human development could be thwarted by the controlling and conditional socialization processes external to the person that I described in Chapter 2. In this way, it looks outside the person rather than within the person for an understanding of how problems in living arise.

Second, the practitioner informed by humanistic and existential perspectives needs to understand the world from the client's unique point of view, as opposed to seeing them as representative of a diagnostic category. As already noted, the emergence of this line of thought was explicitly influenced by humanistic psychology, and most notably by the client-centered school of thought developed by Rogers. In the cultural context of the time—when it was assumed that the therapist was an expert on the client's mental world—considering that people might be their own best experts represented a challenge to the establishment of the day. Rogers originally referred to his approach as non-directive therapy. He did so because he believed it was the therapist's task to follow the client's lead, thus challenging the then-dominant therapist-directed approach of psychiatry and psychoanalysis, which was to direct the course of therapy by using interpretative methods to derive solutions for the patient. In 1951, with the publication of *Client-Centered Therapy*, Rogers turned the notion of the therapist as the expert upside down, arguing that the therapist should follow the client and help them to uncover their own solutions. So whereas the medical model requires the therapist to know what questions to ask in order to determine what is best for the client, the person-centered practitioner aims to help clients understand for themselves what they need and how to move forward in life.

Third, Rogers used the term *fully functioning* to describe what therapy freed people to move toward. It was not a description of the absence of negative qualities, but a description of positive qualities, for example, being more able to live in the present in a more existential fashion, being less defensive and open to experience, and as a result having trust in themselves to know their own best directions.[5]

In summary, the person-centered approach is about changing the social environment, respecting people's self-determination, and living more authentically. In the following sections I will unpack in more detail each of these three characteristics.

Social environment

In the previous chapter, I described Rogers's personality theory and went on to show how it underpins his theory of helping relationships. For Rogers, it followed that if people are less than fully functioning because of their social environment, then providing them with the optimal social environment would be necessary and sufficient for constructive personality change. Given the optimal social environment, the person's intrinsic motivation toward becoming more fully functioning would do the rest. It makes sense that if it is through the introjection of conditions of worth that people become distressed and dysfunctional, then social environments that counter this previous conditioning will be healing. In his groundbreaking 1957 paper, Rogers described six conditions that he held were necessary and sufficient for positive therapeutic change (see Box 3.1). He was not describing behaviors that one person does to another but rather a way of being in the world and with other people that changes the nature of the social environment.[6]

Box 3.1 The six necessary and sufficient conditions for constructive therapeutic change

1. Two persons are in psychological contact.
2. The first, whom we shall call the client, is in a state of incongruence, being vulnerable or anxious.
3. The second person, whom we shall call the therapist, is congruent or integrated in the relationship.
4. The therapist experiences unconditional positive regard for the client.
5. The therapist experiences an empathic understanding of the client's internal frame of reference and endeavors to communicate this experience to the client.
6. The communication to the client of the therapist's empathic understanding and unconditional positive regard is to a minimal degree achieved.

Importantly, Rogers wrote, "No other conditions are necessary. If these six conditions exist, and continue over a period of time, this is sufficient. The process of constructive personality change will follow."[7]

This constructive personality change is initiated by the self-righting process that results from being in an unconditionally accepting environment. But for this to happen, the client must *perceive* themselves to be in such an environment. Importantly, what Rogers proposed in his statement was that not only must unconditional positive regard be communicated by the therapist (condition 4), but it must also be perceived and experienced by the client (condition 6). If you have ever had therapy yourself, you might ask yourself how much your experience of it is described by these six conditions, especially whether you perceived yourself to be empathically understood and unconditionally and positively regarded.

In person-centered therapy, unconditional positive regard is understood to be the healing factor.[8] As we saw in the previous chapter, this is because if people's problems arise from their introjections of conditions of worth, resulting in their conditional self-regard, then experiencing unconditional positive regard can begin to reverse this prior conditioning.

Unconditional positive regard is, however, a hugely misunderstood concept that is often conflated with "liking" someone, but it is not about liking. Positive regard refers to a warmth and kindness that one has toward a person as a reflection of one's general attitude toward humanity. Unconditional positive regard refers to the consistency of this regard over time. The therapist does not fluctuate in their regard for the other person. Rather, their level of regard is consistent regardless of what the other person does or says. As an example from life outside the therapy room, think of a friend who sends texts. One day they end their messages with two *X*'s, and another day with none, as if they are withdrawing their warmth from you at times to express some silent disapproval. Sometimes, as shorthand, the term *acceptance* is used to convey the idea of unconditional positive regard. Certainly unconditional positive regard involves acceptance, but acceptance does not necessarily convey the notions of warmth and consistency.

Unconditional positive regard is an attitude of the therapist, but it must somehow be expressed. It is no good for the therapist to just sit there, smiling and nodding, which unfortunately is sometimes the misplaced caricature of the person-centered therapist. The client needs to feel that they are understood in order to know that they are unconditionally positively regarded. Unless we feel truly understood by another, how can we be sure that they are accepting of us? Unconditional positive regard is communicated through empathy (condition 5). As Rogers wrote,

> Empathic understanding is always necessary if unconditional positive regard is to be fully communicated. If I know little or nothing of you, and experience an unconditional positive regard for you, this means little because

> further knowledge of you may reveal aspects which I cannot so regard. But if I know you thoroughly, knowing and empathically understanding a wide variety of your feelings and behaviors, and still experience an unconditional positive regard, this is very meaningful. It comes close to being fully known and accepted.[9]

Empathy is the therapist's attempt to show their understanding. That is to say, to demonstrate that they are able to sense what the client's experience is like: to understand the client's perceptions from their point of view—their ideas, meanings, and emotions—and, importantly, communicate this such that the client feels understood. In one of his posthumous articles, Rogers wrote that empathy was often misunderstood:

> It is regarded as passive when you just sit back and listen. To be really empathic is one of the most active experiences I know. You have to really understand what it feels like to this person in this situation . . . To really let oneself go into the inner world of this other person is one of the most active, difficult, and demanding things that I know.[10]

Empathy means that we are able to see the world from the other person's *frame of reference* as if we were the other person, but without ever losing the "as if" condition.[11]

The term *frame of reference* is important. As a form of therapy, Rogers's approach is grounded in the client's perception—their reality—because it is thought that only if perceptions change will behavior follow. Rogers argued that the only way we can understand another person's behavior is to see the world through their eyes. Then, even the most seemingly bizarre behavior will make meaningful sense.

But to truly have an unconditional attitude and the ability to empathize with others is rare. These qualities can however be developed. Being more congruent, Rogers maintained, leads to the development of a greater attitude of unconditionality toward oneself and others and the ability to empathize with others. Congruence of the therapist (condition 3) means being aware of one's inner experiences, thoughts, and feelings without denial and distortion and being able to express these openly and honestly, when appropriate, but also knowing when to hold back. It is important to understand that Rogers did not mean that congruence is an all-or-nothing variable, rather that it is a sliding scale, one that we can move along from moment to moment. No one is completely congruent all of the time, but the therapist must be more congruent than the client in those moments of therapy.

Incongruence of the client (condition 2) is explained as consisting of an incompatibility between underlying feelings and awareness of those feelings, or an incompatibility between awareness of feelings and the expression of feelings. For example, someone who appears anxious to an observer but is unaware of feeling anxious would be said to be incongruent in terms of their underlying feelings and their awareness of those feelings. Someone who is aware of their anxiety but says that they are feeling relaxed would be said to be incongruent between awareness and expression. Incongruence is likely the result of psychological development when there has not been a unitary actualization tendency as discussed in the previous chapter.

Empathy, unconditional positive regard, and congruence are sometimes referred to as the "core conditions." However, this term may have become unhelpful because it implies that these three conditions are more important than the others, when, in fact, the theory can only be understood by taking into account all six conditions. The therapist is not a magician, and Rogers understood that these three conditions are not enough by themselves. Notably, condition one (two persons are in psychological contact) refers to a precondition that if not met, would mean that the following five conditions were redundant. By psychological contact, Rogers meant whether or not the two people are aware of each other and that the behavior of one impacts on the other. So, for example, if someone were in a catatonic state, it would be difficult to judge whether there was psychological contact. A client who is in a highly dis-associated, agitated, or angry state may not be able to engage with the therapist sufficiently to be in contact. For the relationship to exist, there has to be some degree of exchange between the parties in such a way that they impact on each other.

Thus, rather than referring to the core conditions, it is more useful to think of conditions 3, 4, and 5 as therapist attitudes or the "practitioner conditions." As I've described above, each of these three conditions plays its own role. The theory suggests that unconditionality of positive regard allows the freedom for change.[12] For the client to experience unconditional positive regard, however, the therapist has to do more than merely sit passively. Their unconditionality and positive regard are transmitted through their empathy. But empathy is not an act that can be performed; it must be real and genuine and is only truly possible in someone who is congruent—who knows themselves well and is more fully functioning. Listening empathically is a process that involves the attempt to seek to understand others, is effortful and challenging, and involves risks of misunderstanding and the continual seeking of clarification.

Rogers believed that if the six conditions existed—but only if all six were present—then constructive personality change would occur, and the more present they were, the more marked the constructive personality change of the client would be. Rogers's work firmly established this encounter between two persons as the heart of the therapeutic process, not a formulaic treatment. In the prevailing therapeutic culture of the 1950s, this was one of Rogers's revolutionary contributions, and it remains radical today. In the face of competence-based manuals, person-centered therapists press home the idea that the conditions must be considered as a whole, not individually. The helping relationship, while it is dissectible in theory, can only exist in person-centered practice as an indivisible entity. The conditions, then, are attitudes to be held, not skills to be applied according to diagnosis. These factors further distinguish person-centered practitioners (and their training) from practitioners of other therapeutic approaches. The essence of person-centered therapy is the congruence of the therapist—their authenticity as a human being—and that requires deep and meaningful personal growth and development, however these are attained. In other words, what Rogers described in the three practitioner conditions is a way of being, not a way of doing.

It is hypothesized that these six relationship conditions are helpful because people are assumed to move in social, constructive, and self-organizing directions toward growth, development, and integrated functioning. For Rogers, the relationship conditions were about empowerment and liberation; he trusted that people would move in constructive directions if given the opportunity. But if this assumption is not held, what would be the purpose of offering an unconditional relationship? Positive regard for another when offered with an intention and a wish to change the recipient in a specific direction is no longer unconditional; it is conditional. Sometimes we can fool ourselves into believing that our regard is unconditional, but with greater congruence in ourselves, we come to recognize our self-deception and that what we have is actually a disguised and manipulative form of conditional regard.

Provided that the conditions of unconditional positive regard, empathy, and genuineness are interwoven, they lead inevitably to the practitioner taking a non-directive approach in which the client is viewed as their own best expert, who can be trusted to find their own ways forward. There is no need for external direction. The imposition of direction from others undermines the ability of people to find their own direction.

Self-determination

Imagine you have a challenging decision to make, such as whether to leave a relationship, begin a new relationship, take a new job, or leave a job. Whatever it might be, where do you seek the wisdom to decide? Certainly, you might ask friends or relatives for their thoughts on the matter, but do you ultimately look to them to tell you what to do, or do you look within yourself? The phrase "the client is their own best expert" refers to this looking within ourselves. But while we know that such decisions are ultimately ours to take, we are often not skilled at looking within ourselves. Therapy helps you learn how to look within, which involves overcoming a lifetime of having learned to look outside yourself.

The idea that the client is their own best expert is complex. It is based on the tendency toward actualization that is the foundation of the person-centered therapeutic approach. That's not to say that when people come to therapy they are not feeling confused, lost, or disoriented. As organisms, we have a felt sense of what is right for us, colloquially expressed as "knowing in one's gut." Because of this, within the person-centered approach is the assumption that people have it within themselves to know what their own best directions in life are, but that this only becomes clearer for people when they are in types of relationship that facilitate their ability to listen to their own inner wisdom.

Self-determination, as understood from the perspective of the person-centered approach, is not about controlling, restricting, molding, or shaping people; it is about creating the right social environment to facilitate people becoming empowered and liberated to find their own directions. The person-centered approach is known for the non-directive attitude that Rogers advocated early on in his career. Rogers wrote the following:

> It is the client who knows what hurts, what directions to go, what problems are crucial, what experiences have been deeply buried. It began to occur to me that unless I had a need to demonstrate my own cleverness and learning, I would do better to rely upon the client for the direction of movement in the process.[13]

Nat Raskin, one of Rogers's colleagues, wrote in 1947 that non-directivity was not a "matter of acquiring technique, but of gradually embracing the conviction that people do not have to be guided into adjustment, but can do it for themselves when accepted."[14] Non-directivity is an ideological position that arises from the practitioner's conviction that humans are intrinsically motivated toward personal development, differentiation, and cooperative relationships when in optimal social environments.

As already noted, Rogers's work is better known for his statement about the necessary and sufficient conditions for therapeutic constructive personality development. In this he hypothesized that providing a positive and unconditionally regarding, empathic, and genuine relationship is the right social environment to facilitate people's movement toward constructive personality development. These relationship conditions provide a safe, non-threatening, non-judgmental social environment that allow a person to function freely, be self-accepting, drop their defensive strategies, and be self-determining. This is more complicated than it sounds because respect for someone's right to self-determination has to be for its own sake, not to achieve another desired goal.

At the heart of Rogers's approach was the focus on the inner resources of the person and how, under the right social conditions, the person will be intrinsically motivated to self-organize, seek out knowledge to satisfy their curiosity, and pursue goals that are meaningful to them. This ontological view of human nature is what underpins the non-directivity of the person-centered practitioner. Non-directivity is a much misunderstood concept. It does not mean "no direction"; rather, it means the practitioner is not imposing their own direction, but helping the client to find theirs. It is as though the client is in a darkened room where there is a thread leading to the door, and they must first find that thread and then, slowly, little by little, learn to follow it until they reach their destination. The therapist knows that if the client is in touch with that thread, they will get to where they need to be, but this is not to say that either the client or the therapist knows where or what that destination is. To be our own best expert is to look within ourselves, to trust in our actualizing tendency, and to follow its thread knowing that it will take us where we need to go.

The idea of the client being their own best expert is axiomatic, therefore, to the person-centered approach and is one of the ways that the approach contrasts with the medical ideology, which holds that it is the doctor who is the best expert on the patient. Rather than looking within themselves, the patient must look to the doctor, who has the knowledge and expertise to diagnose and prescribe the correct solution.

As I write about the medical model, I switch from using the word *client* to using the word *patient*. This is deliberate, of course, as Rogers is known for having introduced the term *client*. At the time this was a revolutionary thing to do as it represented the non-medical ideology of Rogers's new approach. Today, alternative words are often used instead of *patient*, and there is debate over what is the best language to use. But in that debate, the specific meaning of the word *client* as seen from the person-centered perspective is often not understood. I've heard the argument that people who attend for medical treatment are patients and that it is therefore misleading to call them anything else. I don't have much to disagree with in this argument except when it comes to person-centered therapy, as I don't consider it to be a branch of medicine.

I've also heard the argument that what matters is what people want to be called. As one therapist said to me, "I've asked patients if they would prefer to be called clients, but they don't mind what I call them." That particular therapist was not a client-centered therapist, so I have no argument against their doing as they think best. I recognize that it is true that people seeking help don't necessarily care whether they are referred to as patients or clients. But when it comes to person-centered therapy, it does matter. The words we use reflect how we think about the help we offer. The term a therapist uses is important—not because of what the patient thinks, but because of what the therapist thinks. Each of the different terms reflects a different ideology on the part of the helper. The term *patient* implies the language of medicine and puts the therapist in a doctor-like position in which they have expertise on what is best for the patient. It portrays someone seeking help because they are damaged, impaired, and deficient. Whether they realize it or not, psychotherapists who adopt the language of medicine presumably also adopt the assumptions of medicine and thus put themselves in a position in which they feel a need to diagnose in order to provide the right treatment.

In the person-centered approach it is the client who has expertise on what is best for them. Psychological problems are not illnesses to be cured, but states of self and social alienation. In this way, the choice of language matters. The debate is not so much about the word actually used in conversation or about which word people seeking help prefer; it is about how it signifies the way in which the therapist thinks. If, as a therapist, you use the word *client* but really you are thinking *patient*, this does not make you person-centered therapist. It would be better to use the term *patient* but be thinking *client*.

A person-centered therapist simply does not think of the person they offer help to as a patient. Therefore, words like *client* will be more accurate in describing their activity and less misleading to others. The important part is how they, as a therapist, think about what they are doing. In practice, it is not often a big issue in the therapy room. I can see how those who don't know the logic behind it all might see this as a lot of fuss over nothing, as people seeking help generally don't seem to mind which word is used. As a therapist I would not step in to correct or explain to a client that they were using the wrong word. In person-centered therapy it is the client's frame of reference that the therapist tries to stay in, so a person-centered therapist might even use the word *patient*, but they would do so with an awareness of the meanings it has for the client and for their therapy together. It might, for example, convey the all-too-common expectation that the person expects you, as a therapist, to be like a doctor, to ask them questions, to tell them what is wrong, and then to provide the treatment.

The person-centered approach is critical of the medical model, but only when it comes to what we would see as problems in living that have been incorrectly medicalized. We are not critical of the medical model for its own sake, only when it is applied to issues of distress and dysfunction that are understood to arise via the theoretical mechanisms described in the previous chapter. For example, I began this section by asking about leaving a relationship or taking a job, which are common issues that confront us all at one time or another. I imagine the idea that one should look within oneself to work out what to do in those situations seems intuitively obvious, but where is the line drawn? When do the problems in living that are behind our distress and dysfunction become medical problems?

Rogers used the term *non-directive therapy* in his early writings, but he found it a misleading term because it seemed to some to imply that there was no direction. Subsequently, he called it client-centered therapy to better capture the idea that there is a direction, namely the client's. The therapist may offer a non-directive way of being, but that is only in order to facilitate the client's direction. To return to my earlier metaphor, for the client, finding their direction is like seeking a thread in a darkened room and trying to follow it wherever it goes. The client is reaching out in the darkness, stumbling, but eventually finds a thread to grasp and follow. It is not an easy process: it requires inward reflection and self-awareness as the client struggles to listen to their inner wisdom. This is very different from the more clumsy interpretation of Rogers's approach, which would entail asking the client what they want out of therapy at the outset and expecting them to know.

Rogers's pioneering research involved listening to recordings of therapy sessions in order to understand what happens during psychotherapy. He observed a general tendency for clients to change in ways that mean they are becoming more self-directed, for example, by becoming more trusting of themselves (see Box 3.2).[15]

Box 3.2 Ten ways in which people become more self-directed

1. People move in a direction that is away from facades. No longer willing to put on a metaphorical mask, they become more willing to be open about who they are, what they think, and how they feel.
2. They are no longer driven by "oughts" and begin to live life as they see it rather than how they have been instructed to by others.
3. They are no longer willing to do what others expect of them and move away from living a life driven by others' expectations.
4. No longer willing to spend their days pleasing others, they begin doing what pleases them.
5. They begin to choose their own paths in life and their own goals.
6. They become aware that they are not fixed in who they are, but that life is an adventure where things change in new and exciting ways and where one is always learning.
7. Their eyes are opened to the complexities of the world and of themselves as part of it. No longer content with the old certainties, they begin to embrace the richness of life.
8. They move toward openness to experience, seeking to learn and to change and to enjoy the challenges ahead.
9. They become more accepting of others. As they become more open to themselves, they become more open to others.
10. They become more trusting of themselves, daring to feel their own feelings and trust their own sense of themselves and their uniqueness in the world.

Thinking about the 10 statements shown in Box 3.2, to what extent would you say these describe you right now in the way you live your life? Importantly, these are not fixed states of being but are fluid and changing. Rogers described how people move from having what he described as an *external locus of evaluation* to an *internal locus of evaluation* as they become more able to evaluate experiences for themselves. In this way, Rogers's view was that good therapy was a process of learning and change that involved becoming less rigid in our perceptions and opening up to new experiences, and ultimately learning to look within ourselves. In this way it can be said that the client knows best.

The idea that the client knows best does not mean that the therapist does nothing, but rather that they must be the companion alongside the client in the darkened room. Their role is to create the social environment for the client that allows them to look within themselves. The practitioner is not imposing their own direction, but trusting in and helping the client to find theirs. Non-directivity has attracted a significant amount of attention within the field. Brian Levitt suggests that "at its most basic, non-directivity implies being responsive to the client's direction. It implies that individuals have the capacity and right to direct their own therapy and lives."[16]

Non-directivity is a complex concept. A distinction was proposed by one of the leading scholars in the person-centered tradition, Barry Grant, who made an important contribution when he distinguished between two forms of non-directivity: instrumental and principled.[17] Instrumental non-directivity is a technique that is used by a therapist in order to achieve a predetermined outcome: but If being non-directive in that way doesn't seem to achieve the outcome, the practitioner would switch mode to something more directive.

In contrast, principled non-directivity is when the therapist has no intention other than to create a therapeutic relationship (as defined by the six necessary and sufficient conditions described above). Principled non-directivity characterizes the person-centered approach. It requires the therapist to trust in the client's self-healing capacities and their right and capacity for self-direction. There is no planned outcome. The objective of principled non-directivity is not to make something happen; it is to simply accept and respect others just as they are without wanting to change them.

Principled non-directivity, therefore, is based on the radical ontology that the human organism is by its nature directional and socially constructive and can be trusted. However, what it means to practice in a principled way can be a matter of interpretation. Grant wrote the following:

> The paradox of principled nondirectiveness is that a therapist who wholeheartedly lives the attitude may at times appear to be extremely directive. A client may request direction, advice, interpretations, or instructions, and the therapist may offer these. The decision to do so does not depend on a determination of the client's needs, best interests, diagnosis, or learning style. It rests, rather,

> on whether the therapist wants to honor the request, judges himself or herself competent to honor it, and believes it moral to do so. The therapist has no stake in having things come out one way rather than the other.[18]

Grant was making a helpful distinction, but it needs to be emphasized that in making this comparison he is showing what person-centered is and what it isn't. Instrumental non-directivity is never person-centered, but it is what a lot of therapists, and I would add, coaches, do under the mistaken belief that they are basing their work in Rogers's theory. There is not a choice of how to be non-directive because for the person-centered therapist or coach, there can only be a principled approach to it. Instrumental non-directivity is ultimately a directive form of practice.

Having established what is meant by non-directivity, a common question is how it relates to Rogers's six conditions, including the three therapist attitudes. As we have seen, Rogers believed that human nature is basically trustworthy. Seen this way, it is important to understand that the non-directive attitude is not something that "sits alongside" the relationship conditions of empathy, genuineness, and unconditional positive regard. It is not something "additional" that the practitioner has to do. Rather, non-directivity arises out of these conditions. The qualities of unconditionality, positive regard, empathy, and genuineness come together to create the fundamental non-directive attitude of the practitioner, which because of their trust in the agency of the client, means that they do not intervene and have no intention of intervening. Jerold Bozarth wrote this of client-centered therapy:

> The therapist goes with the client, goes at the client's pace, goes with the client in his/her own ways of thinking, of experiencing, or processing. The therapist cannot be up to other things, have other intentions without violating the essence of person-centered therapy. To be up to other things—whatever they might be—is a "yes, but" reaction to the essence of the approach. It must mean that when the therapist has intentions of treatment plans, of treatment goals, of interventive strategies to get the client somewhere or for the client to do a certain thing, the therapist violates the essence of person-centered therapy.[19]

In creating an empathic, positively regarding, unconditional, and congruent social environment, the practitioner is not trying to change the person. They have no agenda for the person whatsoever. By this, I mean that they do not seek to make the person feel better, be more confident, have stronger feelings of self-worth, or any of the many other ways in which therapists or coaches from other schools of thought might aim for the client to change in a specified way. This can be hard for those new to the approach to understand. Surely the therapist or coach must be trying to get the client to change in some way or other? But they are not, because the theory is that in an accepting, positively regarding, and unconditional environment, people will change in constructive ways. Having goals for how the client should change inevitably brings some element of conditional regard that would paradoxically thwart this very process.

Unlike other psychologically based interventions, the person-centered practitioner is not doing anything to the person. Grant used the phrase "taking only what is given"[20] to describe how the client-centered practitioner is not trying to add to, explain, or interpret the words and actions of the client. They seek purely to understand and show that understanding in a way that is empathic, genuine, positively regarding, and unconditionally accepting. The practitioner's only agenda is for themselves to create a social environment that is characterized by these three conditions. The practitioner trusts that, given the optimal environment, the client will change toward becoming more fully functioning. Clues for understanding the world of an individual client cannot be found in books, theories, frameworks, categories, taxonomies, or systems. Here Rogers uses empathy as the keystone for understanding the narrative of the client—the foundation of relationship—not as an instrument of interrogation.

In contraposition to person-centered practice, other approaches use empathy as yet another technique to be introduced at the appropriate time, for a designated purpose of, for example, information-gathering or trust-building. But in person-centered psychology, empathy is the beginning and end of everything. It allows for the therapist or coach to be within the client's frame of reference, to see the world from their point of view. Students often ask if it is okay to ask questions in the person-centered approach. But of course, in truth, there is nothing prohibited about asking questions. It can sometimes be helpful and appropriate to ask questions.

The important learning is about what questions are for. Typically, in other schools of therapy or coaching, questions are used to understand another person's experience from the questioner's frame of reference. A therapist may want to know certain information to make sense of the client's experience in terms of, for example, how well they fit a particular diagnostic category or theoretical framework or to check out an interpretative hunch that they have. This is more likely true of closed- than open-ended questions. The person-centered therapist, however, would rarely use closed-ended questions, although there are exceptions, such as when trying to ascertain risk. For example, therapists working within a professional code of ethics will be obliged to ask questions about suicidal thoughts once disclosed to ascertain the possibility of them being acted upon. Open-ended questions, on the other hand, are often quite appropriate in person-centered therapy in helping the client to explore issues in more depth: "Could you say more?" "What was that like for you?" But such questions used too frequently and without empathy and genuineness can also become platitudinous. For the person-centered therapist, such open questions would be used as an expression of empathic understanding and to help see the world more clearly from the client's frame of reference.

The basis for the non-directivity in the person-centered approach is the actualizing tendency. While non-directivity seems logical given that theoretical assumption, others have made the case for it purely on ethical grounds. But non-directivity detached from its theoretical base is no longer within the scope of the person-centered approach because there would be no reason to expect that it would lead toward more fully functioning behavior.

Fully functioning

Condition 2 of Rogers's six necessary and sufficient conditions is the congruence of the client. *Congruence* is a much misunderstood term, however, often thought to refer to speaking honestly about one's thoughts and feelings. But outward behavior is only one facet of congruence. Barrett-Lennard, one of the foremost proponents of Rogers's theoretical system, wrote about congruence:

> It implies consistency between the three levels of (a) a person's primary experience, (b) their symbolized awareness, and (c) their outward behaviour and communication. The concept is theoretically centred on consistency between the first two of these levels, this being considered the main determining condition for congruence between awareness and communication.[21]

This means that outward behaviors are not necessary expressions of congruence, but may be expressions of incongruence if the person has not symbolized into awareness their primary experiences. Seen like this, congruence is ultimately about self-awareness and self-knowledge.

As congruence deepens, the actualizing tendency is given a release such that the person moves in the direction of what Rogers referred to as fully functioning:

> "The fully functioning person" is synonymous with optimal psychological adjustment, optimal psychological maturity, complete congruence, complete openness to experience . . . Since some of these terms sound somewhat static, as though such a person "had arrived" it should be pointed out that all the characteristics of such a person are *process* characteristics. The fully functioning person would be a person-in-process, a person continually changing.[22]

In a later paper, Rogers described three characteristics of the fully functioning person: they are open to all of their experiences, that is to say, they are sensitive to the world around them, other people's reactions, and their own internal feelings, reactions, and meanings; they live existentially, able to be fully present in the moment; and they are able to trust their feelings and reactions to guide them in their actions.[23] Such a person has a non-defensive attitude and is able to listen to others empathically and unconditionally, communicate clearly and effectively, and respond to situations creatively. Thus, the fully functioning person is someone who is accepting of themselves; values all aspects of themselves, their strengths and their weaknesses; is able to live fully in the present; experiences life as a process; finds purpose and meaning in life; desires authenticity in themselves, others, and societal organizations; values deep, trusting relationships; is compassionate toward others and able to receive compassion from others; and accepts that change is necessary and inevitable.

In this way, Rogers was describing people at their best and moving away from the then-prevalent deficit-based model of human experience, that is to say, rather than focusing on what was wrong or lacking in a person, looking to instead conceptualize what people are striving to become. Soon after I first came to Rogers's work, I heard the term *fully functioning* and learned how he had used this to describe the direction of change in therapeutic and other interventions, but the full significance of the idea did not hit me immediately. I had heard the term, I understood what it meant, and yet I didn't really understand. I had not yet shifted my worldview. As a novice therapist I was still entrenched in an illness ideology. I continued thinking about reductions in, for example, depression, anxiety, and posttraumatic stress. As I have said, becoming a person-centered therapist is about a shift in worldview, part of which is conceptualizing people in terms of their becoming fully functioning. This worldview is about the language we use to describe ourselves and others that recognizes our potential for growth and development, but in finding that language we must go against the grain of all our years of entrenched learning of the more familiar language that underpins the illness ideology.

For instance, recently I turned on the radio to hear a conversation about mental health in children and young people. The discussion was around the incidence of various psychiatric disorders and the availability of help and medication. But we rarely hear such conversations framed in terms of young people's opportunities to be themselves, lead authentic and meaningful lives, and find their direction in life and how we can create a society that genuinely offers those opportunities. One might say that surely that is simply a different conversation. But that is the point. From the person-centered point of view it is the same conversation, using language from a growth model rather than a medical model to talk about the same experiences.

What strikes me when I listen to such conversations about mental health is that those speaking, often senior psychologists, do not seem to realize that they are promoting a particular ideology—an illness ideology—that might help in one way, but in another be a cause of much distress and suffering. In response they might say that one has to use a language that others will understand, and I would agree with that but also add that as scholars and practitioners, we must be able to traverse these different languages and do what we can to challenge an illness ideology where it is applied thoughtlessly and unnecessarily. In the person-centered approach we need to be able to step into a different frame of reference altogether.

In terms of understanding the process of becoming fully functioning, Rogers's theory proposes that when a person develops a self-structure that is congruent between self and experience, they become more able to engage in organismic valuing. Rogers sums this up:

> As the individual perceives and accepts into his self-structure more of his organic experiences, he finds that he is replacing his present value system—based so largely upon introjections which have been distortedly symbolized—with a continuing organismic valuing process.[24]

Able to evaluate experiences in this way, people perceive themselves as the locus of evaluation. But for this to come about, we must first look to the concept of unconditional positive self-regard. In his 1959 chapter, Rogers held that in a social environment characterized by unconditional positive regard, people will develop unconditional positive self-regard. Unhindered by defenses and distortions, they will then self-actualize in a direction consistent with their actualizing tendency toward becoming fully functioning human beings.

Rogers discussed creativity being an outcome of this process of becoming more fully functioning: engaging with life in a creative way and being able to adapt and survive under changing circumstances. Such a person

> would not necessarily be "adjusted" to his culture, and he would almost certainly not be a conformist. But at any time and in any culture he would live constructively, in as much harmony with his culture as a balanced satisfaction of needs demanded.[25]

Importantly, given one of the oft-cited criticisms of the approach, Rogers did not see the fully functioning person solely in individualistic terms, but as someone who was constructive socially.

In later papers, as Rogers optimistically discussed the emergence of people who are more fully functioning as a result of changes in society inspired by the humanistic movement—the "persons of tomorrow"—he described how they would be closer to nature and more ecologically minded, seeing themselves in alliance with nature as opposed to the current mindset, which is one of conquest over nature.[26]

The fully functioning person, however, is not a static state. All of us have, to varying extents, self-actualized incongruently with our actualizing tendency. For some, there is minimal incongruence, while for others it is more substantial, and the more we struggle to hear our inner voice, the more we can be said to be in a state of incongruence. According to this view, the various psychological problems we may experience are manifestations of the internalization of conditions of worth.

In essence, what the theory is saying is that, deep down, each of us possesses an inner wisdom about how best to lead our lives. Each of us has a different best path to take in life, depending on our intrinsic characteristics, strengths, and interests. We all know people who don't seem to have found their path in life. Perhaps we know someone who could have been a brilliant teacher, a compassionate doctor, a talented carpenter, an inspired artist, a great sales director, or any number of other careers, but for one reason or another never found their path in life to take them there. They might be good at what they do but feel that what they do is "just not them." Of course, it's not just about our employment, but this is the major way in which we come to express ourselves and our unique talents in our culture, and it is one of the underlying reasons for whether or not we experience satisfaction in life.

Thus, most of us realize only a fraction of our full potential. We grow up to develop an image of ourselves that we show to the world. We use psychological defenses to stop ourselves from hearing the truth about this image. We don't want to hear evidence that we are not as clever, attractive, witty, handsome, or liked as we tell ourselves we are. For this reason, we don't really get to know ourselves properly. We hide from knowing ourselves because the pain of self-knowledge is too great. We do this in different ways, for example, by distorting the reality of our experiences in ways to fit what we already think of ourselves and the world or by denying events that have happened (see Box 3.3).

Box 3.3 Reflection: Become aware of how you distort and deny

If you were to be really honest with yourself, are there aspects about yourself that you know to be true but you don't like to admit to? Take a few moments to just let your answers come to mind, and write down whatever pops up. Now think about the things that you usually do to stop yourself from confronting these truths about yourself. Typically, people will do things like blame others, eat comforting food, or get busy doing something else when situations arise that challenge them with information that is inconsistent with how they want to see themselves.

Box 3.3 asks you to be really honest with yourself, and in this way is asking you to reflect on aspects of yourself that are on the edge of your awareness. But what about those aspects that are so denied and distorted that they are out of your awareness? In an unconditional and accepting social environment where we feel valued, we can begin to drop our defenses; those aspects will then come into awareness, and we can begin to confront the truth about ourselves. The person-centered approach is focused not just on the alleviation of distress, but on helping to facilitate people to become more fully functioning. For Rogers, a fully functioning person displays attitudes and behaviors in which they are open to experience, able to live in an existential manner aware of the fluid and changing nature of experience, and able trust in themselves to know their own directions in life.

In this regard, Rogers observed that one of the key process changes to occur in more fully functioning individuals is a movement toward increasingly living in the "here and now":

> It involves an increasing tendency to live fully in each moment. Such living in the moment means an absence of rigidity, of tight organization of the imposition of structure on experience. It means instead a maximum of adaptability, a discovery of structure in experience, a flowing, changing organization of self and personality . . . It involves discovering the structure of experience in the process of living the experience. To open one's spirit to what is going on now, and to discover in that present process whatever structure it appears to have—this to me is one of the qualities of the good life, the mature life, as I see clients approach it.[27]

At the time Rogers was writing, in the 1950s, the idea that clinical psychology and psychotherapy should be concerned with helping people flourish was an innovative proposition. The idea of focusing on well-being is no longer controversial, and in contemporary terms, his concept of fully functioning might be described as a form of eudaimonic well-being. In this way, Rogers has come to be recognized as one of the forerunners of modern positive psychology, a topic that I will return to later.

...

To me it seems that only when we are working with each of the above three characteristics in mind can we consider ourselves to be applying the person-centered

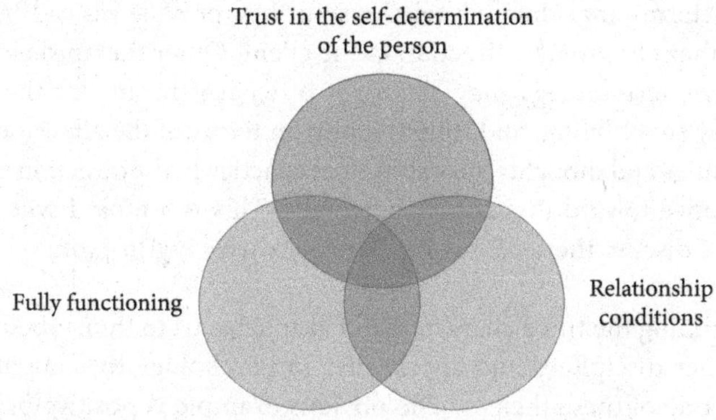

Figure 3.1 Three characteristics of the person-centered approach

approach. That is to say, being person-centered is not only about providing the relationship conditions, but about understanding that the power of those relationship conditions is helpful only because of people's innate tendency toward self-determination and that their direction of change is toward becoming more fully functioning (see Figure 3.1).[28]

The concept of fully functioning is a positive psychological one, as already mentioned, but it is important to note that it is different from many other ideas in positive psychology. This is because it refers to the outcome of an innate process toward certain human qualities that are thought to represent the natural human state, such as becoming more open to experience, more autonomous, and more socially constructive. Fully functioning refers only to a direction of change specified in Rogers's theory, not to other ideas of becoming happier in terms of a life of pleasure and the avoidance of challenging feelings, or fitting better into society's structures, which, as we have seen, may actually be at odds with being more fully functioning.

Having established that the person-centered approach is about the above three characteristics, I hope to dispel some of the confusion that results when the term *person-centered* is used incorrectly to refer to only one of these characteristics. Consider the fable of the three blind men encountering an elephant for the first time. One of them, reaching out and touching the elephant's trunk, exclaims, "I understand the nature of this animal. It is like a snake." The next, touching a leg, cries out in reply, "No, it is like a tree." The third reaches out to touch the ear and exclaims that it is like a fan. Different versions of the fable abound, but the point here is to remind us of the need to see the whole of something. The person-centered approach can be misunderstood when only one part is seen. For example, there are many therapists who value the therapeutic relationship but do not have the conviction that clients can be trusted to be self-determining; thus the relationship they provide instead becomes a vehicle for them to provide direction to the client. Other therapists influenced by psychiatric terminology may lose sight of what it means for the client to become fully functioning, and thinking only in terms of the alleviation of distressing feelings and thoughts, may shift their practice in the direction of helping the client move toward these other outcomes. This is a topic I will return to later when I discuss the tensions for therapists working in more medicalized contexts.

Understanding the three characteristics also helps us to think about how we relate to other disciplines and approaches in psychology that might specialize in only one of these themes. The obvious example is positive psychology, which focuses on the positive, not on the social environment and respect for self-determination. That is not to say that there are not positive psychologists who focus on all three characteristics, simply that as a field of study and practice, it is not defined by them.

The characteristics themselves can be broken down even further when we consider the social environment created by the six necessary and sufficient conditions. Only when all six are taken together do they create a climate of change. Many therapists will say that they are influenced by Rogers's statement about the six conditions, but in a way that is no longer person-centered. Judith Beck, the president of the Beck Institute for Cognitive Behavior Therapy, for example, in describing the complexities of cognitive behavioral therapy (CBT) and how it incorporates the principles of evidence-based treatment manuals, adds that "effective CBT therapists also use excellent Rogerian counseling skills, adapting them as needed for some individuals. They demonstrate empathy and positive regard. They foster a strong therapeutic relationship."[29]

It is true that CBT is often caricatured as interpersonally cold, though it is often not like that at all. Cognitive behavioral therapists do value the role of the relationship, and many practitioners use some ideas derived from the person-centered approach. But note in Beck's quote the lack of any mention of unconditionality and congruence. This might be missed by a casual reader. It is certainly possible to pick out aspects of the person-centered approach and incorporate them elsewhere, but it is not possible to incorporate all characteristics of the approach into other forms of therapy, given that the emergent property of the whole is non-directivity. Seen this way, one can—using the analogy I introduced in Chapter 1—swoop in and take a piece of the theory back to one's own nest. But in doing so, the piece is untangled from the rest of the theory in which it belongs and, in transit, it loses its original meaning. Empathy without unconditional positive regard or congruence is not quite empathy as the person-centered practitioner knows it, and unconditional positive regard with the intention to change the person is a form of instrumental directivity.

As Rogers's biographer, Kirschenbaum, notes, much of Rogers's thinking has been so deeply incorporated into theory and practice in the wider disciplines of psychology and therapy that these ideas now seem like common sense, such that many scholars and practitioners are likely unaware that this is what they are doing or recognize quite how radical his theory actually is. Recent years have also seen the emergence of new therapies and approaches to coaching that echo and replicate, in a new language, what are essentially Rogers's ideas. I am not accusing anyone of plagiarism or intellectual theft as these newer therapies and approaches to coaching are not part of the historical timeline of the person-centered approach but have developed independently, their authors, one assumes, being ignorant of Rogers's work and that of the person-centered approach. But it adds confusion as one needs to be thoroughly knowledgeable and understanding of the person-centered approach to see the similarities and the differences. One of the key learnings is to understand that Rogers's main concepts of empathic understanding, congruence, and unconditional positive regard are separable only in terms of their role as theoretical building blocks. In practice they are tightly intertwined as the strands are in a single rope. When all three are simultaneously and fully held, the medical ideology is fully challenged and the approach can be said to be truly person-centered.

Empathy in the absence of congruence and unconditional positive regard can be the tool of tricksters and used for manipulation. Only when coupled with congruence and unconditional positive regard, bringing honesty and no ulterior motive, is empathy beneficial. In turn, unconditional positive regard without congruence and empathy is not knowing one's own boundaries and becoming a target for victimization by believing anything because one does not know oneself and what one believes or stands for. Transparency and congruence without empathy and unconditional regard is not knowing when to keep quiet and listen and being too self-interested, and is likely to be felt as judgmental. These are all traps that novice therapists can fall into as they find their voice as a therapist, learning to balance holding congruence, empathy, and unconditional regard equally and in tension with each other. What emerges, then, is something that is more than the sum of the parts. The relationship has presence, authenticity, depth; it is growthful, accepting, compassionate, meaning-centered, and spiritual. Such a relationship creates the right social environment so that the process of therapeutic change will be automatic, needing no external direction, and movement will be toward realignment of self and experience, leading to more fully functioning behavior.

Rogers began his career as a clinical psychologist, and his early writings were concerned with therapy, which he developed in the three ways described above. He began to formulate his ideas around non-directivity and self-determination in the 1940s, consolidating his theory around the optimal conditions in the

1950s and describing his ideas about the fully functioning person in the 1960s. Therefore, much of his writings were in the language of therapy and about one-to-one relationships, but beyond the 1960s, having established his framework, his attention expanded to encompass other ways his ideas could be applied.

He considered how the same optimal social environment could be facilitative of growth in a range of contexts. Rogers's approach was about helping people move toward their potential, with no distinction made between helping people move toward their potential and helping them with what might be considered mental health problems—all could be understood from within the same explanatory framework. But as the profession of therapy has become more aligned with an illness ideology, increasingly Rogers's approach is out of step. The profession is no longer recognized as a force for positive change in the way that it once was.

I mentioned earlier that Rogers used the term *counseling* to describe his work because of the resistance from the psychiatric establishment to his use of the word *psychotherapy*. But if Rogers were writing today, I wonder if he might be more drawn toward the term *coaching*.[30] Like therapy, the coaching profession includes a wide range of activities and approaches. But unlike therapy, which has become dominated by the language of disorder and deficit, coaching is focused on positive psychological functioning and the development of potential. Indeed, many ideas in the world of coaching are similar to those of Rogers or, indeed, can even be traced back to his or other similar humanistic schools of thought, although this is not always acknowledged or recognized.

Seen from Rogers's theory, therapy and coaching are about a self-righting process, helpful to people whose tendency toward actualization has already been usurped and thwarted. Of more importance, it might be argued, is that the helping professions expend their energy on upstream interventions to facilitate people's development in the first place, such that the eventual need for self-righting—and interventions by psychotherapists, clinical psychologists, and others—is reduced. This is a topic I will return to later when I discuss the positive psychology movement.

Concluding comments

This chapter draws out the three strands of theory and practice that make Rogers's theory unique: its emphasis on the social environment, the self-determination of the person, and the movement toward fully functioning. It is the combination of these three characteristics that defines the person-centered approach. In this way, the application of Rogers's approach is not about doing something to people, at least not in the way that one usually thinks of when talking about psychological interventions. Rogers proposed that the optimal social environment was one that was experienced as unconditional, positively regarding, empathic, and genuine. In the person-centered approach, the practitioner is not trying to change the person and has no agenda for the person whatsoever, but they trust that, given the optimal environment, the person will move toward greater congruence. This is an automatic process given the right social environment for human nature to do what it does—self-right—and, in that process, trusting in people to self-direct.

In this way, it is an approach that is about the importance of the social environment. However, it is not a social determinist philosophy, but about respecting people's right to self-determination, which is what makes it a radically different form of practice from most other psychological interventions. This can be difficult to understand if looking at the person-centered approach from outside its paradigmatic stance. It can be challenging not to see therapy or coaching as doing something to another person, but imagine if you truly believed that people would only move toward becoming more fully functioning if they experienced themselves in the optimal social environment. It follows naturally that you would stop cajoling, advising, and directing, as you would realize that such behavior raises the other's defenses and defeats your aim for them to change. Instead, by having no aim for the other person, you become able to offer yourself in such a way that the person has no need for their defensive behavior and thus feels free to look within themselves.

Chapter 4
Reconceptualizing psychopathology
Conditions of worth versus breakdown and disorganization

It might seem odd that *psychopathology*, the term used to describe the study of mental disorders, appears in the title of this chapter. To use this term in the context of the person-centered approach may seem contradictory because the person-centered approach doesn't consider the problems in living that people have to be disorders in the usual medical model use of that term. As we have seen in the previous chapter, the person-centered approach is not about treating illness. It rejects the idea of mental disorder, based in an illness ideology that there is something wrong and broken inside the person for which they require expert diagnosis, cure, and treatment if this is not the case.

Rather, the person-centered practitioner is interested in facilitating a process of growth. As mentioned earlier, Rogers thought that moving a person from one side of a diagnostic line to the other was a limited way to think about the outcome of therapy and instead proposed a process of change that he described as having seven stages.[1] The number of stages was arbitrary, used simply for descriptive purposes, because he was trying to convey the fluidity of the process, of movement along a continuum as the person becomes more fully functioning.

Stage 1 is described as the period when a person is in a "state of fixity and remoteness of experience." Feelings are unowned, and problems are not recognized. This is the point at which people are most maladjusted but do not recognize themselves as such; they are unlikely to seek help and may blame others or see others as having problems. As the person moves along the continuum, there is increasingly a loosening of the constructs they hold about themselves, others, and the world, and an increasing ability to describe their feelings until eventually, at stage 7, they deeply experience and understand these feelings and have a sense of ownership and a trust in themselves and an ability to express themselves. The person's self-structure has become fluid and open to revision with experiences that present new information. Change may be along this continuum, but the process is not necessarily linear, although Rogers did posit that once someone is at the sixth stage, it becomes irreversible.

The Humanistic Psychology of Carl Rogers. Stephen A. Joseph, Oxford University Press. © Oxford University Press (2025). DOI: 10.1093/9780197790632.003.0005

There is no need for diagnosis, as already explained, and the seven stages are not intended to be used diagnostically, as the practitioner does not make use of them to inform their choice of treatment, but they are helpful as they give a language to understand the process of change, how people move from fixity of their self-structure to a loosening and fluidity. The process gives us a positive psychological way of relating to what might otherwise be thought of as psychopathology (see Figure 4.1).

It is not, therefore, that person-centered practitioners do not have a way of thinking about problems in living—they have their own terminology and theoretical ideas for how to describe the ways in which people struggle. But because the idea of mental disorder based in an illness ideology is rejected, critics of the approach can misunderstand it as saying that it does not address serious psychological problems, only life's wear and tear, and that client-centered therapy is for the worried well. For this reason, it is important to address how the person-centered practitioner views what others consider disorders. This is not to condone the illness ideology but ultimately to challenge this misperception about the approach and show that psychological problems can be understood in a non–medical model way.

Stage 1. In a state of rigidity and remoteness from experience, unable to recognize problems, feelings are unowned, self-structure is fixed, and unopen to change. Communication is about external events and people.

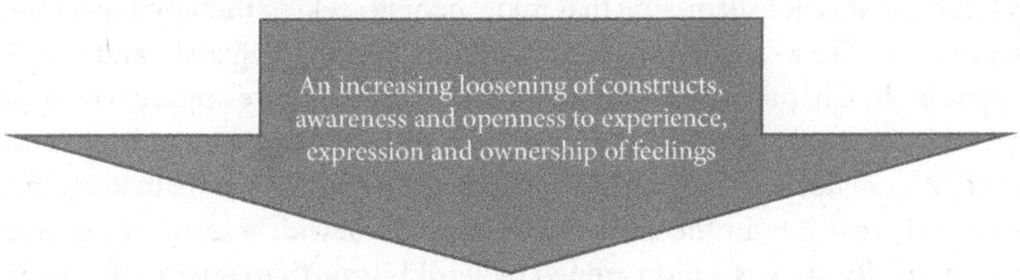

Stage 2. Describes feelings but does not recognize them or own them.

Stage 3. Will talk about self but as an object and in the past tense.

Stage 4. Increasingly experiences feelings in the present but is unsure and distrustful of them.

Stage 5. Increasingly experiences feelings in the present, with an ownership of them.

Stage 6. Accepts feelings and experiences and desires to understand them.

Stage 7. Experiences clear internal communication, flow of expression, fluid self-structure, ownership of feelings, openness to change, reduced anxiety and other bodily manifestations, and contentedness.

Figure 4.1 Summary of the seven stages of process

It is important for the person-centered practitioner to be able to bridge that gap in their own mind between the person-centered theory and medicalized terminology. Clients who come to therapy rarely know much about the different approaches to therapy and do not speak in terms of wanting to explore their conditions of worth or becoming more fully functioning, but they do talk about feeling depressed, anxious, or traumatized.

Those who criticize the medical model and the use of diagnosis are sometimes misunderstood as saying that psychological distress is not real and that people who report difficulties are exaggerating. This is not what it means to be critical of diagnosis. No one is denying that many people experience psychological suffering. What critics of diagnosis mean is that such problems in living are not illnesses in any true medical sense.

To the end of his career, Rogers was set against the medical model of psychiatry. Rogers and his colleague Ruth Sanford wrote the following:

> The single element that most sets client-centered psychotherapy apart from the remainder of this comprehensive textbook is its insistence that the medical model—involving diagnosis of pathology, specificity of treatment, and desirability of cure—is a totally inadequate model for dealing with psychologically distressed or deviant persons.[2]

The idea that therapy is a branch of medical practice has become dominant in our culture, so it is not surprising that many people seeking therapy expect their therapist to act like a doctor, ask them questions, make a diagnosis, and provide a treatment. In Chapter 1, I discussed that it might be more appropriate to see the person-centered approach not as a form of healthcare but as educational practice. We are not so much curing or treating a person as we are helping them to learn and grow. But for the moment, therapy is still widely seen as healthcare.

The *specificity myth* is a term coined by Jerold Bozarth to refer to this widely held assumption of the illness ideology that different psychological conditions require different treatments. Bozarth argues that the wider mental health education and treatment system is founded on the pretense that there is scientific support for the effectiveness of treatment for specific dysfunctions. In contrast, person-centered theorists like Bozarth believe that the specificity myth comes at the expense of offering more relational therapies. Bozarth's conclusion was that effective therapy is due to the relationship between the therapist and the client, and the client's inner and external resources, which implies that techniques in therapy are largely irrelevant.[3] This is a major concern when one realizes that this is the basis on which training and credentials across the psychological and psychiatric professions are judged. Today I would largely agree with Bozarth's view, but when I was a young doctoral student unfamiliar with this alternative view, it seemed self-evident to me that different conditions required different treatments. Just as a doctor needs to be able to distinguish between a heart attack and indigestion, surely we needed to untangle the different manifestations of psychological suffering? Indeed, my doctoral thesis was based around that idea, and thinking back to that time helps me to understand how pervasive this idea is.

In the late 1980s, I was a student at London's Institute of Psychiatry researching the psychology of trauma. The term *posttraumatic stress disorder (PTSD)* had only been introduced recently, in 1980, by the American Psychiatric Association. At that time there were only a handful of us in the United Kingdom who were familiar with the term and the new research that was emerging. *PTSD* is the term used by mental health professionals to describe reactions that cause clinically significant distress or impairment in social, occupational, or other important areas of functioning in people who have experienced a traumatic event. It refers to a familiar constellation of psychological reactions often experienced by people in the aftermath of traumatic events that involve some form of confrontation with death and injury, such as major disasters, technological accidents, road traffic accidents, criminal victimization, sexual assault, war experiences, disease and illness, and political violence.

Typically, people with a diagnosis of PTSD are highly aroused and anxious. They are likely to experience highly distressing thoughts, images, and dreams, while simultaneously trying to avoid anything that triggers recollections of what happened to them. PTSD consists of four symptom clusters. First, people experience distressing recollections, including images, thoughts, and distressing dreams. They may even feel as if the event is happening again, often having "flashbacks," such as feeling as though they are back in the burning car or can smell the body odor of their assailant. Second, people experience problems with avoidance. When they encounter reminders, they may experience distress and feel shaken up. As a result, they often try to avoid these reminders, such as thoughts, feelings, conversations associated with the trauma, and activities, places, or people that bring back memories. Third, people have negative cognitions and disturbances in mood. They may experience changes in beliefs about themselves, others, and the world, leading them to feel that others cannot be trusted or that the world is a dangerous place. Fourth, there are problems of emotional arousal. They may experience difficulties falling or staying asleep, episodes of reckless or self-harming behavior, irritability or outbursts of anger, hyperalertness, an exaggerated startle response, and difficulty concentrating. When the above problems last for more than a month, a diagnosis of PTSD can be made.

It was exciting as a new student to be at the forefront of a new line of inquiry into this clinical phenomenon. As we were at the Institute of Psychiatry, not surprisingly, my research, that of my peers, and that of the staff around us was into topics of clinical concern. We were all studying topics such as anxiety, depression, schizophrenia, and, in my case, PTSD, trying to understand the nature of each of these disorders, their causes, and how best to treat people who were suffering from them. I got to know the details of the diagnostic category of PTSD, and I began writing about the topic and researching alternative ideas about how the symptom criteria should be arranged. It was a largely unquestioned assumption for me at that point in my career that this was important work because we had to understand the nature and presentation of this condition to be able to refine our research tools for developing and testing new treatment procedures. There was debate about the relationship between the intrusive and avoidant components of posttraumatic stress disorder and how they should be conceptualized, a topic I spent much time on. There was also debate about the specificity of some symptoms as they had an overlap with other clinical disorders. Guilt, for example, was included as a symptom of PTSD but was also common in depression. Future definitions of PTSD would therefore remove the symptom of guilt in an attempt to create clear differentiation between these two disorders. This type of work appealed to me in the same way that a jigsaw puzzle would engross me. Even now I feel tempted to prolong this section to go into the detail, but instead I will return to the thread of my discussion about how I was immersed in a worldview based in a medical ideology.

I enjoyed the intellectual challenge of thinking about the nature of PTSD and how best to conceptualize it, and for a while it was a main interest of mine. However, I did not question the validity of what I was doing. It seemed obvious to me that this should be the starting point for investigation into any clinical issue, and so the *Diagnostic and Statistical Manual of Mental Disorders*, which described the different psychiatric diagnoses, was a useful resource. If different disorders required different treatments, then reliable and valid diagnosis was vital for scholars and clinicians to communicate with each other about what they were doing and what worked and to develop their procedures.

As I settled into this new environment I began to wonder about a career in clinical psychology. A clinical psychologist was, as I understood it then, someone who had a knowledge of a range of clinical conditions and was able to offer whatever was the most appropriate treatment for each, in the way I have described above. I was full of admiration for such people. By the end of my doctorate, I had taken up a post as a lecturer in social psychology, but I was still thinking about a clinical career. For two or three years in a row, I toyed with a half-completed application, but I never submitted it. As a PhD student, many of my peer group had followed that path and were carving out successful careers in clinical psychology, and I felt the pull to do the same. And yet, I also felt a battle within myself as time went on. I was reading more and more psychotherapy literature and beginning to understand in greater depth the differences between clinical psychology and the traditions of psychotherapy, especially those of the humanistic and existential schools, which greatly appealed to me. These seemed to be approaching the topic of trauma and helping in a different way, in which it wasn't so much the technique—the specific treatment used by the therapist—that was important, but the human relationship of warmth, empathy, and wisdom about life and suffering. As I immersed myself more deeply in my reading about humanistic and existential psychology, I felt I was discovering ideas and perspectives that had been lacking for me up to that point and that I now began to see were lacking in the profession of clinical psychology.

Later in my career as a person-centered psychologist, I looked back at this time and I could see that the person-centered approach was not taken seriously by clinical psychologists because it seemed of no relevance. Person-centered therapists were told they lacked the theory and skills to work with people suffering in these ways. The major texts of that time on PTSD did not reference person-centered theory or therapy. This was not surprising because client-centered therapists do not adopt the language of the medical model and the assumption that specific conditions require specific treatments. Therefore, there was little written by person-centered scholars that might show they had the ability to work with such clients.

Thus, my question was whether Rogers's theory could explain the development of PTSD. Extending that question, could Rogers's theory also explain all the other conditions? Person-centered therapists tend to avoid psychiatric terms because of their theoretical position in relation to the medical model. But the consequence is that others, and perhaps the therapists themselves, do not know if the therapy they offer is useful to people who are diagnosed with that condition and who seek help for it. Thus, it seemed a valuable exercise to be able to understand if and how person-centered theory might be applied to understanding these different psychiatric conditions. Confronted by critics who misunderstand the approach, we have to enter their frame of reference and use their language to articulate how the approach can provide an explanation for psychopathology, especially as those critics are often in positions of power and influence over funding and employment. But the idea that one theory alone could account for so much diversity in the presentation of people's suffering—is that possible?

A transformation in my thinking and worldview took place gradually over about five years, the result of which ended up in my 2005 edited book with Richard Worsley, *Person-Centred Psychopathology*, in which we asked our contributors to write about the person-centered approach in relation to psychopathology, and more recently the *Handbook of Person-Centred Therapy and Mental Health*.[4] The problem as I saw it then was that if you are within a dominant culture that adopts the medical model, and you don't, your voice will go unnoticed. This was certainly the case for person-centered practitioners when they were told that they were not equipped to work with trauma patients. We needed to spell out how the person-centered approach could be applied to such concepts as PTSD, not by condoning the concepts but by dismantling them and reimagining them anew from a person-centered perspective. As when you are in a foreign country, it is helpful to speak the language. Since then we have seen others tackle similar exercises, such as Pete Sanders and Andrew Hill in their influential book *Counselling for Depression*, recently updated by David Murphy.[5]

I have touched upon how psychopathology is considered from the person-centered perspective. Here I will go into more depth, beginning with a discussion of how Rogers's theory proposes that problems in living are usually considered as either arising from conditions of worth or through the process of breakdown and disorganization.

Psychopathology arising from conditions of worth

As we have seen in chapter 3, problems in living are expressions of alienation that arise through the thwarting of the actualizing tendency, as expressed famously by Rogers in his example of the potato shoot in a darkened room and how it would grow to be several feet in length but be spindly and thwarted in its development.

None of us can escape the influences of the world around us. Whereas the theory of the tension between the actualizing tendency and conditions of worth is universal, the specific nature of that tension is unique to each of us. In the same way that each acorn has the potential to be the best oak tree it can be, no two acorns germinate in the exact same environment. No two oak trees are identical. And no one oak tree is ever the perfect expression of the potential that was held in its acorn: every tree will have been thwarted to some degree, through drought, lightning, wind, and so on, but it will be the best expression of its potential that it could be, given its circumstances. It is the same with people.

Rogers did not deny that human behavior is often destructive, but for him such behaviors were not innate but the result of hostile interpersonal environments that thwarted the inherent tendency toward actualization, diverting it away from its otherwise socially constructive and agentic direction. In essence, as we have seen, when the infant behaves in accord with introjected values, as if those values were their own, they are considered to be acting in a way that is consistent with a condition of worth. The infant is now no longer acting on their intrinsic, organismic valuing of experience. Gradually, the distance between personal valuations and feelings is increased and a state of incongruence between organismic experience and self-concept arises. Such incongruence will often manifest in ways that those using psychiatric language would describe as symptoms of anxiety or as depression (see Box 4.1).

Box 4.1 Case study: Depression as seen as an expression of conditions of worth

As a child, Fiona's conditions of worth were to do well at school. She learned to work hard at school to please her parents because to do otherwise, she believed, would result in the loss of their positive regard for her. This is not to say that Fiona was aware that this is what she was doing. She had introjected the values of her parents so that she came to value herself only insofar as she succeeded. Although she grew up to be successful in her career, she felt that something was not quite right. She didn't enjoy her work, and as she began to listen more closely to herself, she began to realize that, deep within her, the values she was living were not her own but those of her parents, or at least the messages that she had introjected as a young girl about what was important. Throughout her adult life, Fiona had tried to live up to these values that she had internalized in childhood, and although successful in her career, her satisfaction with life was low, and she was often irritable with those around her, had low mood, and would drink heavily to help her cope with her feelings. It was through her diagnosis of depression that she entered counseling, through which she began to realize that the things that mattered to her—her freedom of expression and creativity—she had left behind long ago in childhood in favor of the things that seemed to matter to other people. She felt that while her career had been relatively successful, what she was doing had little meaning or interest for her, and she increasingly felt that she had wasted her life. In this example, Fiona's experience was initially identified as depression—a way of describing her feelings and thoughts—but ultimately what she was going through was an expression of how thwarted she felt as a person, incongruent within herself, leading a life that wasn't authentic.

People's conditions of worth are held so strongly and deeply that their actualizing tendency becomes usurped, such that they self-actualize in a direction

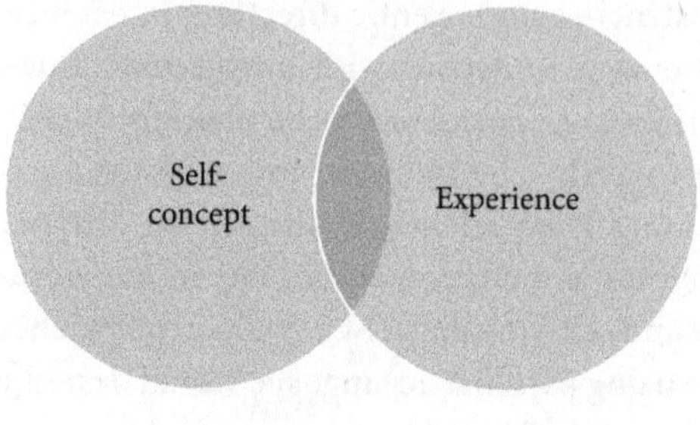

Figure 4.2 Congruence

The greater the overlap, the more the congruence. The less the overlap, the more the incongruence or maladjustment.

consistent with their conditions of worth as opposed to the actualizing tendency. Rogers said the following in his 1959 chapter:

> This, as we see it, is the basic estrangement in man. He has not been true to himself, to his natural organismic valuing of experience, but for the sake of preserving the positive regard of others has now come to falsify some of the values he experiences and to perceiving them in terms based only on their value to others. Yet this has not been a conscious choice, but a natural—and tragic—development in infancy.[6]

This quote from Rogers captures the essence of the theory and how it explains people's difficulties in living. Incongruence between self-concept and experience is considered to be the single source of maladjustment. This can be illustrated as a simple Venn diagram, where the greater the overlap, the more congruence there is between self and experience; the less overlap, the greater the maladjustment (see Figure 4.2).

In other words, person-centered theory is about how people become estranged from themselves. At first glance, this seems a narrow definition that readers might think excludes the numerous conditions for which people often seek help, such as low self-esteem, depression, anxiety, worry, and stress. But for the person-centered theorist, these are simply the different ways in which people experience their incongruence. It should be noted that while Rogers's views on human nature differed greatly from the traditional Freudian views, when it came to Freud's theory of psychopathology, Rogers's theory describes a similar mechanism. Experiences of incongruence are threatening to the self-structure, leading to anxiety and triggering denial and distortion in how the person sees themselves and the world. Distortion is a defensive process in which experience is changed so that it is brought into awareness in a way that is consistent with the self-structure. Denial is another defensive process in which threatening experiences are not allowed into awareness. In this way, the self-concept is maintained as part of the self-actualization processes working against the tendency toward actualization.

Incongruence and resultant processes of denial and distortion give rise to the wide variety of presenting issues. In Box 4.1 I gave a brief example of the problems faced by Fiona, but such examples are limited in conveying the depth and richness of the idea. It can be hard to understand how what seems like such a simple idea can lead to such a variety of complex presentations. But imagine that conditions of worth are the layers of an onion, built up through social interactions starting in infancy, before the infant has even acquired language, as they learn how to behave to elicit responses. Over the months and years, and throughout our lives, each of us has our own unique buildup of layers of conditions of worth: to work hard, to please others, to be strong, or whatever they may be. Think of all the subtle and not-so-subtle messages we have introjected from parents, caregivers, religious leaders, and others, whether they are given intentionally or unintentionally, and the information stored within us, whether we're aware of it or not, about what we have to do to be valued. We are deeply conditioned when we are young to see the world and ourselves in a particular way, and we learn to behave in a way that is consistent. It is a way of seeing the world that we can spend the rest of our lives trying to shake off, although we will never fully succeed.

As we enter adulthood, these conditions of worth are so tightly packed, so deeply introjected that we may not even realize that they are conditions of worth. To us, it is just who we are. Now imagine how idiosyncratic this process is, how no two people will ever have the exact same layers of conditions of worth, and how, because of that, there are myriad ways in which people will experience themselves and be experienced by others (see Box 4.2).

Box 4.2 Reflection: Being aware of medicalized language

It is commonplace to use psychiatric language and other labels when describing people's problems in living. For example, words like *narcissistic*, *psychopathic*, *depressive*, or *obsessive*. Such labels will often describe very well the behaviors of people, and because we all know what these words mean, they give us a common language. They may also convey the message that this is an illness, or it is just how the person is and it is something in their genes that is fixed. Think about times you have used such terms to describe yourself or someone else. Reflect on the implicit assumptions and hidden meanings that you are conveying—do you really agree with these? Experiment with using person-centered language instead. Ask yourself, what are the conditions of worth that might lead a person to behave in the way that they have? What is the nature of the person's self-concept that would lead them to say that or act in that way? What defensive processes are being used to protect the self-concept?

It is not important to the client-centered therapist what those differences between people look like because the root cause is the same and the therapy is the same for all, so there is no need to classify behaviors into diagnostic categories. But of course, if one were to look at the ways in which people think, feel, and behave and to use traditional techniques of statistical analysis, these behaviors would probably look similar to existing categories. There would be those who have eating problems, issues of depression, anxiety, self-esteem concerns, and so on. But from the person-centered perspective, such a classification system is not only unhelpful therapeutically, it is also damaging because it medicalizes what are not medical issues, as we have seen. Classification gives us no more information as person-centered practitioners than we already have if we pay attention to the client and what they tell us. Indeed, if we look to the client to tell us about themselves, we have more information than if we look at the client through the lens of classification.

Styles of processing

However, while we do not want to fall into the trap of diagnostic systems, it is interesting to think about how there may be different patterns in how conditions of worth lead to the behaviors that they do. One theorist who has offered a classification system of this nature is Margaret Warner, who describes what she calls "styles of processing." This refers to the different ways in which people process information and respond to the world around them. For Warner, severe psychological distress and dysfunction is not well explained by conditions of worth alone. She notes that incongruence might arise in the absence of conditions of worth, for instance in situations where there is rapid change, or even that some individuals may have developmentally or biologically based difficulties in their ability to process experience.[7] While not ruling these possibilities out, I think Warner misrepresents her contribution to theory by positioning her ideas as an alternative to conditions of worth rather than a theoretical description of how conditions of worth actually express themselves, which is how I would propose we think about these different styles. I would argue that conditions of worth affect and distort an individual's natural tendency to process experience. Similarly, David Murphy and Louis Hook, writing in the journal *Person-Centered & Experiential Psychotherapies*, argue that Warner's conceptualization of processing is already implicit in Rogers's theory and that there is a danger in adapting therapy to fit her ideas that we take a "a step closer to becoming a specificity-diagnosis-treatment model."[8]

With their words of caution in mind, it is interesting to examine Warner's framework for the development of capacities relating to processing and self-cohesion. She describes three kinds of difficult process that psychotherapists are likely to encounter, which she refers to as fragile process, dissociated process, and psychotic process.

Fragile process

> Clients who have a fragile style of processing tend to experience core issues at very low or very high levels of intensity. They tend to have difficulty starting and stopping experiences that are personally significant or emotionally connected. In addition, they are likely to have difficulty taking the point of view of another person while remaining in contact with such experiences.[9]

She describes clients who experience "fragile process" as having difficulty holding experience in attention at moderate levels of intensity. Thus, they are likely to have difficulty when confronted with another's point of view without feeling that their own experience has been annihilated. For example, someone who is talking about something meaningful to them, who is interrupted by another person offering them advice, will easily lose their train of thought, possibly becoming ashamed or angry. Not surprisingly, in personal relationships, clients with fragile process are likely to feel violated and misunderstood a lot of the time. Other people often experience them as being unreasonably angry, touchy, and stubborn. This is particularly likely given the fact that they often feel the need to defend their experience to avoid feeling that it has been annihilated.

Dissociated process

> Clients who experience "dissociated process" go through periods of time when they quite convincingly experience themselves as having selves that are not integrated with each other. Sometimes, they experience a disunity of self that feels "crazy" to themselves and to others. At other times they may have periods of forgetfulness for the minutes or hours when alternate personality parts have been dominant. They may go for years without being aware of such parts by keeping very busy and leading quite restricted lives, only to have past experiences return in times of crisis.[10]

At a time of crisis for a client with dissociated process, new parts of their personality may emerge, to the confusion, surprise, and shock of family and friends. Dissociated process seems to be related to early childhood experiences in which the person lacked the comfort and protection of parenting figures. Young children who go through such experiences are likely to develop trance-like patterns of coping that allow them to survive.

Psychotic process

> When clients have a psychotic style of processing, they have difficulty forming narratives about their experience that make sense within the culture, or which offer a predictive value in relation to their environment. Clients experiencing psychotic process . . . [have] impaired contact with "self," "world" and "other." Such clients often experience voices, hallucinations or delusions that are neither culturally accepted nor are easy to process.[11]

These difficult processing styles can exist in varying combinations with each other and can operate at differing levels of intensity. In my view, these different ways in which people process experiences describe the ways in which conditions of worth may manifest. But it is possible that these different processing styles do arise through other means than conditions of worth, as Warner suggests. In that case, however, I don't see that person-centered therapy would necessarily be the only way or best way to help people. That is because the theory underpinning the therapy is about how unconditional positive regard from the therapist creates the environment in which the client can begin to dissolve their conditions of worth.

As I noted at the beginning of this chapter, a common challenge from its critics is that the person-centered approach has no theory of psychopathology. It clearly does, but the difference is that it doesn't start with the category and work backward to find an explanation for that category. Rather, it seeks to understand the myriad ways in which its theory of personality development can be applied. There is no need for expert diagnosis in the person-centered approach because each client is unique in their way of expressing incongruence and best met with empathic understanding rather than being seen as part of a category. This is not to say that the ways in which people's problems manifest cannot be categorized in a meaningful way, just that it is not therapeutically useful to do so. However, it may be of scholarly interest to the therapist to have an understanding of the broad ways in which people's incongruence manifests. The seeming simplicity of Rogers's theory belies a far more powerful explanatory force than is generally recognized.

It is important to see how the concept of conditions of worth can explain a range of problems in living. Imagine that day after day, year after year, a young child introjects extreme conditions of worth, layer after layer, and consider how damaged they will be decades later, as a young adult, shaped by all those years of conditioning. It's similar to how a tree hit by lightning, blown over in the wind, and parched in drought will grow misshapen and twisted. Moreover, we can't easily introspect our conditions of worth because they are the basis of who we think we are and the eyes through which we look at the world, so we are unaware of these layers of dysfunction. Instead, we protect our self-concept with denial and distortion.

Recent years have seen new interest within the psychiatric literature into developmentally adverse interpersonal trauma. It has been recognized that people who have experienced severe neglect and abuse earlier in life are at risk for various psychological problems in living. Different types of complex trauma have been identified, but if we consider the experiences of a child who is subject to interpersonal abuse it is helpful to consider the ways in which complex trauma can be another way of describing the introjection of layers of conditions of worth?

Rogers's theory allows us to understand the myriad ways in which personality develops, such that authentic becoming and the full functioning of the person are thwarted, giving rise to those experiences characteristic of what psychiatrists call complex trauma. By thwarted, I mean growing up in a context in which empathy is minimal—indeed, one in which the child more often experiences the opposite of empathy, where genuineness and authenticity are replaced with dishonesty and alienation, and where unconditionality gives way to control and coercion. That is surely the definition of severe neglect and abuse.

Having considered the problems in living that arise through mechanisms of denial and distortion to maintain an incongruent self-structure and protect it from threat, now I will turn to consider what happens when those very mechanisms come under such severe threat that they themselves breakdown.

Psychopathology arising from breakdown and disorganization

While the vast majority of concerns with which people present to psychiatrists, psychologists, and therapists can be formulated and understood using the concept of conditions of worth, not all problems in living can be explained this way. One example that cannot be easily formulated as resulting from conditions of worth is posttraumatic stress. Here we have to turn to another portion of the theory from Rogers's 1959 chapter: his hypothesis that new experiences that are incongruent to the self-structure can lead to "breakdown and disorganization."

As mentioned, I began my career as a trauma psychologist, and it was only later that I came to understand the significance of Rogers's approach when I realized that he had essentially provided a description of trauma processes decades before the language of trauma became mainstream.[12] Clearly, trauma does not directly result from an internalization of conditions of worth in childhood, but from exposure to a traumatic event. I came to realize that person-centered personality theory provides a much more sophisticated framework than I had first understood, which easily explained the development of posttraumatic stress and allowed it to be recast not as a disorder, but as a normal and natural process in which a person works through the significance of trauma.[13]

In essence, for a fully functioning person, the self-concept is flexible and adaptable in the face of new experience. Most of us, however, are less than fully functioning, and we maintain our self-structure with a process of defense until we experience a threat that is overwhelmingly incongruent with it—at which point the process of breakdown and disorganization described by Rogers is instigated:

1. If the individual has a large or significant degree of *incongruence between self and experience* and if a significant experience demonstrating this *incongruence* occurs suddenly, or with a high degree of obviousness, then the organism's process of *defense* is unable to operate successfully.
2. As a result *anxiety* is *experienced* as the *incongruence*is subceived.* The degree of anxiety is dependent upon the extent of the *self-structure* which is *threatened.*
3. The process of *defense* being unsuccessful, the *experience* is *accurately symbolized* in *awareness*, and the gestalt of the *self-structure* is broken by this *experience* of the *incongruence* in *awareness.* A state of disorganization results.
4. In such a state of disorganization the organism behaves at times in ways which are openly consistent with experiences which have hitherto been distorted or denied to awareness. At other times the self may temporarily regain regnancy, and the organism may behave in ways consistent with it.[14]

Rogers's 1959 theory describes the process of breakdown and disorganization of the self-structure. Any number of experiences could provoke this, depending on the nature of the threat they pose to the self-concept.

Rogers's description of how people process information that is threatening to the self-structure explained PTSD, but as his work was done years before the term PTSD was introduced, no one had yet made that connection. It was a lightbulb moment for me to realize that here was an alternative way of thinking about trauma. The nature of traumatic events is that they will demonstrate incongruence to most people because there are common distortions in the self-structure. One aspect of the self-structure in which there is high degree of discrepancy between self and experience is in the denial to awareness of existential experiences, for example, that we are fragile, that the future is uncertain, and that life is not fair. Traumatic events abruptly and obviously present us with experience that leads to a breakdown of these aspects of the self-structure.

Rogers's description is consistent with the social cognitive theories of posttraumatic stress. For example, one of the most influential theorists is the social

* Subception is the process in which a stimulus is experienced without being brought into awareness.

psychologist Ronnie Janoff-Bulman, who has discussed how the experience of trauma has a shattering effect on people's "assumptive world."[15]

Importantly, Rogers's description accounts for the phenomenology of PTSD, including why some people are vulnerable to PTSD while others who experience the same trauma seem to be resilient, because that depends on the degree of discrepancy between self and experience. He discusses the anxiety that is experienced as the incongruence is subceived. However, the hallmark signs of PTSD are the re-experiencing and avoidance phenomena. Rogers describes the disorganization that results when the self-structure breaks down. He writes that the person attempts, on the one hand, to accurately symbolize in awareness their experience (intrusion) and, on the other, to deny their experiences and hold on to their pre-existing self-structure (avoidance). This account of the phases of intrusion and avoidance is similar to that of the information processing theory proposed by Mardi Horowitz, a leading theorist in the field of trauma. Horowitz's information processing approach is based on the idea that individuals have mental models, or schemata, of the world and of themselves that they use to interpret incoming information. He also proposes that there is an inherent drive to make our mental models coherent with current information, which he refers to as the completion tendency.[16]

The pivotal part of Rogers's description of breakdown is that the event demonstrates incongruence between self and experience. Here is the notion that it is how a person perceives the event that is important. It is in the nature of incongruence between self and experience that this will always be idiosyncratic to the person. We all have different experiences in life, and consequently an event that demonstrates incongruence to one person may not do so to another.

Thus, Rogers's theory provided a theoretical explanation for the characteristics of PTSD, but it did so in a way that reconceptualized it as a natural and normal process. Instead, we could talk about posttraumatic stress as a process rather than as an outcome, one that was intrinsically motivated towards growth and development—a topic that I will return to later. But it is important to note that experiences that are extremely threatening to the self-structure, when not subject to satisfactory processing, could ultimately be distorted, leading to psychosis.

As noted, in a "healthy" individual, the self-concept is flexible and adaptable in the face of new experience. When it is under threat, though, the organism protects itself further by making the self-concept rigid and inflexible—the individual retreats into a well-defended, rigid set of certainties about themselves. As it becomes more rigid, the person relies more and more on past experiences—the certainties—and as a result, more and more current experiences will be distorted or denied. At extremes, such a person may seem out of touch with reality. The processes of defense become entrenched, and psychological tension builds up so that under certain circumstances (trauma, or the accumulation of threat), the self-concept effectively "breaks" under the pressure. As we have seen, the resulting state of disorganization will be experienced idiosyncratically by the individual as posttraumatic stress, anxiety, depression, confusion, and chaotic thinking. These expressions of self-structure tension and collapse can be extremely distressing but are indicative of a need to process—to reconcile self and experience. However, insufficient processing might present to observers as symptoms of mental "illnesses," including "psychoses." Rogers and Thomas Holdstock wrote the following:

> The continuing estrangement between self-concept and experience leads to increasingly rigid perceptions and behaviour. If experiences are extremely incongruent with the self-concept, the defence system will be inadequate to prevent the experiences from overwhelming the self-concept. When this happens the self-concept will break down, resulting in disorganisation of behaviour. This is conventionally classed as psychosis when the disorganisation is considerable.[17]

This provides a non-medicalized way to understand psychosis, and what makes this different is that from the person-centered point of view there is always meaning in these apparently chaotic and disconnected experiences, and empathic understanding helps the person to make new meaning.

. . .

In Rogers's theory, problems in living are explained as arising through these two mechanisms described above, conditions of worth or breakdown and disorganization. But of course, it also needs to be stressed that both mechanisms are always in operation in people's lives. We have our developmental experiences, and we have what happens to us; how we are affected by what happens to us depends on how our formative influences shaped us. (see Box 4.3).

Box 4.3 Using Rogers's theory to conceptualize problems in living

Consider the life experiences of someone you know who may have experienced, or who is experiencing, problems of depression, anxiety, posttraumatic stress, psychosis, or another commonly diagnosed condition. Take some time to conceptualize the experiences of that person using the ideas of conditions of worth and breakdown and disorganization. What are the kinds of experiences they had as a young child that are important? What are the conditions of worth that might have been introjected? What are the events that have since happened to the person? How would those have shattered their beliefs and assumptions in such a way to lead to breakdown and disorganization?

I do not mean to assert in this chapter that the ways in which people experience distress and dysfunction can always be boiled down to these two psychological mechanisms described by Rogers. That is a question for further research to address. I simply mean to say that these are the only two psychological mechanisms in Rogers's theory. It seems likely that sometimes there are problems that are genuinely biochemical in causation but that biochemical explanations are much more widely applied than is credible and the person-centered view deserves greater recognition as a valid alternative.

As mentioned above, the person-centered approach begins with its theory and looks to the myriad ways that it can be applied, in contrast to mainstream psychology, which traditionally starts with the diagnosis. But in more recent years, the term *transdiagnostic* has become widely employed by mainstream psychology to describe mechanisms that are present across various disorders. While the term *transdiagnostic* in the context of the person-centered approach is paradoxical as it recognizes the validity of diagnosis, it is nonetheless an interesting development because it acknowledges that some theories and forms of therapy may explain and help across different diagnoses. For some, it might even seem that it is an implicit admission that the evidence points toward the specificity myth discussed by Bozarth.

People seek therapy for all sorts of problems. I don't think that the person-centered approach has the solution to all these. After all, it only offers a way to help people become more congruent—to learn to be themselves. That statement might lead some to conclude that person-centered therapy cannot help with problems of depression, anxiety, self-esteem, or many of the other common difficulties clients bring to therapy, but the person-centered approach contributes an understanding of how all these common difficulties may, at their root, be due to a lack of congruence between experience and the self-structure or through the breakdown of the self-structure. These are probably the underpinning causes for a much wider range of problems in living than is currently understood by mainstream psychology and psychiatry, but such a claim calls for much further theoretical work and empirical evidence to substantiate it.

The person-centered approach is only ever about helping people become more congruent, which, in turn, leads them to be more fully functioning. Insofar as people's problems in living arise due to incongruence, as it is understood within Rogers's theory of personality development, person-centered therapy may be helpful. For the person-centered therapist faced with a client requesting help to deal with what they consider to be depression, anxiety, trauma, or any other condition, offering therapy only makes sense if the client's issues can be formulated within person-centered theory. It is a mistake to treat a psychological problem medically, but I would also caution that it would be a great mistake to treat a medical problem psychologically. The task for the person-centered practitioner is to approach each person with this in mind and to understand that their only business is in creating a climate that nurtures authenticity.

Concluding comments

In recent years it has become more widely accepted that distress and dysfunction in people often arise not from something wrong within them but from what happened to them. Surprisingly, for many this represents a radical shift in their thinking, but not so for the person-centered psychologist, who has always taken this view. In this chapter I have talked about my journey into the person-centered approach's understanding of psychopathology and how I came to realize that it offered a more parsimonious and non-medical approach to understanding trauma. Only when I had replaced one way of thinking with another did I fully understand that this was an approach that did not sit alongside other medically based approaches to therapy and clinical psychology, but was an alternative. It is important to show the person-centered approach's broad applicability and reconceptualize the ways in which mainstream psychiatry, and society, talk about human suffering, in terms of alienation and thwarted potential, to offer more humane and just ways of offering help. Further research and scholarship is encouraged to understand the ways in which Rogers's theory can be used to account for different problems in living.

Chapter 5

Issues in person-centered practice

One treatment for all cases

The consequence of understanding psychopathology from the person-centered view is, of course, that there is one "treatment" for all cases. There is no need for diagnosis because there is only one approach to the therapy for all the ways in which personality has been thwarted in its authentic development. As we saw in the previous chapter, dysfunctional and distressing behavior is consistent with and arises out of the environment, communities, families, and relationships in which people live, work, and learn and the messages these institutions convey about what is takes to be valued. For that reason, the person-centered approach is about creating a new environment characterized by Rogers's six necessary and sufficient conditions, which include the three therapist attitudes of congruence, empathy, and unconditional positive regard. These describe the therapist's approach with all clients regardless of their presentation. As John Shlien wrote,

> Client-centered therapy has only one treatment for all cases. That fact makes diagnosis entirely useless. If you have no specific treatment to relate to it, what possible purpose could there be to specific diagnosis? Nothing remains but the detrimental effects.[1]

This idea—that it is about the relationship between the therapist and the client and that the nature of this relationship is the same for all—can be hard to grasp when one is used to thinking in terms of a medical model, but as Rogers said in his conversation with Martin Buber, "if therapy is effective, there is this same kind of meeting of persons no matter what the psychiatric label."[2] When relationship conditions exist such that people feel unconditionally regarded, their innate tendency toward the actualization of their potential is no longer thwarted but is released so that they are free to move in the direction of greater congruence. A summary of the theoretical process underlying client-centered therapy is shown in Figure 5.1. It should be noted that those who seek therapy do so because their incongruence has, in some way, caused them difficulties in life for which they are seeking solutions. But not everyone who is incongruent seeks therapy. One of the defining features of incongruence is a lack of self-awareness,

The Humanistic Psychology of Carl Rogers. Stephen A. Joseph, Oxford University Press. © Oxford University Press (2025). DOI: 10.1093/9780197790632.003.0006

Person has conditions of worth developed in childhood

⇓

Leads them to deny and distort experiences to fit self-structure/incongruence,

⇓

Incongruence causes problems in living that result in the person seeking therapy

⇓

Client-centered therapy/six necessary and sufficient conditions

⇓

Client experiences empathic understanding and unconditional positive regard

⇓

Experiences less distorted and denied/greater openness

⇓

Organismic valuing process in the client

⇓

Conditions of worth begin to dissolve/client experiences greater unconditional positive self-regard

⇓

Greater congruence

⇓

Movement toward becoming fully functioning

Figure 5.1 Theoretical process of client-centered therapy

so the more incongruent a person is, the less likely they may be to admit to themselves or others that they are having problems. Often, only when an event in a person's life causes some breakdown and disorganization in their self-structure do they seek therapy.

I have described the person-centered view on why diagnosis is generally unhelpful and unnecessary. I would also add that the same criticisms of diagnosis can apply to the use of "formulation," which is often offered as a nonmedicalized alternative to diagnosis but actually also often involves the therapist taking an expert stance if it is done with the intention of offering an appropriate intervention. There is still an agenda.[3] Certainly one can understand a person's problems using person-centered theory, but the person-centered therapist has no agenda for their client.

Clients will, however, usually have their own agenda, often expressed in terms of seeking treatment for a specific condition or set of feelings. Sometimes clients will arrive and use the language of illness to describe their needs. As we saw in the previous chapter, that does not mean that the therapist cannot help, but they should not assume they can. If a client who arrives seeking help is using language that implies suffering from a form of illness, such as talking about their depression as a chemical imbalance, the person-centered therapist has no skills or expertise to treat the person for what they are describing. Only if what the client is describing can be understood as a state of incongruence may person-centered therapy be helpful. Person-centered therapy is more clearly a fit when people describe themselves as feeling lost, looking for direction, trying to make sense of an experience, or wanting to get to know themselves or when they use other such language that implies a search for greater authenticity and agency in life. But this is not always the language that people use when they seek therapy.

The nature of person-centered therapy is that it provides the mechanism for people to look deeply within themselves, to move past their self-deceptions, and to confront themselves openly and honestly. As desirable as that is for leading a more fully functioning life, it is not always what people have in mind when they first arrive seeking help to feel less anxious or depressed or to cope better with a difficult situation. Person-centered therapy may help them do that, but it may also take the person down new roads that they had not expected. They may not be seeking to dismantle and rebuild their sense of themselves and the world, but that is the direction in which they have embarked. Therefore, it is the therapist's responsibility to be clear with clients about what may be ahead and how therapy can lead to deep-seated changes.

If a client believes they are suffering from a chemical imbalance and wants help with that, this is not something the person-centered therapist can do; indeed, in such a case it would seem unethical for the therapist to offer therapy without reaching some understanding with the client about what they are going to be engaged in. Depending on what the client seeks help for, there may be an ethical imperative on the therapist to discuss, at the outset, any clash between their frame of reference as a therapist and that of the client.

Person-centered therapy is only ever about helping people become more congruent. In this way it is vital that person-centered therapists understand how the theory can be applied to understanding their client and why being able to view different psychiatric and psychological conditions from the viewpoint of person-centered theory is so important. They must be able to reconceptualize psychiatric disorders in person-centered terms to look at the same phenomenon from a different angle, the growth model perspective.

But while the nature of psychiatric conditions remains contested, surely not all problems in living are due to incongruence. To offer therapy, we must first know the person, hear what they have to say about themselves, and be able to formulate their problem in a way to show that it is due to incongruence. The point is that whatever a person is seeking help for, unless the therapist can understand it as a form of incongruence, therapy should not be offered for that condition. Understanding mental health problems in this way is unique to the person-centered approach. It seems essential to me that if person-centered theory cannot explain how the client's experiences of distress and dysfunction arose, and thus also the mechanism for how they can be alleviated, therapy should be contraindicated. Offering a therapy for which there is no theory underpinning it in relation to the client's needs would be unethical. That said, even if the therapy is not being offered to provide help for a "condition," it may be offered to help the person live a more fully functioning and authentic life despite their situation. For example, while person-centered therapy would not be helpful for a person suffering from a disfiguring injury—in that case, they would need to see a medical specialist—it might be helpful for that person to talk to someone about how to move forward in their life now that they have this injury.

While many psychiatric conditions might be recast and understood in person-centered terms, others may not. For example, many people describe themselves as being neuroatypical or neurodivergent and being different in some way that may be a cause for concern to them in how they are able to function in society. The person-centered approach does not offer help for any condition if it is not seen to arise through conditions of worth or the process of breakdown and disorganization. As neurodivergence would seem to be an expression of natural and normal individual differences, it is not appropriate to talk of treatment for that as a condition. While this also opens a wider discussion on the medicalization of human experience and difference and how neurodivergence is discussed in mainstream psychology and psychiatry, people nonetheless may seek help for themselves or for their children.

From this perspective, we would not talk of treatments for neuroatypical conditions, but we would recognize that everyone, regardless of individual differences and diversity, can be subject to conditions of worth or affected through breakdown and disorganization. Everyone, given the right social environment, will be able to move toward more autonomy and socially constructive ways of living. A person-centered view is that regardless of individual differences, therapy can help people explore themselves and how to lead and manage their lives in society. Indeed, we might recognize how some conditions of worth might be intensified in relation to neurodivergent states.

In essence, person-centered therapy is only ever intended to help people develop greater agency in their lives and move toward more congruent or authentic functioning. That might not be what the client is asking for, but it must be how the therapist is able to understand it; otherwise, we need to refer the client elsewhere. This point, that the person-centered approach is only ever about helping people become more congruent, cannot be emphasized enough. It is never a treatment for any of the psychiatric or other conditions that are discussed in mainstream psychology and psychiatry unless those conditions can be reconceptualized as an absence of congruence. In such cases it may well be helpful, although it is still never a "treatment" because the approach does not condone the medicalization of what is seen as incongruence. We might think of this as a form of positive psychology or coaching if we wanted to use more contemporary terminology, but it is what person-centered therapy has always been.

The person-centered approach is, as we have seen, a very different way of thinking about psychopathology, one consequence of which is that opportunities for employment as client-centered therapists are often harder to find and may require working in settings that are themselves not person-centered.

Non-directivity in directive settings

I think client-centered therapy has an important role to play in society as a bulwark against the pervasive influence of the illness ideology on so many aspects of our lives. But this means that working as a therapist is challenging for those interested in the person-centered approach because it requires a different worldview. Clients often expect to be treated like patients. They may be easily frustrated if the therapist doesn't treat them in the same way a doctor does and may expect to be asked questions by someone holding a clipboard who will provide them with advice. It takes a skillful therapist to work in a client-centered way with people who have such expectations without leaving them feeling frustrated. But it is not only clients who have such expectations. Other professionals often also expect you, as the therapist, to be the expert in the same way that a medical doctor would be. It is important to clarify that the person-centered therapist rejects the label of expertise in this sense of being like a medical doctor, not in other ways. They are, of course, expert in their own field of non-directive therapy and in understanding psychotherapeutic processes.

But there are few contexts in which helping relationships exist where expertise in the non-directive approach is expected and in which the therapist will be supported in their practice. Colleagues may simply assume that you approach therapy in a non-directive way because you lack the knowledge of more directive techniques—that client-centered therapy is a sort of beginner's therapy. Often those in management will think the same and make demands on you to adapt your therapy to what they believe therapy should be. How to be a non-directive therapist in directive contexts, if it is ever truly possible, is an ongoing question.

Danish therapist Lisbeth Sommerbeck has offered some helpful advice on how to maintain one's non-directivity in a directive psychiatric setting.[4] Over many years she worked successfully as a therapist, finding ways to overcome the challenges, but toward the end of her career, in an article entitled "Being Nondirective in Directive Settings" she described how, with a change in management, she found it increasingly difficult to carry on:

> I was requested to become as directive and as much of an expert on the client as the other professionals in the setting and thus, as I saw it, in practice prevented from working as a client-centered therapist . . . the request to be a case manager was more than enough for me to realize that my long career as a nondirective client-centered therapist in a directive setting had come to an end. It was with a mixture of relief and sadness, but more the latter than the former, that I opted for retirement and sent in my resignation. But of course other nondirective practitioners may live up to the challenge, where I gave up, and find ways of also becoming nondirective case managers, however much this sounds like a contradiction in terms.[5]

Sommerbeck recognized that it is all about the context in which you work. It should always be remembered that the person-centered approach is countercultural—it goes against the grain. The aspiring person-centered therapist may need to be creative, flexible, and highly entrepreneurial to find a way to practice client-centered therapy that allows them to be financially independent. Private practice is an option, but the other contexts in which they can be truly client-centered are limited.

Not surprisingly, many therapists succumb to pressures to incorporate more directive ways of working into their practice that satisfy these external demands on them. If so, they may want to cling onto the self-identification as client-centered therapists, but therapists must be seen by their actions, not their words, and few of those who practice in this way—juggling competing philosophical viewpoints—can really be considered person-centered.

This issue of how to be non-directive in a directive context has interested me for many years. As a university educator, I work in a directive institution, but under the current management my colleagues and I have been able to teach in a student-centered way. We are aware that the opportunity to work in this way could come to an end under a different regime, but for the moment we feel fortunate to be able to carry on as we are. When that changes, like Sommerbeck, each of us would have a choice to make: whether to compromise our principles or find a new path in life. Such is the choice faced by all those who take the person-centered approach. We live in a society that is hostile to, and generally doesn't understand, what we do. Psychiatric and educational settings are the most obvious contexts for this discussion, but the issue is pervasive in any setting where there is some form of helping relationship.

So far I've discussed the challenges of being person-centered in a non-person-centered context, but this issue is so much more complex. Often the context is not clear-cut. Social workers often align themselves philosophically with the person-centered approach and talk about the conditions of empathy, unconditional positive regard, and genuineness as essential communication skills. But when it comes to actual practice, it is hard for social workers to be person-centered, write David Murphy and colleagues in the *British Journal of Social Work*. They refer to the distinction I made earlier between principled and instrumental non-directivity, arguing that whereas the person-centered approach is about a relationship as an end in itself, social workers inevitably have other agendas to pursue through their use of the relationship, such as facilitating engagement with the client in order to find out what they want, to develop rapport, and to gain compliance. Thus, social work is a form of instrumental practice in which the relationship has a utilitarian function. Principled non-directivity is untenable for most social work practice. Murphy and colleagues conclude the following:

> While it might seem to some that we are splitting hairs, the political importance of this discussion is that the use of the term "person-centred" belies the function of modern social work in which the relationship is for the utilitarian purposes of compliance and externally imposed direction on the service user. Social work is not person-centred; it is state-centred. We urge all those involved in social work—educators, students, experienced practitioners, service users, employers and policy makers—not to attempt to transfer person-centred psychology into their models, as the true meaning and validity are lost in the process of translation. The danger is that, if we continue to use the term "person-centred" as if social work was based on the psychotherapeutic principle of self-determination, we serve to diminish the potency of the theoretical principle of the actualising tendency and obscure the true nature of the modern social work profession.[6]

Social work has ways of working that are relationship-based, but that in itself does not make it person-centered. This is not to criticize social work for what it does but to caution readers about how the term *person-centered* can be used misleadingly. Not only social workers, but also clinical psychologists, educators, and many other professionals use terms that transform the meaning of what they actually do into something they find more palatable. None of us in the helping professions would like to think that we are part of the problem, but that is an issue we all must confront as a possibility: that we use language to deceive ourselves from seeing what we are truly doing.

Use of techniques

Previously, in discussing the notion of principled non-directiveness, I noted that it may seem appropriate for a therapist to answer a question, or to offer some exercise or technique, not because they believe it will achieve a desired goal they have for the client, but purely because it may be a way of respecting the client by responding to their request. At one point in my career I worked in a medical setting, and I would often have a clipboard on my knee and a short well-being questionnaire at hand, simply to meet client's expectations. I felt it was my responsibility to meet the client where they were, not to expect them to jump immediately to where I was.

As Barbara Brodley and Anne Brody, two renowned experts on the person-centered approach, wrote in response to the question of whether goal-directed techniques can be applied,

> the answer is NO if they are the result of the therapist's having a diagnostic mindset, and YES if they are the result of the client's questions or requests, and if the therapist is able to participate in applying a technique while integrating such participation into his or her maintaining the therapeutic attitudes.[7]

I have discussed how Rogers's theory can be applied to understanding trauma, but even so, readers may still be puzzled about what trauma therapy from a person-centered perspective looks like. The answer that it is no different from any other instance of person-centered therapy can seem confusing. Surely it has to be different? While it is the same in the sense that the therapist endeavors to hold the therapist attitudes of congruence, unconditional positive regard, and empathic understanding how this unfolds in the relationship from one client group to another may look different. But the process of change remains the same. Rogers suggested that accurate symbolization in awareness of experience was necessary for the reintegration of self and experience to take place—resulting in a relaxation of its rigidity and its defenses. Newer experiences, previously discrepant with the self-concept, may be tentatively admitted, and the process of integration begins. This is the process of therapeutic change.

For people with various issues of anxiety and posttraumatic stress, a more directive therapist might advocate some form of exposure therapy. The evidence is clear that exposure therapy can be helpful, but the mechanism through which exposure works is not incompatible with Rogers's theory. Indeed, it is essentially what Rogers himself proposes when he talks about helping a person to accurately symbolize their experiences. To process trauma, the self-structure must be reconciled with experience, which can take place through the safety of a therapeutic relationship.[8]

But the way in which the therapist engages with the client in facilitating the process of exposure—whether in a directive, expert-led way or in a client-centered way—is key. In the former, the therapist directs the process and decides what intervention should be administered and when. But even the most directive therapist realizes that the more they ignore the pace and direction of the client, the less likely the intervention is to be helpful. Emotional processing and working through trauma require a person to mentally "relive" the trauma-related events, but forcing people to do this when they are not ready and are unprepared is dangerous and is poor therapeutic practice. All therapists, regardless of their approach, recognize the need for a collaborative and informed way of working.[9]

Seen this way, many directive therapists may seem on the surface to be client-centered and may think of their work as informed by these principles, but this is only surface deep if they themselves have an agenda, whether or not they choose to push it. The client-centered therapist has no agenda. It is important to understand that exposure therapies set out to achieve the process of accurate symbolization, but person-centered theory adds the idea that there is no need for the therapist to push the client because the client will be intrinsically motivated to increase congruence between self and experience and to accurately symbolize their experiences in awareness when the right social environmental conditions are present. This is what makes person-centered therapy different: the belief that the actualizing tendency will—when the social environment is supportive—lead the person to accurately symbolize their experience. Thus, there is no need to direct the client toward engaging in various cognitive behavioral exercises, as the client will find their own best way to engage in retrieving, remembering, and re-evaluating their experiences.

It won't be exposure therapy in a recognizable way, as if done according to a manual, but the process involved will be the same. I remember one client who, after several sessions, told me he wanted to bring some photographs to the next session. He turned up with a shoebox full of pictures of his family and his now-deceased wife, and over the following weeks he took out one photograph at a time, laid it on the table for us both to see, and shared his memories. This was what he needed to do to symbolize his experiences. Would it have been helpful if I had suggested this and instructed him to do it? Maybe, although I don't think such an instruction is ever helpful unless the client is also ready.

Client-centered therapy can offer traumatized clients an unconditionally accepting relationship in which the client does not feel pushed to move in any direction other than their own. People are not linear in how they express themselves but will at some times approach their feelings and at other times retreat from them. The client-centered therapist needs to be aware of this process and not think that the client ought to be doing anything differently, and certainly not push them to do otherwise. Within that safe therapeutic relationship, the client will be processing their emotions and working through what they need to.[10]

The client-centered therapist is able to offer a social environment that serves to slowly dissolve the conditions of worth, with the consequence that the self-structure is gradually broken down and the self is reintegrated with experience to rebuild a new self-structure consistent with the actualizing tendency. Traumatized clients, however, have already had aspects of their self-structure abruptly shattered. The task of the client-centered therapist is therefore to help the client rebuild their self-structure by reintegrating self with experience. As we have seen, person-centered theory suggests that as the client comes to develop a self-structure with more congruence between self and experience, they should also become more fully functioning. Such movement toward becoming fully functioning in traumatized clients might be described in current terminology as posttraumatic growth, a topic I will return to when I introduce positive psychology in more detail. (See Box 5.1 for a summary on reflections working with trauma.)[11]

Box 5.1 Ten principles for working with trauma

1. Clients might not want to talk about their trauma, particularly early on, before the relationship has developed. The client-centered therapist will not push the client to talk. They will be careful to note the process, but without implying that the client should do anything differently than what they are doing.
2. Clients will likely feel more comfortable talking about their experiences when the therapeutic relationship has developed and they feel accepted and understood by the therapist. This takes however long it takes. Reassurance from the therapist that it is acceptable to talk before this trusting

relationship has developed will not speed up the process. Feelings on the part of the therapist of frustration and of wanting the process to move more quickly than it is will likely only serve to slow down the formation of the relationship.

3. If a client does begin to talk about their traumatic experiences, it is not the therapist's task to direct the content of the narrative. The task is purely to try to understand the client's experience and communicate to them that understanding and to stay with the client in their experience.
4. Psychological contact is the prerequisite for client-centered therapy to take place. If the contact is not present, client-centered therapy is not taking place and the therapist needs to use other grounding techniques to regain contact, for example, through reflecting to the client about their body language or describing items around them in the room.
5. As the client explores the meaning of their experiences, the therapist's task is to help the client to hear their own meanings so that they can reappraise and re-evaluate for themselves. It is not the client-centered therapist's task to provide the meaning for the client.
6. As the client feels intense negative emotions of fear, despair, sadness, and so on, it is not the client-centered therapist's task to try to remove these feelings. The task is to stay with the client's experience.
7. It is not the therapist's task to direct the client to exercises or activities, but if the client asks for, or clearly indicates in some way that doing something might be helpful, offering that activity as an empathic response to the client may be appropriate. Importantly, however, the therapist does not push the client to do the exercise or activity and presents it to the client only as an expression of empathy, not as a goal-directed technique.
8. Although theory states that the client will move in growthful ways given the right social environment, the therapist does not set this up as an a priori expectation for the client so that they feel they are failing if they struggle to find positive meaning. Posttraumatic growth can be a gradual and slow process. It is also important to understand that growth is a process rather than an outcome.
9. Although it is useful for therapists to have a knowledge of the literature on the general reactions of people who experience trauma, the therapist should not assume that this knowledge necessarily applies to each and every client.

10. Therapists can help provide clients with the social environment conducive to recovery, but they cannot make them recover. Therapists should endeavor constantly to make sure that, in their interactions with clients, they do not take responsibility away from their clients, who must, in the end, take responsibility for the progress of their own therapy. Clinicians can create the therapeutic context conducive to posttraumatic growth, but only the client can achieve growth.

Person-centered theory states that if the client is not engaging in whatever process or activity they need, this must be because the social environment is not supportive enough for them to feel unconditionally accepted and thus able to drop their defenses. If the client seems stuck, this does not mean that it is time to try doing something different; it is simply time to work harder at what you *are* doing: being empathic, genuine, and accepting. Ultimately it is not about the use of techniques but about the therapeutic relationship that one develops through the holding of these attitudinal conditions.

In this way, person-centered therapy allows for a variety of possibilities to be realized in practice, but it is not an eclectic approach.[12] In a controversial paper published in the journal *Person-Centered & Experiential Psychotherapies*, Stephen Ong and colleagues showed that the person-centered approach is not eclectic and that it can't be eclectic without losing sight of its fundamental philosophy.[13] In short, the person-centered approach has a distinct ontological position, namely the underlying image of the human being as a proactive person driven by the actualizing tendency, such that clients are trusted to be their own best experts. A more eclectic approach to therapy implies that the therapist can shift their orientations in such a way that they step away from one ontological position to another to suit the client's wants and needs. Simply put, in stepping away from the ontological position that clients are their own best experts, such as integrating methods that denote the therapist as the expert, the therapist is no longer working in a person-centered way.

Ong and colleagues argued that it is simply not possible to have a consistent ontological position on human nature when practicing as an eclectic therapist. In an eclectic approach, giving the client what they want may initially be pleasing to them, but it is not necessarily consistent with the overarching goal of person-centered therapy, which is to foster the process of connection to the organismic valuing process. But, importantly, Ong argued that while Rogers's approach is not eclectic, it is inherently pluralistic in the many ways that a therapist can relate empathically in the therapeutic relationship.

However, the idea of the therapeutic relationship based on Rogers's theory is not to be confused with the idea of the "therapeutic alliance," which refers to how the client and therapist work together to develop a bond of trust and confidence as they agree to tasks to achieve the client's goals. The alliance is, in itself, an instrumental technique used by other therapists to provoke trust—it is not part of the person-centered repertoire to build alliance as a technique. The therapeutic alliance is thought to effect therapeutic change, with research suggesting it to be one of the best predictors of client outcome. The concept of the therapeutic alliance, however, derives from psychodynamic theory and is therefore grounded in a different paradigm, one that is more goal-directed and instrumental than the non-directive, humanistic theory of Rogers.

This is not to say that the person-centered therapist does not build an alliance, but it arises indirectly rather than instrumentally. For example, Steven Ackerman and Mark Hilsenroth found that a positive therapeutic alliance is facilitated through an environment in which empathy and acceptance are present.[14] An alliance will emerge spontaneously out of the therapeutic relationship. Research has shown that the therapeutic alliance mediated the association between the therapeutic conditions and outcome.[15]

The important point is not what one does, but how one does it, and whatever one does should remain consistent with the philosophy of the approach. What we do is grounded in the self-organizing principle and the belief that people can be trusted to find their own best directions. As already discussed, the distinction between directive and non-directive helps to make clear what the approach isn't but is less clear on what it is. While the term *client-centered* reminds us what it means in practice, it doesn't specify what to do, only how to *be* in terms of the three attitudinal conditions. In this sense, it seems possible to bring various modes of expression, tools, and techniques into therapy and other practices and maintain the non-directive/client-centered attitude. I am not the first to reach this conclusion, and what I say will not bring an end to debate about what is and isn't client-centered because ultimately the decision about where to draw the line across this fuzzy category is a personal one.[16]

However, while I think the theory is flexible enough that the use of tools and techniques can be used at times as expressions of empathy, this is very different from using them with the intention of providing a treatment. In the reality of day-to-day practice, I would say that if committed to the ideas and values of the person-centered approach, a therapist is rarely inclined toward offering tools and techniques. In situations where therapy with a client does not seem to be going well, there may be temptation to reach for some technique that one knows, but experienced therapists are more likely to double down on providing empathic listening and reflect on the quality of their unconditional regard and their own blocks to congruence.

We may find the same in everyday life with friends and relatives: that instead of listening empathically and offering an unconditional acceptance, we stray into advice-giving, interpretations of their and others' behaviors, and collusions with their frame of reference, all in an attempt to help, although it often does not (see Box 5.2).

Box 5.2 Listening to friends and family

In some situations in life we have good advice to share with others, but often we don't really know what is best for others—whether they should take that new job or take a chance on a new partner, for example.

Think back to a time when a friend or relative was sharing an emotional problem with you. Ask yourself whether you were able to listen empathically and unconditionally, trusting in them to move toward their own solutions, or if you felt inclined to offer advice and try to solve the problem for them. Was what you did helpful to them?

The next time you find yourself in a similar situation, notice any tension within you between the pull you feel to offer solutions on the one hand and to stay empathically with the person, trusting them to find their own solution, on the other.

Concluding comments

This chapter aimed to reflect on various real-life issues that often arise in classroom conversations as students seek to put into practice their new learnings. It can be a challenge to read about the theory and then to practice as a therapist, often in contexts that are not receptive to the non-directivity of this approach. A main message of the chapter is that the person-centered approach was developed only to facilitate people becoming more congruent in their lives and that it is not a treatment for psychiatric disorders in the traditional sense. Unlike other therapies, it is not a system that requires tools and techniques, but these are not ruled out insofar as they can be expressions of empathy. Understanding the idea of non-directivity and how it relates to the use of techniques is essential to becoming a person-centered therapist, but while this is an important conversation, even more important is to consider the therapist's way of being, the topic of the next chapter.

Chapter 6
Putting the theory into action
A way of being

The previous chapters described the characteristics of the person-centered approach and its application to psychopathology, but putting these abstract ideas into practice requires some elaboration and discussion. As an educator in this approach, I am familiar with how challenging it is to learn to be a person-centered practitioner. The caricature of the client-centered therapist is that of someone who sits and nods, smiles and repeats what has been said. It is understandable that people reach for such caricatures because it is so difficult to understand what it is to be a client-centered therapist. All other schools of therapy instruct students on what to do, in ways that describe behaviors and activities, whereas the client-centered approach says to be empathic, genuine, and unconditional. Imagine seeing your first client and being armed only with that information! No wonder students crave instructions for what to do in more concrete behavioral terms.

For those new to the approach, there is always the question of "What do I actually do?" Our ideas about human nature are at the core of how we practice as therapists. Practicing person-centered therapy is about trusting the client to know what is best for them, to know what they need to focus on. If anyone thinks that seems like a step too far, they would probably also find Rogers's theory about the tendency toward actualization too far-fetched. But unless we truly believe that there is an inherent tendency that becomes thwarted by conditional regard, what would be the rationale to think that unconditional positive regard would be healing? The more common assumption in Western culture is to think that human beings are innately socially destructive rather than socially constructive, in which case it would be better to adopt other approaches that offer ways of directing people to more desirable outcomes. To be a person-centered practitioner, therefore, means taking a deep dive into yourself to figure out what you really think about human nature.

For this very reason, in our therapy training program at the university where I teach, we make theory an important part of learning to become a therapist, perhaps more than is typical in many programs. A student therapist can practice offering the therapeutic conditions to others, but if they don't actually agree with the theory of why this works, advice-giving, interpretations, and subtle and

The Humanistic Psychology of Carl Rogers. Stephen A. Joseph, Oxford University Press. © Oxford University Press (2025). DOI: 10.1093/9780197790632.003.0007

not so subtle directions will all creep into their practice. Certainly we strive to provide the opportunities for students to reflect on whether this is a course suitable for them at this time in their lives, but some are in a rush to learn how to do therapy at the expense of this more important first task of learning about themselves.

It may be that the student therapist is, on the surface, trying to act like a person-centered therapist, but below the surface the medical ideology still operates: they are trying to change the person, not their social environment. The difference is subtle but profound and is, as I said before, the difference between trying to *give* someone empathy and acceptance and *being* an empathic and accepting person. The person-centered approach is not so much a way of doing but a way of being. And it starts with an image of what it means to be human.

Those of us who take this approach see people as intrinsically socially constructive, and for that we are often seen as fools, naive to the ways of the world and the true nature of people. I find Rogers's theory compelling, intellectually, but as discussed previously the theory does not say that people are good or bad in a moral sense, simply that they are striving to actualize in a constructive way for themselves, those around them, and even the species. But more often this tendency becomes usurped and they self-actualize in ways that lead to selfishness, corruption, dishonesty, and hurtfulness.

Rogers's theory is about how people's intrinsic nature is often thwarted and twisted out of shape to make the world we live in full of the good and the bad. What it means to trust in the actualizing tendency is that when people are in the *right* social environment, they will begin to move in constructive directions appropriate to their social context. It doesn't mean that we should be naive to the destructiveness of people around us. The day-to-day reality is that most of the time, people do not experience themselves in growth-promoting climates and instead behave in ways that serve to defend their self-concept that are destructive and damaging to those around them. I don't think that people are born to be destructive but that it arises out of the process Rogers described and can be reversed given the right social environment (see Box 6.1).

Box 6.1 Reflection: Human nature

An important first step to take if you are interested in the person-centered approach is to reflect on the issues discussed here about human nature and to be sure that you can buy into that part of the theory, because this is what underpins the notion that the client knows best. Read each of the following pairs of statements and choose which one in each pair best reflects your own point of view.

1. Human nature is essentially corrupt from the moment we are born.
   or
2. It is only through what happens to us in life that we become corrupted.

1. The aim should be to create a society that tries to control people to force them to behave decently.
   or
2. The aim should be to create a society that assumes that people will behave decently.

How strongly do you believe in your answers? What do you think are the experiences in your life that have led you to your answers?

The client knows best

The statement that the client knows best is commonly said to convey Rogers's approach in a simple way. But as a popular way of communicating a more complex idea, it fails because critics take it to mean that you simply need to ask someone what they think is best for them and that they can tell you there and then.

The person-centered approach to practice is about the "conviction that people have the right to direct their own lives and do not have to be guided into adjustment, but can do it for themselves when in the right social environment."[1] As we have seen, the right social environment is chiefly characterized as one of unconditional positive regard. It is a social environment in which a person has the perception of being free to move in any direction they choose, and for this to happen the practitioner must be non-directive. This is seen as the logical position to take because of the underlying theoretical framework of the approach. But it remains controversial in the wider world of therapy, which has always been dominated by the illness ideology. I've already referred to principled non-directivity as the attitude of the therapist, reflecting their basic belief in the client's resourcefulness for growth and self-direction. Non-directivity is not a technique; it refers to the stance of the therapist in relation to the client. Importantly, it does not mean that the therapy itself lacks direction, but that the direction is determined by the client.

Therapeutic work needs to be consistent with the basic principles of the primacy of the actualizing tendency and the assertion of the necessity and sufficiency of the therapeutic conditions, which allow the therapist to respond to each client in unique ways that are rooted in the context of the immediate experience of the relationship. A therapist's behavior in the session is based on the moment-to-moment empathy of the client's experience as well as the therapist being in touch with their own experiencing in that moment. Person-centered therapy does not mean doing *nothing*, as some critics seem to suggest. It also does not mean doing *anything*, as other critics suggest. Doing anything that the client wants is equally not person-centered. It is a much more organized and deliberate approach involving close attention to the client's moment-by-moment process with a deep trust in their ability to find their own direction.

I wrote in Chapter 3 about how this was like finding a thread in a darkened room. To use another metaphor, it is following a trail left in the forest: the client sees a broken stick and follow that direction for a while, then a half-hidden footprint appears, pointing in a new direction, as they search within themselves and pay attention to the organismic valuing process. Person-centered therapy is a process of working alongside clients as they find out what is important to them, not asking them to decide what they want, which is why empathic understanding is so central.

The person-centered therapist does not introduce new material or prompt the client about how to think about the content of what they say or what direction to go in. This way of relating is different from everyday conversations, which often include agreeing with people, providing them with explanations, or offering solutions. There may be rare and exceptional occasions in therapy when doing one of these things is called for, but on the whole these are not therapeutic ways of responding (see Box 6.2).

Box 6.2 Examples of responses that are not person-centered

The fictional examples below show three typical ways of responding that are not person-centered: agreeing with the client, offering explanations, and providing solutions.

1. Agreeing with the client

CLIENT: I am just so angry at John for what he did. He had no right to say that, and there is no way I am going to do what he wants after this.

THERAPIST: I agree with you. It was wrong of him, and if I were you I certainly wouldn't do what he wants either.

2. Providing explanations

CLIENT: I am just so angry at John for what he did. He had no right to say that, and there is no way I am going to do what he wants after this.

THERAPIST: I think your anger might not be so much about what happened with John, but rather about the feelings you were carrying with you before that. He has just hit a release valve.

3. Offering solutions

CLIENT: I am just so angry at John for what he did. He had no right to say that, and there is no way I am going to do what he wants after this.

THERAPIST: If you don't go ahead with the plan, I think you can still move ahead. But what I would suggest is that you phone John first, let him know how you feel, and see if he will do it on a different day.

Empathic listening is not a passive process, however. It requires active attention to all that is said and all that is not said, including the client's body language and tone of voice. The therapist must be congruent enough to be able to rely on their intuition, their felt sense of what is happening in the client's moment-by-moment experience. The therapist needs to be able to capture and convey to the client their understanding of the breadth and depth of what has been said as well as conveyed by their posture, tone of voice, or any other non-verbal cue. When this is skillfully done, the client may experience the therapist's empathic understanding and unconditional positive regard, opening them to verbalize further and to explore issues in more detail (see Box 6.3).

Box 6.3 Empathic responding

In the following excerpt the therapist responds in a non-directive and empathic way that helps the client who is feeling angry begin to realize for themselves that within the angry feelings are also feelings of fear for his son's welfare.

CLIENT: I am just so angry at John for what he did. He had no right to say that, and there is no way I am going to do what he wants after this.

THERAPIST: You have such anger in your voice . . .

CLIENT: I just blew up when I heard him say that. How could he be so thoughtless?

THERAPIST: You sounded so angry right now as you were saying that, and—I'm not sure about this—you also sounded sort of disappointed, something like that. I'm not sure . . .

CLIENT: I am angry; he let me down. I am really angry with him . . . I am disappointed. I expected more. (silence) He let me down. How could he do that?

THERAPIST: You say you are angry, but anger is not in your voice now. You sound more sad, or . . .

CLIENT: I know he has to go live his own life now. I will miss him so much, and I suppose I had hope that he would go to college, do the usual things. I feel I don't know anymore. I feel frightened for him. I just want him to be okay.

Sometimes, client-centered therapy is misunderstood as agreeing with whatever the client says. This is not the case. Client-centered therapy involves challenging the client, although not in a way that is directly confrontational, as might be the case in other therapies. A therapist who is congruent will at times say what they think or feel about something and disagree with the client, but the skill is doing so in a way that is empathic and unconditionally regarding (see Box 6.4).

Box 6.4 Therapist transparency

This is the fifth session. The client, a woman named Abigail, has been suffering from posttraumatic stress–type reactions after being attacked in the street and is working through her feelings about what happened. In this session we catch up just after she has described her angry feelings toward the perpetrator, and in doing so used some derogatory and racist language. The therapist, first of all, wants to stay with the feelings being expressed, but also feels herself wanting to say something about how she is feeling herself because of the language used.

THERAPIST: I can really feel how angry you are. You were almost shaking right now as you were telling me about what happened. It's like you are asking yourself, Why me? What did I do to deserve this? There is no answer, and all you are left with is a feeling of powerlessness and such rage. That's what it seems like to me.

CLIENT: Yes, that's it. I just feel helpless, and what's the point now?

THERAPIST: What's the point . . . feeling stuck, and wondering to yourself, How do I move forward? Is that it?

CLIENT: I know it's what I'm feeling now, and I will get over it. I just needed to say that and get it out.

THERAPIST: I get that. It was very powerful . . . I also want to say that I felt shaken, too, as you were talking. Some of the ways you described the man who attacked you left me feeling uncomfortable. It's not language I would use. Those are very powerful words that many people would find hurtful.

CLIENT: I know; I feel ashamed of myself saying what I did. I hope you will still want to see me. I just felt so angry.

THERAPIST: You feel you have let me down in a way or that I think less of you now?

CLIENT: I think less of me . . .

THERAPIST: I just wanted you to know that those are words I feel uncomfortable with and wouldn't use, but it's not going to make a difference to my feelings toward you or wanting to work with you. I feel that what we are doing together is important, and I value our time together every week and getting to know you.

CLIENT: Thank you. It's just the way I was brought up; we all spoke that like that when I was younger. And it's like it's still in there, and sometimes the lid gets blown off, but I know it's wrong.

The client therefore does not hear themselves being judged or scolded and does not feel the need to be defensive as a result, and thus is more able to enter into conversation about the disagreement. However, the more unconditionally accepting the therapist is, the less likely they are to feel a need to bring themselves into the conversation in this way, unless they can see it clearly as to the client's therapeutic benefit.

Rogers spoke about this in his 1975 interview with Richard Evans. He said that over the years he had not changed his view on the client as their own best expert, but recognized that he himself had become more willing to share his thoughts and feelings with clients. This was done not to direct them, but because he was aware that doing so might provide the client with some "jolting data."[2] New data that jolts us challenges our existing world views, such that we must somehow reconcile experience with self. Either we defend and distort the meaning of the new data to fit the existing self-structure or we are open to changes in our self-structure to accommodate the new data and develop more realistic perceptions.

To be challenged in this way allows people the opportunity to reach new insights and ultimately to be better equipped to make new choices in life. Rogers's theory holds that other ways of challenging clients that are directly confrontational, which may be promoted by other schools of therapy, will be perceived as threatening to the self-structure and greeted with defensive reactions. In this way client-centered therapy is non-judgmental, a concept that itself is often misunderstood. Therapists do judge—in the sense that they, too, have a felt sense of what is right and wrong, values that are important to uphold, and thoughts and feelings that reflect their experiences—and will be willing, at times, to share their thoughts and feelings with a client. The ability to do this while simultaneously holding the attitudes of congruence, empathy, and unconditional positive regard is important.

In practice, the person-centered therapist strives to understand both the content of what the client is saying and the process they are working through, reflecting back their understanding to the client so that they have a mirror to their experiencing in that moment. This helps the client to hear their own inner voice, go deeper into their process, and become aware of new material that was previously at the edge of their awareness. But at no point does the therapist direct the client as to how they ought to be experiencing. Their role is only to hold the relational attitudes within which the client's own process will direct the session.

Non-directivity is the attitude of the therapist. They have no intentions for the client; their only intention is for themselves—to hold the attitude of unconditional positive regard, express their understanding to the client empathically, be a congruent person within themselves, and be genuine in their relationship with the client. For anyone coming from other perspectives on therapy, it is difficult to really understand this, and hence non-directivity as an attitude may be confused with having an influence. We are all influenced by others—of course we are. Indeed, the point of therapy is to influence. Within a therapeutic relationship the therapist must make choices about what to say, when to say it, and when to stop saying something, and whatever choice is made inevitably can influence the client. But the difference is in the attitude. Imagine two therapists. One has no agenda for you as a client; their only intention is to understand you and help you work out for yourself what you need to do. The other wants you to understand what they think is best for you. Their words might be the same as they greet you when you enter the room and as they listen to you talk, but as the session progresses, the differences in their underlying attitude will be felt.

This is not to say that therapists need to refrain from talking about goals in person-centered therapy. A therapist can focus on goals, tasks, and methods if that is what the client chooses to bring at that moment. What a client brings determines the direction of a session. In therapy, the client often wants to make sense of an event from the past; in coaching, it is more often to look to the future. In this way, person-centered coaching might be more goal-orientated from the client's frame of reference. There are myriad ways in which a therapist or coach can bring their expertise into a session, as long as this is at the client's direction. For example, if the client wants to learn a mindful breathing technique, the therapist might practice it with the client, if appropriate, as an expression of empathy. The process would still always be directed and controlled by the client, and the values and benefits would be assessed by the client.

But it is important to understand that although at times a therapist might judge it appropriate to share some experience or techniques with a client, it is not the therapist's role to just do whatever a client asks. The therapist's role is to help the client develop in such a way that they can go into the world to meet their own needs; their role is not to meet those needs themselves. For example, a client has recently broken up with her boyfriend and is talking about finding a new partner for a sexual and romantic relationship. The therapist will engage with that conversation in a way that will better equip the client to go forward in life outside the therapy room to seek out a new relationship. It is not the therapist's responsibility to provide the new sexual relationship. This is an extreme example, but it makes the point that therapy is about helping the client to develop the agency to satisfy their needs or wants in their lives outside the therapy room, not to satisfy them in the therapy room. Typically, clients look to therapists as authority figures. Rogers described work with one such client:

> I show real acceptance of her desire to be dependent, to rely on me as the authority who will give the answers. Notice that I accept her *wish* to be dependent. This does *not* mean that I will behave in such a way as to meet her expectations. I can more easily accept her dependent feelings, because I know where I stand, and I know that I will not *be* her authority figure, even though I am perceived as such.[3]

Certainly the therapist has a responsibility *to* the client, but they should not take a position of responsibility *over* the client. That is to say that they have a duty to live up to their obligation to the client in the way that they have agreed, but not to see themselves responsible for the client's achievement of their goals. To assume responsibility over the client is not to bring something extra to the therapy, but to take something away from the client, namely the freedom of the person to become who they truly are, to learn to trust themselves and their organismic valuing process, and to become self-directing.

The person-centered therapist does not assume that clients have the ability to self-direct sufficiently from the outset. It is axiomatic to the approach that they don't—the client *is in a state of incongruence*. As I've already mentioned, clients will often *want* to be treated conditionally. They may look to the practitioner to assume power over them, to *medicalize* their condition for them, or to blame them or others for their misfortune. The therapist needs to be fully attentive to the wholeness of the phenomenological world of the client, be aware of the tensions between expressions of a tendency toward actualization and those of a conditional self-concept, and be able to follow the client empathically moment by moment, with unconditional positive regard. Person-centered therapy is about the often gradual and difficult process of movement toward discovering one's goals, wants, and needs. For the therapist to put the onus on clients to articulate these from the outset is therapist-centered and steps outside the person-centered paradigm.

Following the client moment by moment with empathy and unconditional positive regard comes with practice and with the confidence in oneself that develops with practice and greater congruence. The real learning is not about the skills of doing but about oneself. Person-centered therapy is not a way of doing so much as a way of being. Being a person-centered therapist is ultimately about one's own congruence, or authenticity, as a human being. To be able to do the things described above, one has to have developed oneself in such a way that observing the world and others around you in an empathic and unconditional way is not an act, not something that you switch on and off for the duration of a session with a client. In a nutshell, becoming a therapist is about becoming oneself. Greater congruence, according to Rogers's theory, gives rise to an empathic and unconditionally regarding way of being.

Working with cultural diversity

Recent years have seen much more attention from mainstream social scientists, psychologists, and therapists given to issues of diversity. It is true that Rogers in his writings, which are now several decades old, did not address issues of cultural diversity as fully as he probably would have done if he were writing today, and there are instances of Rogers's own practice that might be criticized today. But we must be cautious in criticizing instances of practice that we do not unnecessarily generalize to the theory itself. I believe it is a mistake to think that the approach is not relevant across different cultures. I would argue that attention to cultural diversity is not only baked into the approach but is an aspect of the theory that needs to be made much more explicit.

The first point to make is the person-centered approach was seen as countercultural at the time of its development. This opens a discussion about what it means to fault the approach for being a reflection of Western culture, which is a common criticism from those who are not knowledgeable about the approach. Rogers's theory was a social critique of Western culture at the time, and it remains countercultural today, standing against the medicalization of distress and the oppression of people through conditions of worth.

Second, the person-centered approach is concerned with overlapping and concurrent forms of oppression. *Conditions of worth* is the term used in Rogers's theory, but it deserves to be unpacked in modern terms for those unfamiliar with his approach. A more contemporary term is *intersectionality*, which refers to how discriminatory forces such as racism, antisemitism, misogyny, and homophobia come together in a person's life. Rogers did not use the term *intersectionality*, but his theory gave us a way to think about the conditions of worth in an individual's life and to become practiced at seeing the world through another's eyes and understanding their unique frame of reference, including all the discriminatory ways in which the world around them was telling them they needed to be in order to be valued. *Intersectionality* is a modern term, but the idea is not new to those who understand what it means to listen empathically to a person and to see the world from their unique frame of reference. In saying this I am not denying therapists' responsibility to be aware of the issues and challenges that come with working with people from different backgrounds. After all, that is exactly what is demanded in an empathic relationship.

Third, empathy is a form of cultural sensitivity. The practitioner seeks to understand, through the theoretical lens of conditions of worth, the historical effects of colonization, forced removal, denial of culture and language, racism, sexism, and so on. Critics may not always understand this aspect of Rogers's theory and may think that such historical effects need to be understood instead of, or alongside, his theory, not understanding that his theory is already an analysis of systematic and collective systems and their influence. It is true, however, that Rogers's theory has not always been understood and appreciated in this more sociological sense, and one of the messages of this book is that unless we do so, we cannot fully understand the approach.

The person-centered approach allows us to work with people from diverse backgrounds because it is always about empathically understanding the unique individual and in that way can be said to be a culturally sensitive practice. It should be stressed that as an approach it does not condone forms of oppression but seeks to help people choose for themselves their directions in life. In that way, it is an approach that is equally countercultural in many other societies across the world that also restrict people's freedoms and, as a form of therapy, does not sit easily within many cultures.

At the core of how the person-centered therapist works is empathy, so right from the outset the therapist is trying to understand their client's frame of reference, which inherently involves developing a culturally sensitive understanding of the client's experiences. It is what empathic understanding is all about. If a client does not feel that they are understood, that is not the fault of the theory, but an example of poor practice. It is the therapist's responsibility to do what they need to do to be able to create an empathic environment for their client, and if that involves having an understanding of the client's cultural background, then that is what they would congruently do. The approach is an idiosyncratic one: it is about meeting the person, not about meeting a person as a representative of a larger group of people, such as a particular ethnic group or a diagnostic category. The practice of any particular person-centered therapist may be lacking in cultural awareness, but it is a mistake to generalize this to the theory itself.

The fourth point is that if one agrees with the fundamental theoretical assumptions of Rogers's approach, it is applicable to all contexts and populations. Rogers's theory is intended as a universal statement of the human condition, and as such, we would not expect there to be differences in the general processes as described from one group of people to the next. We look at the influences of the world through the concept of conditions of worth in tension with the actualizing tendency. The theory is presented as a theory of human nature; seen like this, it is either a valid theory or it is not. If it does not apply to one group of people, then it does not apply to anyone. This is a significant theoretical issue that I will return to later, in Chapter 8, but for now the above points are important to consider in the education of therapists and other professionals because it follows that how to educate therapists about issues of cultural diversity differs in the person-centered approach.

Learning to think in terms of intersectionality is important. But for the person-centered practitioner this involves deepening their own congruence such that there is sufficient awareness and overturning of their own prejudices and biases toward others, having the capacity to be genuinely accepting and unconditional in their regard for others, and being able to empathize so that the other is truly understood. This does not come from teaching about others but from learning about themselves.

In other schools of counseling and psychotherapy, it is usual to have lectures on issues of diversity, readings provided around topics of difference, or talks from people of different backgrounds of disability, ethnicity, or class about their experiences. This is intended to be of benefit to the students, to help them understand diversity and reflect on their own positions. An assumption underneath this is that it is informative of what will be helpful in advance of meeting a client who is part of that wider group. That is, in essence, an offshoot of the medical model I described earlier and no different from the idea that one needs to understand the categories of psychiatric disorder and the methods of treatment for each before meeting someone from one of the categories. This is appropriate for those other practitioners who work in a medical model way, but the person-centered approach is all about meeting the individual from their frame of reference, not as a representative of a category. This is not to say that general knowledge gained from reading about different topics, whether in psychology textbooks or fiction, or meeting different people is not useful. It can help to deepen our empathic connection with another. But it can also have the opposite effect of detracting from our empathic connection if we go into an encounter with preformed ideas, such that we see our clients through generalizations or stereotypes about the groups to which they belong.

A way of being

Students want to know how to do therapy, and to be told that this is a way of being rather than a way of doing can be frustrating. Thus, it is understandable that trainers often resort to trying to instruct students how to do it. After all, this is how students are trained in many other forms of therapy. But while you can tell someone the definitions of empathy, genuineness, and unconditionality, give presentations on the research into these concepts, and do practice sessions, becoming the sort of person who holds these attitudes isn't actually something that can be taught.

This is part of the problem of switching one's worldviews when entering into the person-centered way of working. How can you explain a way of being when asked to explain it as a way of doing? One can talk about paraphrasing what clients say, for example, as a way of explaining what to do, and this may be experienced as helpful in the beginning, but one has to tread carefully so as not to focus on doing at the expense of learning about being.

Congruence, or authenticity, is about getting to know yourself, understanding yourself and your conditions of worth, the layers of them, and becoming freer in your attitudes and ways of responding to people: being less rigid, more aware of what is going on inside you and around you, and no longer trapped by your conditions of worth, but able to observe them without being driven by them. In this way, you will learn to accept yourself more unconditionally and, in turn, be accepting and unconditional in your attitude toward others.

Rogers's theory states that in becoming more congruent, people become more unconditional and empathic in their attitudes, so to become a therapist is to become more congruent. I think it is relatively easy to pretend to be a person-centered therapist—anyone can learn some skills that allow them to put on an act that this is who they are for fifty minutes of therapy—but to actually be congruent, genuine, and unconditional requires deeper personal development and growth. Skills can be learned and honed through practice, certainly, but the person must first develop the attitudes of empathy and unconditional regard.

In this way, education to become a person-centered therapist is first and foremost about personal development and growth rather than learning a set of skills. The skills emerge out of the personal development. The foundation for this is Rogers's theory of personality development, which, as we have seen, is about the alignment of experience with the self-structure. Most of us have distorted views of ourselves and the world around us, as learned in childhood and shaped by conditions of worth, so becoming a therapist requires our distortions in self-perception to be challenged.

The self-structure, as discussed by Rogers, develops as a result of incongruence. There is no self in Rogers's theory that exists beyond the conditions of worth from which it has developed. As in Buddhism, moving toward greater congruence is actually a process in which the person strips away their conditions of worth and thus the layers of their self-structure, which, if it were possible to do completely, would leave only the motivation for maintenance and development of the organism.

Becoming more congruent is a continuous life journey. Rogers himself wrote about his own developmental process in various places and contrasted the person he had become later in his life with his younger self, who had been so conditioned by the values of his upbringing.[4] Rogers has to be credited with a revolution in psychotherapy in which it is the person of the therapist and their humanness in relationship, not the technique, that becomes the central component.

But for those setting out on the journey, truly learning what it is to bring oneself as a person to therapy may not be easy to do, or to understand, because they are still so driven by deeply introjected conditions of worth and not yet able to let go of the ways they defend and distort experiences to maintain their own self-structure. A person who cannot yet be themselves in a truly congruent fashion may be no more congruent than their client, which would mean that the third of Rogers's six conditions cannot be met.

The therapist must be more congruent than the client, but therapists are themselves only human. At the beginning, as a trainee therapist, you may only have begun to peek under a layer or two of your conditions of worth. But that may be enough for many clients. With education, greater experience, and effort to become more congruent, more layers will fall away and more clients may be able to benefit. Congruence is not something you have that can be switched on and off; it is the essence of who you are, the extent to which you have self-actualized in a way consistent with the actualizing tendency and not with conditions of worth. Learning to be oneself, congruent, and authentic is a challenging and long-term project.[5]

Because of this, congruence is not something you leave behind in the consulting room, and that is what Rogers meant when he talked about a way of being. It is a way of being that you are when you are driving your car, doing the shopping, talking to a neighbor, or voting in an election. You are who you are, and if you are a more congruent person, you will behave in ways that characterize a more congruent way of being: more empathic, unconditionally regarding, and more fully functioning. I bring this up because a common question among students is how to be person-centered outside the therapy room. It can be confusing because sometimes it seems as though you are expected to behave like a therapist wherever you go and in whatever you do, but this is not so. If you purport to be a person-centered therapist, however, this does mean that you are implicitly making at least a minimal claim that you are more congruent in your disposition than most, and for that reason one would expect certain behaviors from you, in public spaces and in private, consistent with the theory that congruence leads to openness, fluidity, empathy, and unconditionality. In essence, when put together, that means having decency and integrity as a human being.

What makes the difference between this as a way of being in one's personal life and one's professional life is whose frame of reference you are looking at the world from. In your personal life, you choose to be in your own frame of reference except in those instances when you may seek to understand another's point of view. But in a professional working context, as a practitioner meeting a client, it is the client's frame of reference from which you need to be looking at the world, except for those instances in which you might return to your own frame of reference to deal with a complex ethical or other issue that demands your attention and professional expertise.

Learning to work in a person-centered way is challenging, therefore, because often the expectation is to learn the skills, which, although important, come second to learning about yourself and beginning on a road to personal congruence. Unlike other approaches to practice, which can be presented in manualized form and thus learned in a more step-by-step way, the person-centered approach is idiosyncratic because each therapist is bringing themselves as fully as possible into the relationship. It is helpful to look over the shoulders of more experienced therapists when learning, and several books of case studies exist that can be useful guides to learn about practice,[6] to use as inspiration as we find our own voice, and to gain confidence in communicating empathy in a way that is genuine for us. It is about finding your own voice (see Box 6.5).

Box 6.5 Reflection: Learning to find your own voice

When someone is talking about something deeply upsetting and personal to them, it can leave us lost for words. A tendency might be to offer practical advice, and sometimes that will be appropriate, but often all that is wanted is an empathic response, something that shows that you are listening and doing your best to understand. We need to be attentive to the cues.

Listen for the feelings that are described. Angry, sad, jealous, miserable, and powerless may all describe what the person is feeling, but they might not actually use these words. Sometimes people might say they feel one way, but their volume and tone of voice says something different.

Observe the other person. Notice their posture; their movements, whether still or agitated; whether they seem flushed; and their facial expression. Imagine yourself in the same posture and what that feels like.

Notice what is going on within you. How do you feel listening to the person? Pay attention to your body for clues.

Let it all sink into your awareness. When you are ready, share your observations. With practice, you will sharpen your skills at noticing and gain in confidence in expressing yourself.

There are two major stumbling blocks to the application of the person-centered approach. First, professionals are often employed to deliver a service to clients where the agenda is already set in advance with particular goals in mind, restricting the therapist, or coach, or whatever other practitioner from staying with the agenda of the client. This issue is more pertinent in some contexts than others, but having the opportunities to work in a person-centered way is often restricted. Second, adopting a non-directive relational stance is challenging for professionals who are used to offering advice, interpretations, and problem-solving. Without appropriate experience and training in person-centered theory and practice, it is difficult to work effectively in this way, and for the less experienced practitioner, this can easily spill into giving advice, offering interpretations, and using other interventions that are incompatible with the person-centered approach.

Being mindful

Mindfulness practice has been gaining increasing attention in the West over the last forty years, and a range of secular mindfulness-based interventions have been developed in the service of improving psychological and physical health. Mindfulness involves a receptive attention to and awareness of present events and experience and includes the ability for self-regulation of attention (moment-to-moment awareness) and an attitude of curiosity, openness, and acceptance toward one's experiences, including thoughts, perceptions, emotions, and sensations.

Kabat-Zinn, one of the founders of the modern mindfulness movement, defines the approach as paying attention in a particular way: on purpose, in the present moment, and non-judgmentally.[7] Typical formal mindful practices involve attention to and awareness of present-moment breathing, hearing, seeing, thoughts, or bodily sensations. Theoretical and conceptual understanding of mindfulness in a Western context has also been a recent concern of academic disciplines and psychology in particular.[8] Empirical work has shown that mindfulness is associated with a host of well-being indicators and that mindfulness-based approaches provide possible means of fostering self-determination and self-awareness and in this way facilitate the satisfaction of basic psychological needs for autonomy, competence, and relatedness.[9]

Within therapeutic and coaching psychology settings, mindfulness training has been mostly allied with cognitive behavioral therapy as a technique to reduce the risk of relapse following treatment for depression. People are encouraged to view their thoughts as "mental events" that are detached from, rather than an integral part of, the person and their psychological makeup. This detachment then provides individuals with the skills and abilities they need in order to prevent the escalation of depressive thoughts and feelings into full-blown major depression.

There is clearly a synergy between the aims of mindfulness, with its focus on present awareness, and the psychology of Rogers.[10] Relating this back to the discussion in the previous chapter about whether one can use techniques, I would argue that it is not whether one can use them, but how they are used. There are exercises and techniques within the mindfulness literature that a practitioner could use with a client.

I would also go further and say that the person-centered approach is already a mindful approach. It may not use the exact same language as the mindfulness literature, but if one thinks through the concepts of person-centered theory, the notion of present awareness is central to the concepts of congruence and unconditionality. By definition, the therapist conditions of empathic understanding, congruence, and unconditional positive self-regard in the service of staying present with and attentive to the client's moment-to moment process is a mindful practice.

The practice of person-centered therapy requires the practitioner to relinquish any goal for the client. The notion of going with the client in their direction and at their pace, so central to person-centered practice, is often misunderstood as being little more than asking the client what they want from the sessions and then attempting to give it to them. What is actually required, as I've discussed above, is the practitioner paying attention, moment by moment, to what the client says and how they say it, along with their expressions and posture. In short, person-centered therapy requires the practitioner to be mindful of their client, to understand without wanting to change the client's frame of reference. This is perhaps most clearly represented in the person-centered idea of the therapist developing an unconditionally accepting, empathic understanding of the client. Here we can see that the practitioner is required to adopt an attitude of mindful and non-judgmental curiosity about the client's experience, asking, as Rogers put it in 1987 in an article in the *Journal of Humanistic Psychology*, "Can I be sensitive to every nuance of personal meaning and value, no matter how different it is from my own experience?"[11]

Above, I discussed the person-centered approach as a way of being, dependent on the personal development of the therapist. This is usually achieved through personal therapy, personal development groups, and experiential learning within training. I would suggest that mindfulness exercises used within person-centered training are likely to help people develop congruence.[12]

Mindfulness skills training focuses on developing the attitudinal aspects of curiosity, openness, acceptance, and non-judgment—attitudes that converge with the process outcomes of person-centered therapy and Rogers's definition of fully functioning. Therefore, those individuals who are more fully functioning from a person-centered understanding are also likely to show higher dispositional mindfulness.[13]

There is certainly convergence between mindfulness and person-centered practice in their shared goal of facilitating more present-focused living, their association with more autonomous functioning, and their focus on authenticity implicit in the person-centered conceptualization of congruence. It should probably not surprise us, then, when mindfulness practitioners embrace attitudes and values that resonate with those of the person-centered approach. Kabat-Zinn wrote the following in 1994:

> I like to think of mindfulness simply as the art of conscious living. You don't have to be a Buddhist or a yogi to practice it. In fact, if you know anything about Buddhism, you will know that the most important point is to be yourself and not to try to become anything that you are not already . . . It [mindfulness] is simply a practical way to become more in touch with the fullness of your being through a systematic process of self-observation, self-inquiry and mindful action.[14]

Research testing the correlation between psychometric scales of mindfulness and self-actualization are consistent with the notion that there is a similarity between Rogers's views and those of the Buddhist tradition.[15] Indeed, the very concept of congruence, which is so central to person-centered approach, would seem to refer to both moment-to-moment awareness and openness and acceptance toward one's experiences including thoughts, perceptions, emotions, and sensations. Recognizing the similarities between the concepts of congruence and mindfulness promises to be helpful to person-centered practitioners who may have overemphasized the secondary aspect of congruence, the honest expression of thoughts and feelings, at the expense of developing more mindful self-awareness. On the other hand, it may be beneficial for mindfulness practitioners to reflect on the wider theoretical context provided by the person-centered approach and its non-directive stance, to be aware of how mindfulness is often taken out of its original theoretical context and used instrumentally when, in fact, it is better understood as a goal in itself.[16]

My argument is that person-centered practice is already a form of mindfulness. Practitioners holding the attitudinal conditions of empathy, unconditionality, and congruence are already by definition engaged in mindful practice—that is, they are present in the moment, self-aware of inner experiencing, and accepting of themselves.

Concluding comments

My aim in this chapter has been to clarify some of the misunderstandings that often arise in putting theory into practice. Rogers described six necessary and sufficient conditions for constructive personality change that to this day remain the cornerstone of practice in the person-centered approach and that included the practitioner conditions of congruence, empathy, and unconditional positive regard. But Rogers never operationalized these conditions in such a way that there are step-by-step instructions for how to do this because he was describing a way of being rather than a way of doing. But in today's world, where it is commonplace for therapies to be "manualized" so that therapists have steps to follow, workbooks to read from, and tools to deliver, this is what those new to Rogers's philosophy often look for. Ultimately, however, it is about learning about themselves in a journey of becoming a more authentic human being, something that can only come about through deep personal development, to become a person who is empathic and unconditionally regarding in their attitude toward themselves and others.

Chapter 7

Building bridges to positive psychology

Applications to psychotherapy, organizations, and education

As I discussed earlier, one of the unique characteristics of Rogers's person-centered approach was its focus on becoming fully functioning. Forty years later, positive psychology arrived on the scene, and other practitioners, scholars, and researchers turned their attention to the topic of well-being and how to promote human flourishing, but in doing so they showed little awareness that this was a path already well-trodden. Much of my writing since the birth of positive psychology has been about the application of the person-centered approach to positive psychology and its offshoots of coaching, positive organizational scholarship, and positive education.[1] The person-centered approach sits within the wider tradition of humanistic psychology, but in this chapter I want to make the case that, seen more contemporarily, it is also part of the positive psychology movement and, more widely, that of research and scholarship into human flourishing. This is important to recognize because it helps to extend Rogers's ideas into new areas and demonstrate their relevance in today's world.

But more than 20 years ago, when positive psychology was introduced, I didn't pay it much attention at first. It was promoting the idea that psychology had spent its time and energy only investigating what went wrong with people, at the expense of what went right. I completely agreed that it was a good idea for psychologists to redirect their efforts in this way, but having spent the previous several years studying the person-centered approach, my initial reaction was to ignore this new movement as it seemed to offer nothing new. I thought the movement's ideas were not as revolutionary as they seemed to imply they were, but echoed those of the humanistic psychologists from previous decades. I felt irritated by what seemed like an ignorance of the history of psychology and realized later that I wasn't alone in holding such views as many humanistic scholars felt similarly, but I also saw the enthusiasm of my students for positive psychology. They were younger, fresh from their degree courses, and knew little about the history of psychology and the humanistic tradition but were excited and energized by positive psychology.

The Humanistic Psychology of Carl Rogers. Stephen A. Joseph, Oxford University Press. © Oxford University Press (2025). DOI: 10.1093/9780197790632.003.0008

The more I came to understand the new movement, the more I could see that positive psychology was succeeding in bringing ideas about well-being and human flourishing back into mainstream awareness, while humanistic and person-centered psychology were failing to do so, and had themselves become marginalized in the backwater of research and practice. For the past two decades, I have sought to build bridges between humanistic and positive psychology, making the case that the person-centered approach is a form of positive psychology. I would like to claim that my efforts, as well as those of many others, have helped to shift the discussion such that it is common, when picking up a contemporary book on the topic of positive psychology, to see Rogers and other humanistic psychologists explicitly mentioned as pioneers, and many of the ideas from the person-centered approach are now part of mainstream debate and discussion, attracting new research interest. But I feel that my bridge-building has been far more successful in bringing the ideas of the person-centered approach to positive psychology than in bringing positive psychology to the person-centered audience. I hope to redress this balance here, not only to position the person-centered approach as part of contemporary positive psychology, but also to introduce person-centered scholars and practitioners to the ideas of positive psychology and to encourage greater attention to the application of the approach outside the therapy room.

Positive psychology

Positive psychology was formally launched by Martin Seligman in his 1998 presidential address to the American Psychological Association.[2] This led to a special issue of the journal *American Psychologist* in 2000 in which the editors, Seligman and his colleague Mihaly Csikszentmihalyi, brought together a range of scholars with the common interest of how to promote positively valued human experiences, which until that point had been largely neglected by research.[3] Seligman later said the idea of positive psychology came to him in a moment of epiphany while gardening with his daughter, Nikki, who was then aged five, when she instructed him not to be such a grouch. "In that moment, I acquired the mission of helping to build the scientific infrastructure of a field that would investigate what makes life worth living: positive emotion, positive character and positive institutions."[4]

What Seligman realized was that when it comes to understanding problems in living, a considerable amount of time and money had been spent over the years documenting the various ways in which people suffer psychologically, but nowhere near the same effort had gone into understanding what makes life worth living. Seligman therefore resolved to use his presidency to initiate a shift in psychology's focus toward a more positive psychology. But while such thinking was a refreshing change for many, these were not new ideas. The idea of focusing on the positive was an idea that was, as we have seen, always core to humanistic psychology.

Arguments similar to those put forward by Seligman had been proposed decades earlier by the first generation of humanistic psychologists. So it seemed that the ideas long championed by humanistic psychologists were now being put forward again, but in a way that was critical of humanistic psychology for its supposed antiscientific stance and that paid scant acknowledgment to its achievements.[5]

In response, the *Journal of Humanistic Psychology* published a special issue in 2001 containing several articles dedicated to what had become a fraught relationship between humanistic and positive psychology. Tom Greening, the editor at the time, opened by remarking that positive psychology had appeared as if humanistic psychology, with its decades of scholarship and research, had simply not existed and noting that Rogers himself had been a president of the American Psychological Association.[6] Eugene Taylor, in his article in the special issue, refuted Seligman's arguments that humanistic psychology was antiscientific and that it had not generated significant research.[7] It was also argued that positive psychology could learn from the experiential, process-oriented research methodologies common to the humanistic psychotherapies.[8] Certainly it is clear that some of the initial comments by positive psychologists in the early days were unjustified.

As the positive psychology movement evolved, however, and gained a foothold in the mainstream agenda, its leaders came to acknowledge, in later articles, the accomplishments of the pioneers of humanistic psychology.[9] I don't want to reiterate those discussions here because I think the positive psychology movement has largely accepted the arguments that were put forward by its critics and now considers humanistic psychology to be part of its historical lineage. Positive psychology has become a richer and deeper form of scholarship as a result. For example, one important shift that seems to reflect the accommodation of ideas from humanistic psychology is the movement toward more eudaimonic conceptualizations of well-being as opposed to only the hedonic. As a result, it is now more difficult to dismiss positive psychology as superficial, as some of its critics had done, such as Barbara Ehrenreich, in her book *Smile or Die*.[10]

But there is often some truth in messages we don't want to hear, and such was the case for humanistic psychologists when positive psychology arrived. As mentioned, I felt dismissive of positive psychology myself and even irritated by its seeming ignorance, but I came to see that there was also some truth in positive psychology's initial negative portrayal of what humanistic psychology had become. There were aspects of the 1960s counterculture associated with humanistic psychology that were questionable and did no favors to its standing in the eyes of mainstream psychology.[11] But humanistic psychology provides a wide umbrella under which many theories and approaches to psychology and therapy stand, and it has a rich history of scholarship.[12] The person-centered approach stands under that umbrella, but not all humanistic psychologists are person-centered in their approach. There are parts of humanistic psychology that are antiscientific and lacking in evidence. Thus, as I've argued before, it was possibly a politically astute move by the positive psychologists to distance themselves from the perceived embarrassments of humanistic psychology if they were to succeed where humanistic psychology had failed in garnering mainstream attention, funding, and prestige.[13] But in tarring humanistic psychology as a whole with criticism, much of that landed in places that simply didn't deserve it, including the person-centered approach, which has a well-developed evidence base and scientific approach. In that respect, the person-centered approach has much in common with positive psychology, making it, in my view, the original positive psychology.

Whether intentionally or not, positive psychology has helped to bring the ideas of Rogers and the person-centered approach back into the mainstream. The defining feature of positive psychology was the focus on human flourishing, and it provided a corrective to the previous decades of research on the various manifestations of distress and dysfunction. As a result, many scholars and practitioners now dedicate their careers to the study of well-being and how to promote human flourishing. In that respect, I don't see much to disagree with.

However, when I mention my interest in positive psychology to colleagues who are involved in the person-centered approach, often they are dismissive of it, possibly not understanding that it is a serious discipline concerned with how to promote well-being and human flourishing and confusing it with more popular ideas around positive thinking. Or it may be that despite their own dedication to the person-centered approach, they have themselves become ensnared by the illness ideology and lost sight of the original positive psychological nature of the person-centered approach, only emphasizing the other two of the three characteristics I discussed in Chapter 3. For many practitioners of the person-centered approach, its defining characteristics are that the client is expert and that the six relationship conditions are necessary and sufficient. Less attention is given to Rogers's personality theory and the conceptualization of the therapeutic aim to become more fully functioning. So mainstream is the medical terminology for mental health that many person-centered practitioners inadvertently slip into the use of medical terminology to discuss their client work.

I mentioned in my introduction that I thought the person-centered approach was ahead of its time, and in its early days it was, but more recently this important and fundamental characteristic of the person-centered approach—that it is about positive psychology—has been given little attention in the contemporary person-centered literature. The medical model had become commonplace, such that the language of disorder and deficit is everywhere.

A browse through a directory of therapists will show many practitioners who describe themselves as person-centered also advertising themselves as working with a range of different conditions. As discussed earlier, this is understandable in the sense that therapists need to attract clients to stay in business, and so they reach out using language that clients will understand. However, this is not always done with an awareness of the contradictory nature of doing so. Years of having to compete and market themselves in an industry driven by an illness ideology has, I believe, led many person-centered scholars and practitioners to lose sight of the fact that theirs is a growth model. Thus, person-centered practitioners and scholars needed this conceptual reboot from positive psychology as much as anyone else. For many years now, it has been a mission of mine to develop a wider awareness that therapy is not only for alleviating psychological suffering, but also for helping people to become more fully functioning. I used the term *positive therapy* to describe this. It is not a new idea, as I described it in my book *Positive Therapy*,[14] and it was, as we have seen, the vision of Rogers, who used the term *fully functioning* to describe what therapy freed people to move toward.

Some might wonder why such a discussion about the relationship between positive psychology and the person-centered approach is useful or interesting; the answer is that it is important to know how to situate the approach in relation to mainstream discussions within the scholarly and professional community. To see the person-centered approach as a branch of humanistic psychology is correct, but to see it as only that, without reference to its more contemporary synergies, is to miss opportunities for its growth and development. One example of this is the interest in posttraumatic growth, a topic that has become somewhat of a flagship for positive psychology.

In the early 1990s, following an explosion of research into posttraumatic stress disorder in the 1980s, some researchers began to observe that survivors of trauma also reported perceiving benefits and positive changes. The term *posttraumatic growth* was coined in 1995 by Richard Tedeschi and Lawrence Calhoun, two clinical researchers based then at the University of North Carolina. Posttraumatic growth was, and continues to be, defined by those who originated the term as "positive psychological changes experienced as a result of the struggle with traumatic or highly challenging life circumstances."[15]

Posttraumatic growth describes phenomena that were observed in clients following trauma, and the term is used by many psychologists who are not necessarily viewing it in person-centered terms. It simply describes their research and practice into the positive psychological changes often observed in people following trauma, such as an enhanced appreciation of life, shifts in priorities about what is important to them, an ability to form deeper and more intimate relationships, and a recognition of new strengths within themselves.[16] Of course, Rogers never actually used the term *posttraumatic growth*; he was writing decades before it was coined. But his description of breakdown and disorganization, which I discussed previously in relation to trauma, and how person-centered theory proposes that people are intrinsically inclined to reconcile self and experience captures what the person-centered theorist would describe as a movement toward more fully functioning behavior, which can be conceptualized as posttraumatic growth.[17]

A few years ago the journal *Person-Centered & Experiential Psychotherapies* had a special issue dedicated to the topic of posttraumatic growth.[18] The client-centered approach to posttraumatic growth challenges the trauma industry by offering a non-medicalized view, putting the person back in the driver's seat as the expert on what is best for themselves, and, above all, offering a hopeful view that overcoming adversity can also mean positive psychological changes. For client-centered therapists working with traumatized people, this is good news. We don't need to see our clients as broken, disordered, or needing to be repaired or fixed, but rather as benefiting from the healing power of empathic and unconditional relationships. In the therapeutic relationship, clients can process their experiences of breakdown and disorganization through learning to listen to themselves, becoming more self-accepting, and finding new directions.

The point here is to build bridges between client-centered therapy and mainstream positive psychology—on the one hand to build greater awareness and understanding of the person-centered approach, and on the other to help empower client-centered therapists in their understanding and ability to communicate with other professionals. Because these bridges are incomplete, I believe the approach has become isolated and intellectually degraded over the years.

While one obvious application of positive psychology is in clinical psychology and therapy, as this discussion has illustrated, possible applications of positive psychology are much wider.[19] Posttraumatic growth is just one example of a topic from positive psychology, all which are essentially trying to answer the same question of how to promote human flourishing, in all its aspects and in all contexts of people's lives. Moving beyond the clinical context, two areas of particular interest are organizational scholarship and educational practice.

Positive organizational scholarship

Many of us spend our lives working in organizations, and all of us are recipients of the services provided by organizations. It is in all our interests that organizations not only function effectively but also that they operate with concern for people as human beings. Since the beginnings of the discipline of psychology, there have been those who have sought to apply it to organizational life, often in favor of finding ways to boost productivity and performance, but the last decade has seen a new trend in organization studies toward what has been called positive organizational scholarship (POS). Influenced by the ideas of positive psychology, POS is an extension of organizational scholarship to encompass flourishing in organizations.[20] POS has changed the face of organizational studies in recent years, with topics such as hope, optimism, resilience, strengths, grit, mindfulness, and emotional intelligence becoming the focus for empirical work and theorizing. These have acted as stimuli to influence change within organizations toward positive approaches.[21]

However, while some of these terms may be new, as we have seen, the idea of taking a positive approach is not entirely new, and there is much in POS that is reminiscent of an earlier field called "humanistic management," which also sought to promote human flourishing and add value to society.[22] POS brings together scholars from a range of disciplines interested in human flourishing in organizations, and increasingly, organizations are applying their research.

It may seem uncontroversial to propose that Rogers's theory could be applied in POS to fostering better employee relationships, leadership development, and so on. The philosophy of the person-centered approach has applicability in numerous contexts, including in institutions and organizations, with the aim of transforming communication, developing person-centered leadership, introducing innovation management, managing conflict transformation, overcoming resistance to change, and offering process consultation and leadership coaching. It can be applied to individuals, teams, departments, and whole organizational systems.[23] What could be problematic about advocating better human relations and seeking to promote human flourishing in workplaces? Is that not what POS is striving to do? Indeed, I would argue that a humanistic POS would be more radical in its approach to empowering and liberating people. That is because the non-directive aspect of Rogers's theory challenges the contrasting philosophy of most mainstream institutions and organizations, which is that people need external direction. Organizations, generally speaking, operate from bureaucratic procedures and competency and performativity frameworks because, of course, the hidden ideology is not that people need freedom but that they need control and coercion.

Therefore, in most organizations there is little that would be recognized as the genuine application of values and ideas that are person-centered, but as POS becomes taken seriously within organizations, it provides an opportunity for a new vision. On the surface there is a synergy between person-centered ideas and POS. There are clear applications of Rogers's theory in organizations to develop positive relationships, positive human resource practices, and positive leadership and change. In this regard, Rogers's work on the use of encounter groups as a way to manage conflict promises to be helpful. As already mentioned, so much of his thinking has been incorporated into theory and practice as common sense that many scholars who follow in his tradition are likely unaware that this is what they are doing. Indeed, the person-centered approach has a long history of application in the workplace. As long ago as 1992, Fred Massarik wrote the following in his discussion of the humanistic core of industrial/organizational (I/O) psychology:

> Carl R. Rogers' influence on the humanistic in I/O psychology as well has been far reaching. Particularly his approaches to client-centered therapy . . . have affected directly, or have been infused indirectly into numerous styles of interviewing in industry and organizations, for the most eclectic purposes: employee counseling, selection and placement, exit interviews, assessment for promotion or reassignment, and the like. And his views of "the person" and associated concepts relating to people's capacity for growth have left their mark on human resources/personnel policies, professional training and organizational development.[24]

During the 1960s, before POS, the person-centered approach was influential in many early organizational development interventions. Why, then, does this vacuum of humanistic ideas exist in POS? As Alfonso Montuori and Ronald Purser argue, this may be because the 1970s and 1980s onward saw a changing socioeconomic environment in which there was an erosion of the core values informed by humanistic psychology in favor of a more competitive business environment in which managers were seeking change to address the "bottom line."[25] Encounter group and reflective methodologies were seen as no longer relevant. In their place, more utilitarian tools and techniques were introduced, though they still used the language of freedom and liberation that was associated with the liberal humanistic agenda of writers such as Rogers. Montuori and Purser show how Rogers's work was usurped to provide ways of establishing control and the imposition of authority rather than its originally intended means of creating democracy and participation. In short, Rogers's ideas about developing constructive and empathic human relationships seemed like common sense but, once disconnected from their theoretical anchor, actually become mechanisms of control and coercion.

Thus, it is perhaps not surprising—given Montuori and Purser's observation about what we would now refer to as the rise of neoliberalism—that the person-centered approach receives so little mention in contemporary POS, as it emerged after the decades of the 1980s and 1990s, during which core humanistic values were eroded. Positive psychology stepped into the space that was left, adopting the idea that it would be economically productive to look at positive qualities. But I would argue that it did so as part of the neoliberal culture rather than challenging it as humanistic psychology had done. In fact, as I've already mentioned, the leading positive psychologists initially distanced themselves as best they could from humanistic psychology in an attempt to gain credibility, given how radical its ideas were still seen to be by mainstream psychology in the late 1990s. They deliberately chose to play up the utilitarian functions of the new positive psychology to attract attention from funding bodies, organizations, and governments.

Thus, while the pendulum has swung some way back, toward framing organizational development within a more positive framework, it has not swung far enough to create the democracy and participation that the person-centered approach and humanistic psychology once brought to management studies and I/O psychology or swung anywhere close to the potential of POS as a more humanistic discipline. There are, of course, exceptions. Many POS scholars do draw on a person-centered theory of personality, but there is so much more work of this nature that could be done. Relationships as envisaged by Rogers dismantle traditional hierarchical structures, share power openly and transparently, and lead to non-directive dialogue (see Box 7.1).

Box 7.1 Reflection: Thinking about person-centered organizations

This is a POS-inspired exercise that can be used to generate discussion within an organizational setting. The following are polar opposite statements that characterize the way organizations treat their workers. Thinking about the organization that you work in or are most familiar with, choose one concept from each pair that is the closest to your experience.

1. Trusting employees to do their best and offering them guidance and expertise to help as requested
   versus

2. Micro-management of activities

1. Genuinely listening to employees and acting on their concerns and suggestions
   versus
2. Showing no interest in employees' point of view

1. Seeing everyone in the organization as being on the same side in terms of their goals
   versus
2. Seeing conflict and competition between workers and management in their goals

Why do you think the organization is the way that it is? How might you like it to be different, and what steps do you think could be taken to move in that direction?

Positive education

Education is the most powerful institution in the world for shaping the future of humanity because of its influence on how each generation comes to view what matters and what to prioritize and value. Recent years have seen much interest in positive psychology applications to education and the development of the new subfield of "positive education." Positive education was an idea that developed out of the positive psychology movement initiated at the turn of the new century by Seligman and colleagues "as education for both traditional skills and for happiness."[26]

The term *happiness* is used in this definition in a broad sense; positive education programs have been shown to foster a range of positively valued qualities, including curiosity, love of learning, optimism, creativity, and social skills. The argument put forward by Seligman and colleagues was that, in the context of rising levels of depression and anxiety among young people, positive education can provide young people and young adults with the skills they need to increase their resilience, positive emotions, engagement, and meaning in life. Since it was introduced, the influence of the positive education movement has grown considerably.

Many educational theorists have welcomed the movement and are seeking ways to embed positive education into the classroom, on the sports field, and throughout the curriculum in schools and universities. This is done using various positive psychology exercises, such as thinking about three good things (an exercise in which people are asked to reflect on aspects of their life that they are grateful for), and helping young people to use their strengths in new ways. Applications of positive psychology are now widely recognized in schools and higher education, and various scholars continue to explore different applications within these contexts.[27] These institutions provide an opportunity to teach young people and adults skills of well-being that it is hoped will combat rising levels of depression and anxiety and enhance their learning and ability to think creatively. Positive education has been eagerly adopted by the educational sector, and many schools now implement some version of positive education, from introducing an aspect of positive psychology as a lesson within the curriculum to full courses about positive psychology or institution-wide programs. Most notable is the work reported from the Geelong Grammar School.[28]

But while these ideas of positive education are now entering the mainstream educational agenda, the idea that education can be about more than it currently is, and play a greater role in the development of young people, is not a new one. The notion that education is about more than imparting knowledge dates back to Greek and Chinese classics and also appears in more recent literature. This renewed emphasis on the development of the positive psychological qualities of the person and the notion of education as a vehicle for helping people flourish is welcome. But even in this sense, positive education as a renewed interest arising out of developments in psychology is not new; it is similar to that of the person-centered approach of Carl Rogers in his book *Freedom to Learn*.

Rogers saw education as a vehicle for promoting human flourishing and developed his ideas in the context of the contemporary empirical research and theory in humanistic psychology. But it would not be correct to see positive education simply as a revisioning of person-centered education; while both share an interest in human flourishing, person-centered education was based on a distinctive growth model of human nature. Subsequent to his work developing the field of therapy, Rogers went on, in the 1960s and 1970s, to develop what he called person-centered education. Rogers wrote about the person-centered approach as an alternative pedagogy that can underpin educational practice.

In the program we teach at the University of Nottingham's School of Education, our students learn to be person-centered practitioners, but they do so in a person-centered teaching environment. If they are to trust their clients to find their own directions in therapy, surely they must first become people who are able to find direction for themselves in their own lives? As an educator, it is therefore my responsibility to provide a learning environment in which this can take place. In this way, students sit together with staff in a circle, and the agenda and curriculum are developed together, in an attempt to create a truly democratic learning environment, and everyone is responsible for what is to be learned and when and how it will be learned. There is a direction to this that is determined by the topic of that class, so, for example, in theory class, we are sitting together knowing that the aim is to understand Rogers's theory. Everyone brings their own experiences to that, and in the ensuing conversations and encounters with each other, we begin to learn about the theory, but in a way that means we are living it while we talk about it, learning from our experiences of it rather than listening to others talk about it. And in this process, students are not only learning about the theory, but they are also learning how to learn, learning about themselves and their relationships with others, and experiencing the same processes that Rogers describes in his theory.

Intuitively, teaching person-centered theory in a person-centered way makes sense, but Rogers was not just talking about teaching therapy students; he meant all topics across the curriculum can be taught in a student-centered way. Unlike positive education, which is about dropping some additional teaching about well-being into an existing curriculum that carries on as it teaches mathematics, science, and so on, Rogers's approach is about revolutionizing the existing curriculum such that it becomes student-centered. Math, science, everything is done according to student-centered principles. Nothing is added to the existing curriculum; rather, the existing curriculum is overturned in a way that it is now student-centered. Thus, whereas we might talk about positive psychology *in* education, with Rogers's approach we are talking it *as* education. It is a truly revolutionary way of doing positive psychology.

Despite this, his writings on person-centered education have received little attention in the positive education literature. Positive education, while offering a new focus on human flourishing, does not challenge traditional education with its largely teacher-centered approach. Rogers's view on education was that this approach thwarted and usurped developmental processes and stifled creativity and curiosity. In this respect, positive educational theorists can learn from the person-centered approach to become a more radical force for changing lives in education, whether in schools or in further or higher education.

In the same way that positive education arose out of the positive psychology movement, person-centered education developed out of the person-centered approach to psychology and psychotherapy. Early on, even as Rogers was developing his approach to psychotherapy—for which he is best known—he was beginning to turn his thoughts to the topic of teaching and learning. In *Client-Centered Therapy*, published in 1951, he devoted a chapter to the topic of student-centered teaching. Later, in one of his first papers on the subject, he questioned the common-sense view that teaching is equivalent to learning, writing that learning might, in fact, be enhanced if we did away with teaching, examinations, and institutionally awarded measures of competence.[29]

For Rogers, it seemed that educators and the public focused on teaching at the expense of learning. His argument was that only when educators paid attention to the latter would they find effective ways of promoting learning. For Rogers, what was important was the realness of the facilitator and their willingness to meet the student as a person with qualities such as trust, warmth, and respect. In this way, *facilitator* was a better term than *teacher*.[30] In 1969 Rogers published his influential book *Freedom to Learn*, in which he set out his full philosophy of education: in essence, that human beings have a natural urge to learn, that this most readily happens when the subject matter is perceived as relevant to the student, that learning involves change and so is threatening and resisted, that learning is best achieved by doing, and that the most lasting learning takes place in an atmosphere of freedom in which students were trusted to be autonomous learners.[31]

In the revised edition of *Freedom to Learn* published in the 1980s,[32] Rogers wrote that the goal of education was to assist people to learn to be self-determining; take self-initiated action and be responsible for those actions; adapt flexibly and intelligently to new problem situations; internalize an adaptive mode of approach to problems, utilizing all pertinent experience freely and creatively; cooperate effectively with others in these various activities; and work, not for the approval of others, but in terms of their own socialized purposes. To adopt other goals in which the teacher has a predetermined intention that the student should change in any particular direction was seen from Rogers's person-centered perspective as contradictory to the act of nurturing self-determination.

As with therapy, Rogers's approach to education was based on the ontological view that people are born with a natural tendency toward exploration, growth, and achievement of their full potential. Such socially constructive views of human nature, in which the aim of the educator is to release students' innate potentials, have been compared to the way a gardener nurtures seedlings to release their full potential. A gardener can't make the seedlings sprout; all they can do is provide the right environment so that the seedlings will sprout (see Box 7.2).

Box 7.2 Reflection. Your own experience of school

Thinking about your own education at school, would you agree or disagree with the following statements:

At school I was really helped to find out about myself and what my strengths were.

Teachers always treated me with respect and warmth.

Many of my teachers really tried to understand me as a person.

At school I was given the opportunity to try different things I was interested in.
I felt I could be myself at school.

The more you agree with the above statements, the more that would suggest your school had a person-centered climate. Thinking about your answers, in what way do you think school was an influence on the person you have become.

Applied to education, these are the relationship conditions that the person-centered educator wishes to create for their students and the basis for their non-directive attitude. While many educators may agree with Rogers's philosophy, relatively few implement it in the full sense of what he intended, and even where they would wish to do so, it is difficult because the culture of education today runs counter to his philosophy. As I said in my introduction to this book, students are most often treated as if they are passive recipients of information rather than active learners, given a fixed curriculum with the only goal being to pass an exam, and are asked to write essays that regurgitate what's already been fed to them.

The person-centered approach remains of interest to some educators and educational theorists—in particular those interested in theories and processes of learning—who have long acknowledged Rogers's writings and his influence on the development of experiential, reflective, and problem-based learning and the wider field of humanistic and learner-centered forms of education. David Kolb, in his book *Experiential Learning*, for example, lists him as one of the "foundational scholars of experiential learning."[33]

The person-centered approach to education remains a valuable, philosophically based practical approach to education that can be applied in schools and in higher education.[34] However, it is an approach that is today mostly viewed historically as part of an earlier movement of humanistic educational practices. Therefore, in order to help develop its contemporary relevance, I believe it should be positioned within the more recent field of positive education.

Positive education approaches are not always implemented as an end in themselves but as a means to an end, which is to further academic attainment. For example, the idea of character education is considered as a means to help students do better in conventional terms rather than the outcome of an educational process. Indeed, these approaches to character education are used in all sectors, and there has been research into character development that suggests it can improve employability. While positive education can be useful in broadening curricular activities, this is often done in order to arrive at the same traditional outcome, with academic attainment being considered the primary goal.

The person-centered approach to education remains a radical proposition. For Rogers, the person-centered approach is about genuine human relations in which the responsibility for learning is shared, as much as possible, between student and facilitator. Students develop their own program of learning in the expectation that, given freedom and a facilitative environment, they will move in the most constructive directions for themselves. What we are describing here is an ontological stance toward education in which a person's intrinsic motivation is cultivated and their flourishing as human beings arises, by developing autonomy, agency, and self-understanding through the process of learning to learn.

Is it possible to promote a climate of human flourishing without compromising on educational attainment goals?[35] The question is how these dual goals of learning about subjects and learning about oneself can be reconciled. Rogers managed to do this in his development of person-centered education. From the ontological position represented by the person-centered approach, well-being and achievement are not attained at the expense of each other: success in learning about oneself is integral to success in learning about the world and success in life's achievements. Education can be understood as being about the full development of the person and not merely the functional acquisition of facts or the use of memory to recall these facts. In the person-centered approach, one does not exist at the expense of the other because both are so closely intertwined. In 1967, Rogers wrote in the introduction to his paper "A Plan for Self-Directed Change in an Educational System,"

> The title which I first chose for this paper was 'A practical Plan for Educational Revolution.' I felt, though, that this might offend and antagonize too many people. Why is there need for a revolution in education?[36]

I would argue that while positive education has reintroduced some of ideas about the promotion of well-being in young people and adults into the educational agenda, the need for revolution in the way envisaged by Rogers remains. Person-centered education is a form of positive education, insofar as both emphasize the promotion of human flourishing, but it also places a stake firmly in the ground to draw attention to, and create a tension with, the otherwise implicitly accepted ontological stance of mainstream education.

For the person-centered educational theorist, the introduction of positive education takes a step toward a necessary revolution, but it stops well short of promoting a curriculum change that would be fully respectful of learners' self-determination. For the person-centered educator, the goal of education is not only to teach the content of the material to be learned; it is also to produce more fully functioning people who are open to experience, adopt an existential way of living, and trust in themselves to know their directions. The person-centered approach is a powerful alternative pedagogy in which the person is learning to be themselves—to actualize their potential—in ways that seem increasingly important for the world today.[37] In Rogers's theory, what is important for growth and development in young people is that they encounter new experiences that challenge them and that their self-structure accommodates the reality of these experiences; thus, they approach life more resistant to breakdown and disorganization in the future. A contemporary term for this aspect of congruence is *antifragility*, the idea of resilience arising as a result of stresses and shocks to the system.[38]

Rogers wrote[39] that the humanistically oriented teacher feels like an alien within the conventional system, with their wish to share responsibility for the content and direction of the curriculum and to help students find their own program of learning. I hope the person-centered approach, seen now as a form of positive education, will garner new interest and educationalists will begin to look more deeply into the creation of growth-promoting climates.[40]

Person-centered positive psychology

In the ways described above, person-centered psychology and its applications are not incompatible with an interest in positive psychology. The person-centered approach can be seen as a form of positive psychology because of the common interest in human flourishing. But that simple assertion can be misunderstood as a claim that positive psychology is person-centered. It is not, because positive psychology does not necessarily share an interest in the other two characteristics discussed earlier, namely self-determination of the person and their change in this direction as a result of the social environment. The person-centered approach is a form of positive psychology, but positive psychology is not necessarily person-centered.

Seeing the compatibility, I began to think of myself as a person-centered positive psychologist. I began to see positive psychology as an important umbrella for all of us in the person-centered approach to shelter under in order to be able to share our ideas with a larger community and embrace the enthusiasm of the positive psychologists for empirical evidence—to begin to build bridges.[41]

Thus, I would like to invite readers to become more fully acquainted with what it means to be a positive psychologist. It means that you have interests in promoting well-being and human flourishing, whether through therapy or other means. Broadly speaking, this was also Rogers's vision, and in this sense, the person-centered community has allies. But as with all allegiances between different groups, there are points of intersection and points of difference. As we have seen, the person-centered positive psychologist is also interested in ways to change people's social environment, and they see the person as their own best expert, but this is not necessarily so with positive psychology. As a field of study and practice, positive psychology takes no single stance on these other two threads. That is not to say that they are antagonistic to these ideas, simply that the field is not defined by a single stance on these issues. But positive psychologists say they are driven by evidence and good ideas, so it is up to those of us who adopt a person-centered approach to persuade our colleagues, and in turn we must be open to dialogue with them as we sift the evidence. If the evidence supports the person-centered approach, then one must hope that will be the direction in which positive psychology will evolve.

Positive psychology is not necessarily person-centered, as we have seen, but Rogers's theory is, by definition, always a positive psychological approach. Alignment with positive psychology has been beneficial to the person-centered approach in drawing the attention of a new audience and in helping to position the approach more contemporaneously. The positive psychology movement has brought new life to the humanistic tradition and created a greater awareness of Rogers and his ideas among new generations of scholars. In this respect, I am encouraged for the future of the person-centered approach. But I would not want to underestimate the challenges. There is only so much support that can come from alignment with positive psychology. The humanistic ideas of the person-centered approach do not sit well with the conservative ideologies that have increasingly gained power in Western culture and have also come to dominate the psychological professions.

This is where positive psychology can learn from the person-centered approach. It is true that positive psychology did offer something different from traditional psychology because of its emphasis on optimal functioning, but this is not the same as it being a different paradigm from traditional psychology. Mainstream positive psychology has continued to sit comfortably within more controlling, medicalized, and directive visions for society.[42]

I am heartened that the emergence of positive psychology has led to new interest in the person-centered approach as it becomes recognized that the pioneers of humanistic psychology were the original positive psychologists and that person-centered therapy and other applications of the approach are branches of applied positive psychology. As contemporary psychology moves beyond the medical model to look for new ways of thinking and working, the person-centered approach offers an alternative, non-medicalized, non-controlling, and non-directive positive psychological vision for helping people in distress to flourish. A challenge is to develop more upstream interventions in education and workplaces that are about changing people's social environments rather than trying to change the person.

If we are to truly create a society in which human flourishing is in all policy and practice, in a way consistent with Rogers's approach, the unnecessary medicalization of distress must be removed from its center stage position. I believe that positive psychology has been a welcome shift in the everyday business of mainstream psychology, but as Seligman made clear, it was not a paradigm shift.[43] It continues to operate within the same worldview as mainstream psychology. In this way, positive psychology promises to offer an alternative to the medicalization of human experience, yet it does so only in the most superficial of ways by not using the language of medicine, while continuing to condone the essential elements of the medical model.

The first way that positive psychology condones the medical model is by often being seen as a supplement to traditional psychology, which has focused predominantly on distress and dysfunction. That is to say, positive psychology provides the positive to traditional psychology's negative. In doing this, it condones the idea that there is a separation between the negative and the positive, that there is a dividing line between clinical states and the more fully functioning aspects of human experience. It is true that more recent trends in positive psychology explore this issue, often referred to as positive psychology 2.0. However, they largely do this while still condoning the separation of the two. An example would be research into posttraumatic stress disorder and posttraumatic growth, as if these two constructs were not from different paradigms: the medical model and the growth model, respectively. Invariably, such research more often inadvertently medicalizes the construct of posttraumatic growth rather than reformulating the concept of posttraumatic stress as a normal and natural process.[44]

While the person-centered approach can be seen as a positive psychology, it recognizes no division between the positive and the negative, so it might be said to be the original positive psychology 2.0 because it does not conceptualize psychological states in this dichotomous way. In its conceptualization of a universal human tendency toward actualization, which becomes thwarted in non-optimal social environments due to incongruence between the tendency toward actualization and self-actualization, it provides an understanding of human development that is simultaneously about the concerns of traditional psychology and positive psychology.

A second way in which positive psychology continues to condone an illness ideology is that is carries forward the assumption from clinical psychology that different interventions are needed for different states. This assumption runs counter to the person-centered proposal that there is a unitary cause of distress and growth and, thus, a single form of intervention.

The implication of adopting the medical model is that positive psychology, despite its intentions, has implicitly condoned the idea that less than fully functioning human behavior is not so much the result of the social environment but, rather, a deficit in the person themselves (an absence of a strength) and offers interventions that predetermine what is best for people. So while positive psychology shares an interest in human flourishing, it has no clear stance on the other themes that define the person-centered approach and, thus, can be seen to clash ideologically in these other ways by not emphasizing the role of the social environment and not prioritizing the person's right to self-determination.

The need for diagnosis, formulation, and all expressions of expertise over the person dissolve when the social environment, rather than the person, is the focus of intervention. In this way, the positive psychologist may not be using diagnosis in the clinical sense, but if they are developing an intervention suitable for some people but not others, the same logic applies. Thus, much of contemporary positive psychology remains underpinned by the medical model, but that fact is disguised by its language of strengths, virtues, and happiness. In sum, the assumption that different problems or people require different interventions leads the practitioner to take an expert stance, implying that they know what the client needs better than the client knows themselves. By contrast, the growth model holds that it is usual for people to self-actualize in ways that are less than fully functioning. In this way, person-centered therapy effectively posits a unitary cause of distress, but varied expressions of that distress will arise according to the uniqueness of each individual's incongruence.

Positive psychology is sometimes said to have been built on the earlier ideas of humanistic psychology, but I hope the preceding discussion shows that, in general, apart from sharing the same initial premise that it is worthwhile to understand what leads to a good life, positive psychology has not been built up from humanistic psychology but, rather, it has been built up from the illness ideology it shares with clinical psychology.

Positive psychology can now learn from person-centered psychology. If we reflect on one reason for the demise of humanistic psychology being its clash with conservative ideologies,[45] I believe we also learn about the success of positive psychology. One feature of the conservative ideology is its focus on individualism, which has led to the rise of a culture in which positive psychology research has been used to promote mindfulness for schoolchildren to deal with the stressors of failing educational systems, resilience training for workers to help them cope with punitive workloads, and well-being applications to help people manage the stresses of economic insecurity. Positive psychologists might not always be the people behind such interventions, but the technology and tools of positive psychology are used when stressed and overworked employees are forced by their managers to attend well-being sessions or schoolchildren are given mindfulness classes to cope with mental health concerns. The gap that exists between research and practice might blind some to how their research is understood and used and how, ultimately, its implementation may condone ideas about deficit and dysfunction within the person.

In sum, thinking about the demise of humanistic psychology relative to the success of positive psychology,[46] we might wonder if the latter's rise was at least in part due to fitting well with the demands of conservative ideologies and the need for many organizations and institutions to control and coerce people to behave in particular ways, which presupposes an ideological position that runs counter to a growth model. I hope that the positioning of the person-centered approach as a form of positive psychology will lead to more awareness of the need to create more growth-promoting climates not only in therapy, but also in educational settings and workplaces.

Concluding comments

Rogers's approach challenged authoritarian structures, whether in the therapy room, the workplace, or the classroom. In each context it is about designing the social environment such that it supports and promotes human flourishing. Person-centered practitioners might benefit from the reminder that theirs is a positive psychology, and positive psychologists might benefit from a renewed focus on the idea that if the social environment is right, change in socially and personally constructive directions will be automatic.

Chapter 8
The paradox of the person-centered approach
Natural science in theory but phenomenological in practice

Around the time I became seriously interested in the person-centered approach in the mid 1990s, I was attending a conference where I bumped into one of my professors from my undergraduate days. He had experience in the clinical field and was a teacher and researcher I respected highly. I told him about my interest, and I was struck by his response. “Client-centered therapy,” he said, was “the only decent therapy.” Those words have always stayed with me. Looking back, I wish I had asked him exactly what he meant, but sadly he died a few years after that conversation. Most chapters on evaluation open with a discussion about whether psychological interventions work or not. I will come to this, but first of all I propose to challenge the basis on which we traditionally evaluate psychological interventions and discuss the often hidden assumptions that lie behind our choice of what we are evaluating. Following this, I want to reiterate that the person-centered approach is based on a scientific theory of personality and interpersonal relations, a point that can be lost in the understanding of the practice, which is grounded in the paradoxical notion of the client’s subjectivity. The person-centered approach is phenomenological in practice but based in the natural sciences in theory. Understanding this paradox is at the core of what it means to be a person-centered practitioner.

Decency

Whether something is decent or not depends on your own standards of moral acceptability. The principle of respecting others’ right to self-determination, in the way outlined in Rogers’s theory, seems a decent way of relating to other people. But the choice of what we study and how we practice is a personal one. I have come to understand that psychology is not a neutral discipline. It aspires to being a science, and it is, in the sense that it adopts scientific methods, but

The Humanistic Psychology of Carl Rogers. Stephen A. Joseph, Oxford University Press. © Oxford University Press (2025). DOI: 10.1093/9780197790632.003.0009

it does so to address ideologically driven questions. For example, research into well-being usually starts with the notion that it is a good thing to promote well-being. Is it? It probably is, but surely that's an ideological position, no different from deciding on any other goals for a person or for society. Politicians will often turn to economic measures to claim success, ignoring other indicators related to well-being. That's a choice not only about how to evaluate the outcome but one that, in turn, will create the policies that lead to their desired outcome. If we do choose well-being, what aspects of well-being should be the aim of practice and policy? Should we promote meaning and purpose, or joy and pleasure, or religiosity and spirituality? That is not a scientific question but a personal choice that is based in our own values of what's right, decent, or important. Likewise, the choice of any outcome in therapy or other psychological or policy intervention is not scientifically determined but an ideological choice that this is the right thing to focus on. As I've discussed, Western culture is heavily influenced by an illness ideology, which means that much of what passes for practice and policy in therapy and psychology is determined by, and assessed with, concepts grounded in medicine. In their discussion on the nature of psychological wellness and illness, and how these are socially constructed constructs, James Maddux and colleagues wrote this:

> Psychopathologies and mental disorders . . . are abstract ideas that have been constructed by people with particular personal, professional, and cultural values. . . . What people often call "facts" are not truths but reflect reality negotiations . . . it is to acknowledge that science can no more determine the proper or correct conceptions of psychological wellness and illness than it can determine the proper and correct conception of other social constructions such as beauty, justice, race, and social class. We nonetheless can use science to study the psychological phenomena that our culture refers to as "well" or "ill".[1]

Maddux et al. go on to argue that how we conceive psychological illness and wellness has wide-ranging implications for individuals, mental health professionals, government agencies, and society at large because our conceptions determine what behaviors we consider it necessary to explain and the roles and functions of the helping professions. The application of psychological science can never be a politically disinterested process, no matter how much we might want it to be, and which research is most publicized and becomes the accepted "evidence" is similarly politically determined.[2]

When positive psychology was introduced in 2000, it was not because scientific research had shown that this was the way forward. Indeed, given the weight of the scientific research at the time into medical model constructs, the way forward would have been more of the same. Rather, it was the personal vision of one person, Martin Seligman, who decided it was a good idea, which, as I've mentioned previously, he said originated in a conversation with his daughter. What we research and what we promote as the valued and desired outcomes are always choices we make. Through a wider lens, ideology is ultimately the basis of all social policy—whether the focus should be, for example, on economic growth or personal well-being, left wing or right-wing policies—but no one would claim that their ideological position is an evidence-based one, because they choose what they think is most morally acceptable or decent.

A criticism that I have often heard leveled against Rogers's theory is that it is an ideological position. This argument implies, however, that there is a neutral position that others take. But as the social constructionist Vivien Burr wrote, "No human can step outside their humanity and view the world from no position at all, and this is just as true of scientists as of everyone else"[3] (see Box 8.1).

Box 8.1 Reflection: What are your assumptions?

This notion that all views of humanity must come from a position is a powerful challenge for many. It is worth taking some time to reflect on your own position. Whether you are a researcher, practitioner, educator, or in another profession, if it involves other people and you doing something with them, what are the deep-seated and unspoken assumptions that you are making? What assumptions are being made by your profession?

As an example, think of how teachers are often caricatured as if their job is to pour facts and figures into children's empty heads. An alternative is to think of teachers as if they are gardeners carefully tending a plant. In each of these metaphors, what are the different assumptions that are being made about children?

All forms of psychological practice and policy are grounded in a vision of the human being. It is simply not possible to reconcile all the different approaches. Certainly there are many aspects of different theories and practice that are essentially the same but use different terminology, obscuring their similarity, and it can be intellectually exciting to discover this, but there are also many aspects that are simply irreconcilable, such that the "grand" theories of psychology must stand alone and always be in competition for the truth.[4] An approach that is based on a vision of humanity as driven by destructive impulses cannot be reconciled with one that has a more constructive view. And neither of these approaches sits comfortably with the vision of humanity as a blank slate.

That might seem obvious, but those psychologists and psychotherapists who take a mainstream approach to their work may do so without realizing that theirs is also ideological. The reason for this ideological blindness is that from their point of view, it is what everyone is doing. They have no point of contrast. Like a fish in water, unaware of the nature of its surroundings, they are unaware of their ideological position. What the person-centered approach does differently is set out in the first instance what its ideological position is. That makes it look as though it is ideological when everyone else isn't, but that's part of its moral integrity.

The accusation of being ideological is often thrown out as a criticism of ideas that stray too far from the status quo and the social norms of society. Mainstream ideas are rarely seen as ideological; they are just how it is. Rogers's approach is often criticized as ideological. It is, but so are all the other approaches to the application of psychological ideas. The person-centered approach starts with this discussion; it is up-front and honest about this. We talk about this in the classroom. It frightens some students who are training in person-centered psychotherapy to realize that they are being asked to take an ideological position for the duration of their training.

In essence, after 30 years as a psychologist, I think it is important to justify what we do and provide evidence for claims, but ultimately what we do is always an expression of an ideology. That is not a bad thing; we simply need to understand that what we do is not neutral. It can be hard to grasp this simple fact because we see the world through whatever ideological lens we have, without realizing that we are looking through a lens.

We can be non-directive in our relationships if we believe that there is a tendency for growth inherent in each person. As I see it, therefore, the biggest challenge is to look around at the events in the world caused by how humans relate to each other—from our day-to-day interactions to those events of industrial barbarism we have witnessed over the last century—and ask ourselves what we believe about human nature and whether Rogers's theory stands or falls. It is a question that I have pondered for many years, but I always return to favoring Rogers's ideas. Remember, his theory is about the tension between the tendency toward actualization and self-actualization. The more I develop my understanding of his approach, the more I appreciate that while it may be true that people are intrinsically motivated in constructive ways, this is an impulse all too easily derailed. Rogers's theory describes a fragile process in people, one that needs to be carefully nurtured to bring out the best, but rarely does this happen. In my view, Rogers's theory does not struggle to explain the destructive forces in the world.

The lens we look through also determines what counts as research. The medical model, for example, leads to expectations that therapy is akin to treatment for disease. We expect the treatment to cure the person of the disease so that they go from a state of disorder to a state of normality. Seen this way, the methods of drug trial experimentation seem appropriate, but is this really what psychotherapy is? Not if psychotherapy is seen as a journey of personal development, growth, emotional maturity, congruence, and authenticity. Recently I read a thought-provoking chapter written in 1975 by Richard Farson, the then-director of the Esalen Institute in San Francisco, in which he stated the following:

> It sometimes seems to me a pity that psychotherapy derived from medicine, a field where the benefits are expected to last. If it had developed instead out of a different field, say, for example theatre, then we would not expect it to work after it was over, but only while it was going on. We have unfortunately burdened psychotherapy with an expectation on which it cannot very often deliver, that it will change behavior. In the process we have missed its great value.[5]

When we talk about evaluation, rarely do we think in terms of evaluating the ideology, or the fundamental assumptions, of what we do. But that is what I am proposing. In this case, the idea is that we should respect people's right to self-determination. If you agree with Rogers about the innate tendency toward actualization, you will likely also think that is a good idea, but if not, then it will seem like a bad idea. This is not a topic for scientific research; it is an ideological position, a set of fundamental assumptions on which all else is based.

Therapy is research in practice

Beyond ideology, we turn to the scientific method to evaluate whether what we think happens is what actually happens. There are those in the therapeutic world who rail against the scientific method, seeing it as dehumanizing and reductionist. I think that is a misunderstanding, often arising because the scientific method is confused with the subject matter to which it is often applied—in this case medicine. As we have seen, there are reasons to be wary of seeing therapy as being like medicine, but it is important not to conflate the illness ideology with the scientific method. In essence, the scientific method is simply about checking our perception of reality against what actually happens. As I described earlier, in creating an empathic, unconditional, and congruent social environment, the therapist is not trying to change the person, they have no agenda for the person whatsoever, but they trust that given the optimal environment, the person will change toward becoming more fully functioning. This is a bold assertion that needs to be borne out in the real world.

This notion of changing the social environment, not the person, makes the person-centered approach a radically different form of practice from most other psychological interventions. This can be difficult to understand if you are looking at the person-centered approach from outside its paradigmatic stance. But imagine that you truly believe that people will only move toward becoming more fully functioning when they experience themselves in the optimal social environment and that by trying to direct, control, or coerce people to change, you are likely contributing to a less optimal social environment. Unless that seems true to you, I don't believe that you can fully embrace the person-centered approach.

In that sense, each therapy session is a mini-experiment in which the therapist is testing the therapy, but it is only a good experiment—the results of which can be trusted—if the therapist is fully embracing the theory of therapy, truly living it as a way of being. The hypothesis is that given the optimal environment, the client will change toward becoming more fully functioning. To truly test this hypothesis for yourself as a therapist, you must believe it to be true; otherwise, you will want to direct the other person. And that is what often happens. Therapists who have doubts about the approach find it doesn't seem to work for them. Inevitably they find that it is more helpful if they begin to introduce some forms of direction for the client. Such therapists may tell you that they originally trained in the approach but found it didn't work, not realizing that they never adequately put it to the test. Only by being immersed in the therapy can they trust their findings if the approach doesn't seem to work.

But does that mean that the person-centered therapist must be brainwashed into the approach and unwilling to evaluate it critically? No, it does not. It means that in those moments of offering therapy, the person-centered practitioner must be fully immersed in and accepting of its theoretical premises in order to provide it. Only afterward will they have the information they need to critically evaluate the success of what they have provided. It is a scientific theory, and to test it, the therapist must adhere to the six necessary and sufficient conditions.

That is the paradoxical essence of it as a mini-experiment: to rigorously try to show that it doesn't work by believing wholeheartedly that it does. As Rogers wrote in his 1951 book *Client-Centered Therapy*,

> If the counselor feels, in the middle of an interview, that this client may not have the capacity for reorganizing himself, and shifts to the hypothesis that the counselor must bear a considerable responsibility for this reorganization, he confuses the client, and defeats himself. He has shut himself off from proving or disproving either hypothesis. This confused eclecticism, which has been

> prevalent in psychotherapy, has blocked scientific progress in the field. Actually it is only by acting *consistently* upon a well selected hypothesis that its elements of truth and untruth can become known.[6]

It is important to remember that person-centered therapy is based on a scientific theory and, as such, one should put it to the test. Rogers's "necessary and sufficient conditions" statement is a set of instructions for a constructive human relationship and is the starting point for his "if-then" hypothesis building. If the necessary and sufficient conditions are present, then therapeutic change will result. No other elements or factors are necessary. Over the years, a consensus across theoreticians and practitioners suggests that the conditions are indeed necessary. Therapy in which a client doesn't feel understood or accepted, or worse, in which they feel actively misunderstood and devalued, is doomed from the outset. That doesn't mean that positive change in people can't come about by other means—people report personal growth following adversity, or through witnessing the birth of a child, or watching a sunset, or any number of ways—but Rogers's statement only applies to therapy and other intentional helping relationships. Imagine seeing a therapist who is the opposite of genuine, empathic, and unconditional. Of course these conditions are necessary.

But are the six conditions sufficient, or does the therapist have to add something else into the mix? This is a commonly asked question, so it seems important to address it here. It is a question that is often asked from a mistaken understanding of the idea of what sufficiency means in the context of the person-centered approach, one that does not recognise the pluralistic potential already inherent in its practice. As I discussed earlier, the crux of the approach is its non-directivity, so if you undermine that by introducing something else that comes from your need to direct the client, it is simply not client-centered therapy. But that is not the same as introducing your knowledge, your expertise on an issue, technique, or tool, into the session if that is the client's direction. A behavioral therapist, for example, may suggest to the client that they engage in some exposure exercises to help them deal with some traumatic memory. The person-centered therapist won't do this, but if the client needs to go through a process that requires exposure, the client will in their own way, at their own pace, take the therapist there. The client will say things and do things indicative of that need, and if the therapist is truly with the client in their frame of reference and following their direction, the therapy will end up engaging in a form of exposure, but in the client's way and at their pace. Understood like this, person-centered therapy, as described by Rogers's 1957 statement, is infinitely flexible as a way of working. Person-centered practice is, by definition, sufficient; only when caricatured as a therapist sitting and nodding, repeating back the words of the client, and smiling inanely can the person-centered approach be thought of an insufficient.

Methods

As person-centered therapists and scholars, we wish to hear the voices of our clients and to understand the world as it is for them when we enter the therapy room. As Rogers said in his dialogue with Martin Buber, "I feel that when I'm being effective as a therapist, I enter the relationship as a subjective person, not as a scrutinizer, not as a scientist."[7]

Person-centered practitioners are concerned with the client's frame of reference and take a phenomenological approach. They are concerned with how people construct, understand, and give meaning to their experience of the social world. Thus, there is always a paradox at the heart of person-centered practice, which is the fact that it is based in the natural sciences. Practice is phenomenological, but only because it is the expression of Rogers's generalized theoretical claims about human nature.

As discussed earlier, Rogers's main theoretical writings were his 1957 paper in the American Psychological Association's *Journal of Consulting Psychology* and his 1959 chapter in which he developed his theory of personality. In these works, Rogers provided his most comprehensive statements of the person-centered approach, updating and clarifying his theoretical ideas from the 1951 book. He also set out his main theoretical claims about the actualizing tendency being directional in nature; that this direction is always toward greater autonomous functioning and socially constructive behaviors; the therapeutic and relationship conditions that are necessary and sufficient for constructive personality change; how unconditional positive self-regard mediates the relationship between the therapeutic conditions; and the nature and process of becoming more fully functioning. These writings contained a set of scientific hypotheses in a natural sciences tradition that holds that there is a reality external to perception and theory and that the goal of research is to reach as true an understanding of that reality as possible. To this day, it is this postpositive perspective that underpins the practice of person-centered therapy and other applications of the approach.

In this way, Rogers's 1957 and 1959 writings offered theoretical conjecture about the nature of reality and proposed testable quantitative and experimental hypotheses. In short, person-centered therapy rests on the hypothesis that people have sufficient intrinsic self-direction that will be released under the right relationship conditions. If a therapist does not believe this to be the case, then it would make no sense whatsoever to offer person-centered therapy.

At the time Rogers was writing, in the 1950s, the discipline of psychology was developing an identity as a form of the natural sciences. Psychologists assumed that it was possible to make generalized claims about human beings that could be tested using quantitative and experimental methods to establish cause-and-effect relationships. This is an approach to science that claims true knowledge can be achieved only through sense perception and empirical investigation. Rogers's 1957 and 1959 writings were clearly intended as testable hypotheses in this natural sciences tradition, challenging researchers to use their tools of observation. As Bozarth and Motomosa wrote,

> Rogers (1959) was the first investigator to apply quantitative empirical research to the field of psychotherapy. He presented the only formal theory of therapy that delineates a format for scientific inquiry research. His self-proclaimed *magnum opus* identified only six conditions that are *necessary and sufficient* for the therapeutic process . . . The linear construction of the theory is that, if these conditions exist, there will be certain process and outcome changes in clients. The changes include increased freedom to express feelings through verbal and other modal channels; greater unconditional positive self-regard; one's self as the locus of evaluation, and the client experiencing themself less in terms of conditions of worth and more in terms of the organismic valuing process.[8]

Such postpositive perspectives remain the established ones for mainstream psychological research, with the goal to reach as true an understanding of reality as possible. Using this approach, humanistic researchers have, as we will see in the next chapter, generated much quantitative and experimental evidence in support of person-centered therapy.[9] It is also in this sense that I have argued that every instance of person-centered therapy is like a mini-experiment in which the therapist is testing the hypothesis of whether holding the attitudinal conditions of empathy, genuineness, and unconditional positive regard will lead to change in the way described by Rogers, in a particular predetermined direction toward more fully functioning behavior (see Box 8.2).

Box 8.2 Reflection: Test the theory in everyday life

Take the idea that each instance of practicing the person-centered approach is like a mini-experiment and test it out for yourself. If you are not in practice as a therapist, observe how you interact with others in everyday life. See if you notice that other people move psychologically toward more expression of feelings and openness to experience the more empathic and accepting you are. Use the evidence of your own senses to determine the validity of the theory. Think about the paradox that you are both the participant and the observer in the experiment.

The above description of person-centered theory as based in the postpositive tradition is not controversial. But what is unusual about it, compared to other such theories of human functioning based in the natural sciences tradition, is the paradox that Rogers's 1957 and 1959 writings propose a phenomenological way of relating in practice. If each instance of person-centered therapy is like a mini-experiment, the experimental condition is a phenomenological way of human relating.

The person-centered practitioner must be offering the therapy because they believe in the vision of reality proposed by the theory. This is the therapist's frame of reference. But in the moments of therapy, the theory proposes that the therapist must set aside their own frame of reference. The person-centered therapist's task is to meet with the client and enter their frame of reference, to understand reality as the client sees it. In doing so, they disavow power over the client.

Similar to the concept of bracketing used by qualitative researchers to mitigate the potentially deleterious effects of preconceptions that may taint the research process, the therapist must bracket, or put to one side, their own views and theoretical allegiance such that they are not influenced by their assumptions.[10] But to successfully bracket one's preconceptions, one must first truly understand one's beliefs and positions, and then be able to suspend them, which is what I would suggest should be at the core of training to be a person-centered therapist.

I think one does have to be convinced of the validity of Rogers's explanatory theory for it to make sense to work in a non-directive way.[11] The therapist wants to understand the world as the client sees it, without judgment, but they are doing this only because they themselves have a clear theoretical understanding of human relationships, as described in Rogers's 1957 and 1959 writings. I do what I do as a therapist because of the theory. If I didn't think in terms of the growth model and think that people were ultimately driven by a constructive force, I cannot see how it would be ethical or moral to offer the freedom that comes with the person-centered approach. I would instead look to the ideas of someone like B. F. Skinner and his behaviorism, which is about using psychology to control and shape human behavior in ways that are for the common good.

In sum, the person-centered approach is a phenomenological way of relating, but only because it is grounded in a natural sciences tradition with a clear and specific set of hypotheses. This paradox at the heart of the person-centered approach, however, often goes unrecognized. I believe its recognition is important for the development of new research. Although, as I will describe in the next chapter, there has been a tradition of quantitative and experimental research into person-centered therapy, with a wealth of evidence accumulated from the 1940s onward, that searches for order and effects, and conditions and process in personal change, interest in such research has dwindled since the 1990s. Such research into the person-centered approach has become relatively uncommon today. In part, I would attribute this to the relative lack of person-centered researchers based in academia, but also to the perception that the person-centered approach is purely phenomenological, and even antagonistic to scientific approaches.

There are humanistic psychologists who do reject quantitative and experimental ways of knowing, and for other humanistic approaches this may be a valid interpretation of another humanistic theory, but my argument is that this is simply not an option for the person-centered practitioner because their approach is inescapably grounded in the natural sciences tradition. In this way, important research remains to be carried out to seek evidence that supports or refutes the hypotheses underpinning person-centered therapy and theory, to answer the question of whether person-centered therapy provides an alternative to the medicalization of distress, and to develop the concepts of person-centered therapy and their applications. Such new research is important if the ideas of the person-centered approach are to reach beyond its immediate community of humanistic scholars to wider audiences of more mainstream psychologists.

Research "into" and "from" the person-centered approach

Up to this point I have been talking about Rogers's work and describing his theories of personality and of therapy, which are written in the logical positivist tradition. Such theories can only be adequately tested using appropriately matching quantitative tools. Therefore, I have been largely advocating for a scientific and positivist approach to research, which may surprise some readers who see the person-centered approach as synonymous with more interpretive and qualitative research methods. Today, within the social sciences, qualitative methods are widely used and accepted. This was not always the case, but much of this change was due to the influence of humanistic and person-centered scholars bringing their then-new perspectives to the question of how to do research.[12]

In this section I want to make the important distinction between research "into" and "from" the person-centered approach, as I believe that this is at the root of some confusion among person-centered practitioners as to how they can conduct research. Person-centered practitioners who turn to research often do so in a way that embraces the phenomenological way of knowing. Barrineau and Bozarth, in 1989, wrote the following:

> The person-centered research model, then, focuses on the attitudinal values of the researcher in the way that person-centered therapy focuses on the attitudinal values of the therapist. These values are the critical bases for acquiring emerging data. As such, person-centered researchers value the discipline of divesting themselves of personal beliefs and biases to attend to the always new, emerging world of their "subjects."[13]

This is a description of person-centered research,[14] and in this way, the approach is often understood as a form of knowing consistent with a social constructivist approach in which the researcher aims to understand the world as the participant understands it. This is what I would describe as research "from" the person-centered approach.

Research "from" the person-centered approach is valuable, but only in certain contexts in which such research is appropriate to the research question. For example, such questions might include those about the experiences of clients undergoing therapy, how they feel they have changed, or what was felt to be helpful to them in therapy. But the answers to such questions cannot reveal the nature of cause and effect in the way demanded by the postpositivist tradition in which person-centered theory is grounded. Also needed is research "into" the person-centered approach that directly tests the set of scientific hypotheses on which the theory rests. But research "into" the person-centered approach need not be "from" the person-centered approach. While, to some, that may seem like a statement of the obvious, it has been my experience over many years in the classroom, in discussions with students training to become person-centered practitioners, that there is often a misperception that all research must be "from" the person-centered approach. This misperception, I feel, has led to the more traditional methods and research "into" being overshadowed. I have even encountered this view from journal reviewers. It is, however, a personal choice for how to position oneself as a researcher.

In his early career, Rogers was dedicated to the scientific approach. He wrote about his views on research at some length in his 1961 book, *On Becoming a Person*. He saw research as a way to develop a more accurate way of seeing life, but he was also very clear that the choice of what to research and how to interpret and implement scientific findings was a subjective one:

> Science cannot come into being without a personal choice of the values we wish to achieve. And these values we choose to implement will forever lie outside of the science which implements them; the goals we select, the purposes we wish to follow.[15]

This point cannot be emphasized enough, and it is one that I will return to: ultimately, psychological, educational, and other interventions are always ideological, even political. But for the moment the point I am making is that while recognizing this, it is nonetheless valuable to understand scientifically what we do. As I've noted, it is a criticism of the person-centered approach that it is not scientific, and while that is clearly a misrepresentation of Rogers's early writings, it is true of many of the later writers in the humanistic tradition.

That some researchers want to move away from a reductionist scientific approach is understandable, particularly given some of the later writings by Rogers himself. Later in his career, Rogers was open to the developments in humanistic psychology in the 1960s and beyond that moved away from solely experimental and quantitative ways of knowing to embrace more phenomenological and qualitative ways. Rogers wrote about developing a new human science of the person, and he seemed excited by the development of the new and more qualitative methodologies, which are concerned with understanding the meaning of human experience.

In 1985, in a paper entitled "Toward a More Human Science of the Person" in the *Journal of Humanistic Psychology*, he wrote about how humanistic psychologists had moved away from traditional methods based on logical positivism. But he went on to write that conventional science can be used constructively and gave examples of his colleagues' work, stating that the "hypotheses of a person-centered approach, have been tested and significantly confirmed. So, the conventional methods are not to be thrown out, but they are often inappropriate for questions we wish to study."[16] He reiterated this point a few pages later, writing that, for him, the

> reductionistic, linear, cause-effect, behaviorist view of science is not thrown out but it is seen as simply one aspect of science, a perfectly good way of investigating certain questions, but decidedly inappropriate for others. The conventional view of science no longer reigns supreme.[17]

Maureen O'Hara, writing in the *Journal of Humanistic Psychology* in 1995, examines what she sees as Rogers's shift from positivist scientist to radical subjectivist, concluding that he was at the boundary between 19th-century positivism and 20th-century postpositive constructivism.[18] It is absolutely clear from reading Rogers's 1985 paper that he welcomed the developments in humanistic psychology toward new phenomenological methods and the different type of questions that were now being asked, the more critical ideas around the ideas of what constituted science, and the view that knowledge was no longer only to be gleaned from one narrowly defined way of looking at the world. But in my view he did not abandon the conventional methods of the day or ever challenge the validity of the "if . . . then" style of his hypotheses in the 1957 and 1959 writings. Rather, he now saw the traditional scientific quantitative approach as one method among a variety, each suited to its own purpose. So, while I agree with the idea of Rogers as being at the boundary, I would see this not as a shift from being a positivist scientist to a radical subjectivist, but rather a newfound ability to take on board different ideas and seek to accommodate and embrace both. He was not so radical as a subjectivist to repudiate his earlier positivism.

Indeed, a year later, in 1986, in a paper published in the journal *Person-Centered Review*, Rogers reiterated this point that quantitative and experimental methods were no longer the only mode for behavioral science, but that studies of all types were needed to develop the approach.[19] This remains as true today as it was then.

Rogers developed an appreciation of more phenomenological methods and, in doing so, came to see the more restricted value of the traditional approaches and the increased importance of personal accounts. His own output of empirical research ceased in the 1960s. But it is a misreading, as we have seen, to think that he was advocating a dismissal of quantitative and experimental research and that researchers should only do research from a person-centered perspective. He carried on writing scholarly essays and books targeted at professionals and the general public and was engaged in other work disseminating his ideas in different contexts. Although he was no longer active as an empirical researcher himself, he did not repudiate his own writings from the 1950s, which were firmly grounded in the natural science approach and in which he hypothesized that the therapist's attitudinal conditions of empathic understanding, genuineness, and unconditional positive regard—if experienced by the client—would initiate a process of growth leading to greater congruence and more mature psychological responses.

Today, therapists in the person-centered tradition who offer these attitudinal conditions must surely do so on the assumption that Rogers's hypothesis—of a constructive directional tendency within people that will be released within the right therapeutic relationship—is valid. As already noted, it would make no sense to offer a therapeutic relationship intended to empower and free people's self-direction unless we believed that direction was constructive and trustworthy. However one looks at this, it is an empirical question to be answered by the evidence of our senses.

Some might claim that one could offer person-centered therapy even if it were shown that Rogers's core theoretical claims about the actualizing tendency are incorrect. But I would disagree. The practice of person-centered therapy may value each person's way of viewing the world, but the theory behind person-centered therapy is not a social constructivist one that holds all truths to be equally valid; it is a very particular worldview and understanding of human nature and the processes that give rise to therapeutic change. If these hypotheses are ever refuted, then in my view it is no longer useful or ethical to practice person-centered therapy. It is important to see the scientific method for what it is: a deliberate attempt to test our perceptions against the reality of what happens. By advocating for a scientific approach, all I am saying is that it is important that the claims made by practitioners about what they do, or about what the theory says will happen, should not be contrary to the evidence of our senses. We have a responsibility to pay attention to that evidence.

Understanding that person-centered therapy is based on a nomothetic approach grounded in the natural sciences can be a challenge to the assumptions of many who are learning to practice in an idiographic way that values personal experience. Rogers's 1957 and 1959 writings offer testable hypotheses, and only insofar as those hypotheses are supported by evidence is it ethical to offer therapy based on them. That is the paradox of person-centered therapy: it is a phenomenological approach to practice that values each person's frame of reference, but only because of what its theory says about human nature and how change happens.

It is often mistakenly thought that because the person-centered approach emphasizes the uniqueness of each person's lived experience, anything goes and the approach is only interested in qualitative and phenomenological ways of knowing. This is not true. The person-centered approach is founded on Rogers's theory, which aimed to establish generalized laws of human behavior. In this way, every therapy session with a client is an exercise in hypothesis testing: to see if by holding the therapeutic conditions, the client changes in the expected directions. If one's experience is that the client does not change, then either one hasn't held the conditions well enough or it is time to modify or even abandon person-centered theory. One of the benefits of the quantitative and experimental method is that it means we are open to changing our minds about theory because the idea is to try to find evidence that refutes what we think is true. Testing hypotheses should not be about seeking only to validate what one thinks one knows, but to genuinely test to destruction the very ideas that one holds and thus over time move toward better approximations of truth. Rogers's 1957 and 1959 writings propose a version of the truth, and that version leads person-centered practitioners to do what they do and gives those who subscribe to the approach the duty to see if it holds up to scrutiny.

Concluding comments

Person-centered therapy stands or falls depending on the validity of Rogers's tightly delineated hypotheses about the constructive nature of human beings and the causal relationship between the optimal relationship conditions and more fully functioning behavior. I am not saying that all research must follow in the quantitative and experimental tradition. Other phenomenological research can explore new ideas and understandings in a complementary way. But quantitative and experimental methods cannot be dismissed as a form of inquiry into person-centered practice. That finally brings us to the question of evidence-based practice and what support there is for humanistic therapies and the person-centered approach, which is the topic of the next chapter.

Chapter 9
The facts are friendly
Evidence from psychotherapy research and positive psychology

My argument in the previous chapter was that the person-centered approach is ultimately grounded in the natural science tradition and, as such, there is an obligation for those of us who practice in the person-centered way to test what we think to be true against what we can observe in our experience of reality. We must look to see if those clients who experience the conditions of the therapeutic relationship change in the way Rogers describes. We can observe what happens in our practice and, if given the opportunity, conduct research using more rigorous experimental designs to investigate whether clients change in the predicted way. Rogers also hypothesized about why change comes through the conditions of the therapeutic relationship, suggesting that it is because of the development of the client's unconditional positive self-regard, which in turn allows them to drop their defensive positions and move toward greater congruence. This is written in a way that is clearly intended as a testable set of hypotheses. In this chapter I will discuss the wealth of converging evidence from various areas of psychology and psychotherapy research. In his 1961 book, *On Becoming a Person*, Rogers famously wrote that "the facts are friendly," by which he meant that the evidence is supportive, but more than that, we should not be frightened of evidence but look to it for guidance to get ever closer to the truth.[1]

Psychotherapy research evidence

I have heard the criticism that there is no evidence for the person-centered approach. This is not true. In its early days it was the first evidence-based therapy. That it was grounded in empirical research was one of the things that set it apart from other therapies of the time. Rogers was a psychologist, and as such he was well versed in the scientific method; out of his research, he developed the client-centered approach. Indeed, Rogers can be credited with developing psychotherapy as a subject for research. Until that point, psychotherapy had been

The Humanistic Psychology of Carl Rogers. Stephen A. Joseph, Oxford University Press. © Oxford University Press (2025). DOI: 10.1093/9780197790632.003.0010

a mysterious undertaking that took place behind closed doors in secrecy, but Rogers wanted to understand how it worked. To that end, at the University of Chicago Counseling Center, Rogers developed the first research programs to investigate the effectiveness of psychotherapy. His was the first psychotherapy research clinic. It pioneered the use of new technologies that made it possible to record and transcribe therapy sessions, allowing Rogers and his team to subject therapy to the scrutiny of scientific exploration. The Counseling Center was set up to collect permissions from clients and routinely record client interviews. Transcripts were coded and rated and subject to investigation using the statistical methods of the day. A steady flow of research was published, including reports on methodologies to evaluate psychotherapy in a systematic way. This ensured that the first body of empirical research into psychotherapy was almost entirely person-/client-centered.

Outcome studies of this time showed greater psychological adjustment following client-centered therapy using projective measures of the time, such as the Thematic Apperception Test, or the famous Rorschach, as well as counselor ratings of client change.[2] Such assessment methods were common at the time but relied on the researcher's interpretations of meaning in the projective tests or expert ratings of the client by the therapists. Although this has its value, it does not fully embrace the phenomenological viewpoint that Rogers was taking. So Rogers also used a form of self-assessment data called Stephenson's Q-technique. This can be used in different ways, but in essence, participants were invited, before and after therapy, to sort a set of 100 cards, each offering one personal characteristic, into piles: one containing statements that represented how they saw themselves at that time—the self-sort—and another pile of those cards representing how they would have liked to see themselves—the ideal-sort. By comparing how clients' allocation of cards into the different piles changed over time, Rogers was able to create a way of assessing the outcome of therapy. The discrepancy between the ideal at the beginning of therapy and self at the end was used as a measure of change toward greater congruence (see Box 9.1).

Box 9.1 Reflection: Your ideal self

Below are some examples of the personal characteristics that would have been used on the Q-sort cards.

I am responsible for my troubles.
I am self-reliant.
I often feel driven.
I get along easily with others.

> I make strong demands on myself.
> I get anxious easily.
> I am an impulsive person.
> I am ambitious.
>
> If these were printed on cards, which ones would you select to represent how you see yourself now? Would that be different from how you would ideally see yourself? Which cards would you pick to represent your ideal self? Are there other cards not shown here that you would want to be able to include?

Rogers also made use of early video recording technology, most famously in the 1965 film *Three Approaches to Therapy* produced by Everett Shostrom. Popularly known as the Gloria tapes, these were a series of therapeutic conversations between a client, Gloria Szymanski, and three therapists, Albert Ellis, Fritz Perls, and Carl Rogers, demonstrating rational emotive therapy, gestalt therapy, and client-centered therapy, respectively. The video was used widely in therapy training, although Gloria filed a lawsuit in 1977 against its director, claiming that she hadn't given her consent for how it was used. The court did not find in her favor, and Gloria died in 1979.

The video remains widely watched today.[3] Many articles have been written about the Gloria film, and researchers have used it to explore Rogers's style of therapy and understand his theory in relation to his own practice[4] and how the complexity of a client's narrative relates to the type of therapy. In one study, it was found that Gloria's interactions showed more narrative structural complexity—as coded by trained raters—with Rogers than with the other two therapists. For example, there was a greater degree of openness to experiences, evidenced by the quality, variety, and complexity of the narrative process.[5] The use of technology to record therapy sessions remains central to training as a therapist and doing research into therapy.[6] Recent such innovations include the work of David Murphy and colleagues at Vienna University of Technology and the Open Lab at Newcastle University, who have further demonstrated the potential of new technologies by designing an online system and software tool called mPath, designed to support students' reflection on their practice skills.[7]

Awarded the first Distinguished Scientific Contribution Award by the American Psychological Association in 1955, Rogers was acknowledged as the world's leading psychology and psychotherapy researcher. Kirschenbaum notes that as early as 1950, an entry in the *Encyclopedia Britannica* stated the following:

> These first efforts of Rogers to subject his methods of nondirective therapy to scientific test constituted a landmark for clinical psychology. The *Library Journal* acknowledged that the research project reported in *Psychotherapy and*

> *Personality Change* was "the first thoroughly objective study of outcomes of psychotherapy in which adequate controls have been utilized."[8]

Despite this early pioneering work by Rogers and his colleagues, the person-centered approach almost completely disappeared from academic research settings from the 1970s to the 1990s and for a period of time was critically underrepresented in clinical settings. In part this was the aftermath of Rogers's move to Wisconsin and the large study he conducted there into the effectiveness of therapy for patients in a psychiatric hospital diagnosed with schizophrenia. The study was known as the Wisconsin Project and yielded results that were on the whole seen as not supportive of the person-centered approach,[9] although, as mentioned in Chapter 1, the conclusion that the results refuted Rogers's theory is more controversial. Sommerbeck writes that because of various methodological issues, particularly around whether the therapy itself could really be considered as person-centered, it cannot be concluded that the Wisconsin study provided evidence refuting the use of the therapy for this patient group. She uses cases studies to argue that in her experience person-centered therapy is often helpful for people with severe psychopathology. She also points to more recent developments in what is called pre-therapy, which is a way of working with people developed by Garry Prouty. Pre-therapy involves the use of specific and concrete reflections to help the therapist make psychological contact with people. Thus, several decades after the Wisconsin Project, large-scale, empirical, and robust clinical evidence is still absent as regards efficacy in the treatment of schizophrenia, but there is a wealth of other clinical case material and developments.[10]

In part, the absence of empirical evidence for severe psychopathology was a result of Rogers leaving academia after the Wisconsin Project. While he continued writing, he did not pursue original research himself. In addition, wider interest in the approach dwindled, with fewer research-minded scientists focusing on his hypotheses. Since the 1960s, the person-centered approach has been increasingly less influential in university departments, where such research work is often conducted.

Exacerbating this perception of a lack of evidence was the introduction of the *Diagnostic and Statistical Manual of Mental Disorders* (*DSM*) by the American Psychiatric Association in 1980, which motivated clinical research to focus on evidence for treatment for specific diagnostic categories. Because the person-centered approach is not based on differential diagnosis, the past research evidence for the person-centered approach was now seen as lacking relevance. It didn't provide information about how well the therapy performed against those new psychiatric categories. This put person-centered researchers in a bind. On one hand, there was a need for evidence to show that the therapy was effective. But on the other, doing such research would condone the use of psychiatric language in a way that contradicted the therapy. At this point, research into person-centered therapy stalled. With minimal attention from university departments, there was little research being conducted to address this, and few researchers in the person-centered approach took up the baton to produce new research that sought to explore diagnostic categories.

Up to this point, studies with the rigor required to show strong evidence of causal change over time as a result of therapy or other intervention based clearly on Rogers's theory were lacking.[11] However, over the past two decades evidence has been gathering, with several meta-analytic studies concluding that person-centered therapies are associated with large pre–post client change, that change is maintained over early and late follow-ups, and that person-centered therapies in general are clinically and statistically equivalent to other therapies.[12] And although the approach does not rely on diagnoses to guide the course of therapy, there has been an increase in studies that have considered the effects of therapy for clients with specific diagnoses, such that the National Institute for Health and Care Excellence (NICE) in the United Kingdom has included Counselling for Depression (CfD)—essentially person-centered therapy—in its guidelines for the high-intensity treatment of depression and as an alternative to CBT.[13]

One of the most widely used instruments in person-centered psychology research is the Barrett-Lennard Relationship Inventory (B-L RI), which was developed to assess Rogers's theoretical proposition that unconditionality of regard, congruence, and empathy are important therapeutic conditions. It is an inventory of 64 items to assess these attitudinal constructs of self-regard, conditionality, empathy, and congruence.[14] (See Box 9.2.)

Box 9.2 Example items from the B-L RI

My therapist wants to understand how I see things.
My therapist nearly always knows exactly what I mean.
I feel that my therapist is real and genuine with me.
My therapist is friendly and warm with me.
I feel that my therapist really values me.
My therapist is openly himself/herself in our relationship.

These are example items from the client form of the B-L RI, assessing the relationship qualities of empathy, congruence, and unconditional positive regard as defined by Rogers. Respondents are asked to rate each item to indicate the extent to which it conveys their experience of their therapist.

The B-L RI was originally developed in 1957 by Godfrey Barrett-Lennard, and it remains the most widely used and researched measure of the facilitative conditions described by Rogers as important for constructive personality development.[15] However, there are now several versions, including a shorter form with 40 items and a newer 12-item version developed by Shun Chen and colleagues.[16] The B-L RI score consists of four subscales: level of regard, empathic understanding, congruence, and unconditionality of regard. The subscales can be summed to produce an overall total score that has been referred to as "facilitativeness." Research has shown that the scores of the B-L RI have a statistically significant correlation with a range of psychological and behavioral outcomes. The B-L RI has been translated into more than 20 different languages, including Arabic, Chinese, Dutch, French, German, Greek, Hebrew, Italian, Japanese, and Spanish. This instrument has been used extensively for more than 60 years, and research using the B-L RI overwhelmingly supports Rogers's relational conditions as determinants of greater psychological functioning.[17]

Overall, there is an abundance of research supporting humanistic therapies,[18] and Rogers's therapeutic conditions, with a variety of outcomes.[19] Conclusions of the most recent meta-analyses of the therapist's conditions of positive regard,[20] congruence,[21] and empathy[22] all suggest these variables are associated with client change. It is widely accepted that these facilitative conditions are common factors that make psychotherapy effective.[23]

Rogers wrote his 1957 paper as an integrative statement about therapeutic personality change in any successful therapy. Thus, he was saying that all psychotherapies are effective, provided the necessary and sufficient conditions are present. In a 2016 review of the evidence regarding the therapist's contribution to psychotherapy, Kevin Keenan and Shawn Rubin concluded the following:

> The research evidence overwhelmingly supports the conclusion that good psychotherapeutic outcomes are associated with therapists' strong relational qualities. First among these relational qualities are the facilitative conditions postulated by Rogers (1957) more than half a century ago . . . What is of particular note in the recent literature is the development of theory and research that suggests that these relational qualities are most effective when they are intrinsic to the person of the therapist.[24]

Evidence from social and personality psychology

I have been discussing research that is specifically about person-centered therapy, but support for the approach more generally can be found in contemporary psychological literature. If we look to the wider psychological field, we can see ever more evidence that lines up more broadly with the person-centered approach as a relational form of therapy, as opposed to a technique-based therapy.

In a review of the research evidence supportive of humanistic therapy, Mick Cooper and I discussed the fact that much social psychology is relevant but typically overlooked. Social psychological literature over many years demonstrates that close, supportive interpersonal connections have healing potential, that it is helpful for people to express and process their emotions, and that being authentic in relationships can lead to greater psychological well-being.[25] For example, there is a wealth of psychological evidence showing a strong association between an individual's well-being and the extent to which they are able to express their emotions.

Decades of research show that it is often helpful to talk about one's feelings and that those who hold back from doing so often do worse on various outcome measures. There are many studies exploring this, and investigating the mechanisms through which the expression of emotions may be helpful, for example, in how it allows people to process their experiences, to learn more about themselves, and to reappraise situations.[26] Rogers's hypothesis about the therapeutic relationship would therefore seem to be on firm foundations. Across the profession of therapy, there is greater acknowledgment of the central role of the relationship in therapy, observed and operationalized by Rogers over 60 years ago. Similarly, although developed independently of the person-centered approach, motivational interviewing shares many of the same assumptions[27] and, in turn, provides support for the more process-directed form of person-centered practice.

Beyond the therapy room, the power of relationships to promote human flourishing is now well beyond dispute in the social sciences among scholars and academics of all persuasions. Above, I discussed the B-L RI and its use in therapy research, but we can apply the same concepts to thinking about our personal relationships (see Box 9.3).

Box 9.3 Reflection: Personal relationships

Think about a close friend or family member. How much do you agree with the following statements?

My friend wants to understand how I see things.
My friend nearly always knows exactly what I mean.
I feel that my friend is real and genuine with me.

My friend is friendly and warm with me.
I feel that my friend really values me.
My friend is openly himself/herself in our relationship.

You might also find it helpful to ask yourself the same questions with work colleagues or family members. In thinking about your answers, do you feel you are in growth-promoting relationships?

As Rogers's personality theory makes clear, we need supportive relationships throughout our lives, especially when we are young when unconditional positive regard is essential for us to actualize in growthful directions. Imagine the psychological and developmental effects on a young person whose response would be to disagree strongly with each of the statements shown in Box 9.3.

Evidence for the role of parental conditional regard as a predictor of developmental processes is well established.[28] Other recent research, although not framed from the perspective of Rogers's theory, provides strong longitudinal evidence that school climate—that is, teachers' and students' experiences in a school, including feeling safe, connected, and welcomed—is a strong predictor of well-being, with the researchers concluding that policy and system interventions that focus on school climate may promote students' mental health.[29] Similarly, student-centered learning has been extensively researched, and a review of the literature showed that it is highly effective.[30]

The strongest evidence, however, comes from a field of research known as self-determination theory (SDT). Proposed by Richard Ryan and Ed Deci, and developed over the past 40 years, SDT is an extremely well-researched and well-supported theory of human motivation and development. As with person-centered theory, SDT views the person as an active, growth-oriented organism attempting to actualize its potentialities within the environment in which it functions. The organismic tendency toward actualization is seen as one pole of a dialectical interface, the other pole being the social environment, which can either meet or not meet the person's needs.[31] In this respect, SDT and the person-centered approach are virtually synonymous.

In an article published in 2007 in the *Journal of Humanistic Psychology*, Tom Patterson and I developed the argument that SDT is essentially the same as Rogers's approach.[32] But the similarities between person-centered theory and SDT have been obscured by the differences in terminology. For example, Deci and Ryan's conceptualization of "need satisfactions" consists of needs for autonomy, competence, and relatedness. Research shows that interpersonal support for these basic needs is associated with greater basic psychological need satisfaction, autonomous forms of motivation, well-being, and performance across domains.[33] This can be lateral forms of support, such as peers, colleagues, siblings, or friends, or support from vertical sources, such as teachers, managers, or parents. Essentially, any support a person receives from others that satisfies their basic needs for autonomy, competence, and relatedness is beneficial. This is, we argued, essentially a different way of expressing what person-centered therapists strive to achieve through Rogers's six necessary and sufficient relationship conditions. Essentially, the non-directive relationship is designed to support autonomy (by not encroaching on the person's ability to decide for themselves), competence (by helping the person work things out for themselves), and relatedness (by accepting the person and valuing them as they are so that they learn to relate to themselves and then to others).

Also consistent with Rogers's approach, one of SDT's predictions is that the intrinsic and extrinsic content of people's aspirations differentially affect their wellness. Intrinsic goals are defined as those that arise from within the person, reflecting a human's basic needs for growth, relationships, community giving, and health, whereas extrinsic goals are those that come from the values and expectations of others, such as wealth or fame. Across many studies throughout the world, it has been shown that intrinsic aspirations are linked positively with well-being and that well-being is adversely affected in those whose lives are mostly driven by extrinsic aspirations.[34]

According to Deci and Ryan, intrinsically motivated aspirations energize significant growth-oriented behaviors, including seeking out new challenges, pursuing one's interests, and exercising skills, such that people who act more in accord with their intrinsic aspirations are likely to engage in fulfilling life goals that are most personally satisfying. Similarly, within person-centered psychology, intrinsic aspirations can be considered a measure of the organismic valuing process. It seems that the introjected values of others, reflected in the pursuit of extrinsically motivated aspirations, have less influence as people become more psychologically adjusted.

In short, the extensive research evidence from SDT can be read as providing evidence consistent with person-centered theory.[35] SDT along with Rogers and other humanistic theorists, such as Maslow, all point to basic needs that human beings have for fulfilment and the development of their potential. While there may be slight differences between them in how these needs are described, they all essentially agree on the concept of the actualizing tendency as a basic motivation.[36]

Given that Rogers's career began in clinical psychology and today he is mostly discussed in relation to the world of therapy, it is not surprising that much of this wider evidence is overlooked and that the social psychological nature of his approach is not often considered. Indeed, most social psychology textbooks don't mention him, and if they do, it is only very briefly and not in a way that positions him as a major figure in the history of that tradition. But I think that is where his theoretical work is best situated and where so much evidence can be gathered in support of it. In the opening of their popular textbook on social psychology,[37] Eliot Smith and Diane Mackie identify characteristics of social psychology, including the following:

1. That our view of reality is shaped by cognitive and social processes.
2. That other people influence our perceptions, and they don't have to be physically present to do so.
3. That people are motivated to predict and understand the world to achieve a sense of mastery.
4. That people seek acceptance from others.
5. That people desire to see themselves in a positive light.
6. People's views about themselves and the world are hard to change.

In the subsequent chapters of their book they unpack the evidence for these principles. Although Smith and Mackie do not mention Rogers, these are principles that anyone familiar with his work will recognize as characterizing the person-centered approach. Rogers did not identify as a social psychologist during his career, but in my view his work sits comfortably in this broader field.

One of the reasons why Rogers's work is not central to contemporary social psychology is perhaps that the view of human beings as essentially constructive was for several decades unfashionable and seen as naive. In the decades following Rogers's writings on human nature, psychology took a different turn, with several classic experiments and theories suggesting that human nature was essentially destructive. There was, for example, Philip Zimbardo's 1971 Stanford Prison Experiment. Students who took part in the study were randomly separated into groups of either prisoners or guards. The research was reported to show that the guards soon began to misuse their power and mistreat the prisoners, who displayed signs of distress. The level of abuse and distress grew so acute that the experiment had to be stopped after six days. Such studies were widely reported and have become the staple of many textbooks that present the view that human beings are essentially callous and selfish. Steve Taylor, in his book *DisConnected*, discusses how early psychologists were tailoring their experiments and results to confirm a bleak view of human nature and how contemporary research indicates a much more positive view of human nature as empathic. He argues that human societies have actually been, for the most part, egalitarian and peaceful.[38]

There is much empirical research in the social psychology research that supports Rogers's theory. In more recent experimental research, a study by Guy Itzchakov and colleagues in the *Journal of Personality and Social Psychology* found support across four studies for a core Rogerian hypothesis that high-quality listening allows speakers to be less defensive and thus gain insights about themselves.[39] While it is not clear whether the authors themselves recognized that their hypothesis was a direct test of Rogers's theory and that their study could also be seen as a contribution to the person-centered literature, the authors do recognize the wide-ranging implications of their work and how it bridges different fields of psychology and the social sciences and has implications for political science literature in exactly the way that makes Rogers's theory also so appealing. Rogers's theory lends new hypotheses to be tested by social psychologists, such as whether the effect observed by Itzchakov and colleagues is mediated by a change in the speaker's moment-by-moment self-regard toward greater unconditional self-acceptance. Further, such social psychological research and the greater integration of Rogers's approach within social psychology would be a welcome development.

Measurement of outcomes

Over the years, in an attempt to maintain the approach's contemporary relevance, person-centered practitioners have often compromised their original positive psychological perspective to accommodate the language of disorder and deficit. They have done this in order to establish the effectiveness of therapy against medical model constructs, for example, to claim statistical equivalence with other therapies. However, now that positive psychology has become more widely accepted, the next generation of research will need to take into account the positive psychological potential of the person-centered approach by introducing theoretically consistent measurements of well-being, authenticity, fully functioning, and so on. Understanding the scientific basis of the person-centered approach as a series of testable hypotheses is important in moving forward, but measurement has often been a contentious topic among the person-centered community.

The first point of contention is that, for some, the use of assessments as part of a therapy session is inappropriate as it distracts from the business of therapy itself and is part of an unnecessary "managerialism." Individuals with this view might say that what matters cannot be measured and what can be measured does not matter. Unfortunately, in my experience measurement does matter, not only because those in positions of power think it does and make their decisions about funding, services, and employment on the basis of what has been measured. It also matters because, as discussed in the previous chapter, the person-centered approach is a set of scientific hypotheses, designed to be tested, and there is an obligation to show that Rogers's bold assertions about how people change in relationships are actually borne out in the real world.

The second point of contention is that, for many, the notion of measurement is conflated with assessment and diagnosis. As a result, when we talk about measuring outcomes, some people might immediately think about the illness ideology. For those interested in the person-centered approach, such outcomes might seem inappropriate because they do not measure whether people have become more fully functioning. The more practical-minded may go along with this and engage in research and practice that uses measurement tools based on the illness ideology. I've discussed some of that research above, describing studies that have shown the person-centered approach to therapy to be effective, often in relation to measures of depression or anxiety, or posttraumatic stress. Such research has been important since the question most-often asked about therapy is, does it work? The people asking are rarely interested in whether people feel they have gotten to know themselves better, or been on a spiritual journey, or gained wisdom. What they mean is more likely to be whether the person is better, cured, or repaired. Therefore, researchers and clinicians will often provide some sort of measurement tool to assess the severity of clients' distress and dysfunction to show that, after therapy, those who were above some threshold of disorder are now below it. The use of measurement tools based on symptom reduction implicitly condones an illness ideology incompatible with person-centered therapy, but this does not mean that the very notion of measuring outcomes needs to be rejected. Measurement does not have to be concerned only with the illness ideology.

Because of the dominance of the illness ideology, practitioners and researchers might be less familiar with how to assess a person's well-being or their becoming more fully functioning. However, therapy should be understood not only as leading to the alleviation of distress and dysfunction, but also as promoting well-being. There are many tools available to measure well-being, some of which are suitable for use by therapists. For example, the Warwick-Edinburgh Mental Well-Being Scale that my colleagues and I developed has become a widely used measure. This is a 14-item measure of the range of concepts associated with positive mental health, including both hedonic and eudaimonic aspects, positive affect, satisfying interpersonal relationships, and positive functioning.[40] A more recent tool adapted for use in therapy is the Scales of General Well-Being. One feature of this is that unlike other tools for the assessment of well-being—which are only able to offer an assessment of positive psychological functioning and need to be used in conjunction with more traditional clinical measures—it can be used to understand and assess a general clinical state as well as movement toward greater positive functioning (see Box 9.4). The creators of the scale argue that changing the focus of clinical services from remediation to the nurturing of well-being is a worthwhile goal and that the focus on positive psychological change promises to be important for the future of clinical psychology and psychotherapy.[41]

Box 9.4 Example items from the Scales of General Well-Being

	Not at all true				Very true
I have a purpose.					
What I do in my life is worthwhile.					
I feel close and connected to the people around me.					

Each of the 14 items on the full scale is rated on a five-point scale ranging from 1= *not at all true* to 5 = *very true*, such that scores can range from 14 to 70, with a score of 39 representing a clinical cutoff. Those scoring below 39 are classified as being within a "clinical" population, and those scoring 39 and above are classified as being within the "normal" population.

One of my long-term research projects has been to develop and champion new measures of well-being that can be used in research and practice and that are compatible with the person-centered approach.[42] I am pleased to say that their use has now become a widely accepted practice within the person-centered community. While this has been a topic of interest to me in more recent years, it is one that dates back to the origin of the approach itself.

Rogers himself used various measurement techniques to assess movement and change in therapy. As already mentioned, right from the outset, he and his colleagues at the University of Chicago conducted a comprehensive research program into the process and outcome of therapy using Stephenson's Q-technique. Results from these early studies showed that personality change occurred in a direction that could be defined as an improvement, including increased emotional maturity and change in both the individual's perception of self and in their attitudes toward others.[43]

Subsequently, as Rogers refined his thinking about the fully functioning person and other humanistic psychologists began to study positive conceptions of mental health, many new tools were developed that can be used in therapy and research. One of the first came from Everett Shostrom, who devised the Personal Orientation Inventory (POI), which consisted of 150 pairs of statements. Respondents are asked to choose one statement from each pair that they most agree with. Subscales measured by the POI are Self-Actualizing Value, Existentiality, Feeling Reactivity, Spontaneity, Self-Regard, Self-Acceptance, Nature of Man, Synergy, Acceptance of Aggression, and Capacity for Intimate Contact. The POI can be used to yield two major scale scores. The first is for time competence, the degree to which the person is able to live in the present in a meaningful way without regrets about the past or unrealistic thoughts about the future. The second is for the tendency to be inner-directed in the search for meaning in life rather than externally influenced.[44] The idea that such ideas can be brought into therapeutic work is certainly not new to positive psychology. In 1975, in the *Journal of Personality Assessment*, Donald Tosi and Cathy Lindamood, wrote,

> It is recommended at the present time that the POI be used in counseling and psychotherapeutic situations as a point of departure for greater client self-awareness and self-exploration. The POI does appear to provide meaningful content for therapeutic discussion.[45]

The POI was one of the forerunners of what might now be considered positive psychology measurement, but it was lengthy and its forced-choice format was more cumbersome than that of other measures that were later developed, such as the Feelings, Reactions, and Beliefs Survey (FRBS),[46] which was developed in 1988 to assess aspects of personality that its authors claim were specifically derived from Rogers's writings, such as openness to feelings in relationships (e.g., "I am at ease with people who say how they are feeling") and trust in self as an organism ("With other people I usually behave just the way I feel"). But for the reasons mentioned above, a wariness about measurement has held back progress in the person-centered approach, and for a while, research into the person-centered approach was virtually non-existent. Insofar as such research is going to be conducted, I argue that it is preferable to use tools that are compatible with Rogers's theory.

Thus, in 2006 Tom Patterson, a clinical psychologist at the University of Coventry, and I developed a new 12-item scale to assess unconditional positive self-regard,[47] which Rogers defines as

> when the individual perceives himself in such a way that no self-experience can be discriminated as more or less worthy of positive regard than any other, then he is experiencing unconditional positive self-regard.[48]

This is the idea that people who are self-accepting in such a way that they don't feel they need to look to others for validation and are not swayed by the praise or blame others might give them are more able to find their self-direction in life. In turn, this leads to greater congruence, or authenticity. Unconditional positive self-regard is, however, somewhat of an ideal for most of us. It is something to aspire to, to work toward, and hopefully we dip into it at some points in our life, though the reality is that most of us can go through life rarely glimpsing what it is like to truly accept ourselves for who we are. Investigation into unconditional positive self-regard promises to be a helpful line of research for the future.

Since Rogers popularized the concept of unconditional positive self-regard, it has become a cornerstone of much psychotherapeutic practice. Unconditional positive regard is provided by the therapist, in the understanding that by doing so, the client will in turn develop unconditional positive self-regard. This is facilitated by establishing certain relationship conditions within the therapeutic encounter, through which the client is enabled to achieve positive therapeutic change, evidenced by a decrease in conditions of worth and, by definition, an increase in their unconditional positive self-regard. Although most often considered a unitary construct, this concept actually consists of two factors: self-regard and the conditionality of self-regard. Patterson and I showed this to be the case,[49] with evidence for a clear two-factor solution, with items loading either on self-regard (e.g., "I really value myself") or conditionality of regard (e.g., "Whether other people are openly appreciative or openly critical of me, it does not really change how I feel about myself").

Despite studies that show conditionality and self-regard to be two separate factors, psychotherapeutic practice and theory tend to treat unconditional positive self-regard as a unitary construct. Their results are as predicted from Rogers's theory, namely that those with higher scores tend to have more self-compassion, score lower on measures of depression and anxiety, and score higher on measures of well-being and other indices of positive functioning.[50] Given that the psychologically healthy stance is unconditional positive self-regard and that this is most often treated as a unitary phenomenon, it is assumed that people fall somewhere on a spectrum, with the opposite pole characterized by conditional negative self-regard.

As a unitary construct, however, the other combinations of these two factors—conditional positive self-regard, unconditional negative self-regard, and conditional negative self-regard—get conflated, such that we know that these are less healthy ways of relating to the self but don't know in what way each might contribute to less than fully functioning behavior. Rogers himself did not explicate this much further, and neither have subsequent theorists.

Therefore, rarely is the nature of self-regard experienced by most of us at most points in our lives discussed in relation to the fact that it is composed of two separable factors. The first refers to the expression or withholding of positive regard toward oneself, the positive-to-negative self-regard continuum. The second is the conditional–unconditional continuum, that is to say, the extent to which one's regard for oneself is dependent on the introjected approval from others or not. So, while it is true that the psychologically healthiest people will have both positive regard and unconditionality, there are actually four separate ways in which people may experience themselves:[51]

1. Conditional positive self-regard
2. Conditional negative self-regard
3. Unconditional negative self-regard
4. Unconditional positive self-regard

Research shows the psychological benefits of unconditional positive self-regard, but each of the other three life positions is psychologically unhealthy in its own distinct way, and each represents a stance toward life. There is no intention here to offer anything of a diagnostic system, as it makes no difference to the therapy, as I've discussed, but such a typology of personality structure more helpfully characterizes how a person approaches life at any given time—rather than simply thinking of unconditional positive self-regard as a unitary phenomenon on a spectrum with the opposite pole characterized by conditional negative self-regard—and promises to be an interesting new direction for researchers.

Another new line of research has been into authenticity.[52] The Authenticity Scale, for example, is a tool based on Rogers's concept of congruence. It is a 12-item self-report questionnaire that comprises three components: self-awareness; the ability to take ownership of one's own decisions in life and not be governed by the expectations of others; and an openness and honesty in interpersonal situations.[53] Adopting the Authenticity Scale as an outcome measure for clinical research, prospective research has established that person-centered therapy is related to increased authenticity.[54]

With the introduction of this and other such measures, researchers in positive psychology are now adding to a body of evidence that actively contributes to our knowledge about the person-centered approach. What tools one should use in research depends on the question, but when we are asking if therapy works or questioning the validity of the person-centered approach, it makes sense to design research using tools that are consistent with the theory. More recently, Beth Freire, Susan Stephen, Robert Elliott, and colleagues at the University of

Strathclyde have developed the Strathclyde Inventory, a tool based on Rogers's concept of the fully functioning person. This promises to be a valuable new research tool for the person-centered community. In recent research, Stephen proposed that while such instruments can be used to yield a single score, there may be a hierarchical relationship between the items in such scales that reflects Rogers's description of the process of developing more congruent functioning. Using the Strathclyde Inventory, she describes how as people become more self-aware and able to trust their own experience, they are more able to accept themselves, thus becoming more open to their own experiencing. The more open they become, the more open they become to others.[55]

There are many criticisms of research using tools such as those described above, but these criticisms apply to the field of psychology and the measurement of individual differences as a whole; they are not specific to the application of humanistic ideas.[56] Psychological science is imperfect, but as I said previously, there is a responsibility to ensure that theoretical claims are consistent with experience.

Using tools such as those mentioned above, much new research in personality and individual differences has also emerged over the last decade and is pushing the boundaries of the person-centered approach into new territory that develops Rogers's hypotheses about the personal and social benefits of more congruent, authentic functioning. For example, research has now shown that authenticity is predictive of greater well-being,[57] is associated with greater mindfulness and emotional intelligence,[58] mediates the relationship between mindfulness and well-being,[59] and is associated with the quality of relationships,[60] compassion,[61] pro-social and pro-environmental behavior,[62] self-transcendence,[63] and posttraumatic growth.[64] Other research has reconceptualized posttraumatic growth using person-centered personality theory and shown it to be related to unconditional positive self-regard, and the ability to focus on one's bodily felt sense, as Rogers's theory would predict.[65]

These findings, which are just a snapshot of a growing literature, all provide evidence in support of Rogers's belief that authenticity, or congruence, and unconditional positive self-regard are of central importance to understanding more fully functioning behavior. It would make sense, therefore, to use tools to assess these person-centered concepts of unconditional positive self-regard, congruence, and fully functioning in place of—or alongside—tools to assess concepts such as depression or anxiety. Doing so changes the landscape of research in a way that, I think, can be welcomed by person-centered psychologists and also contributes to positive psychology.[66]

But how we think we ought to offer help to each other in society is not a straightforward, evidence-based question. What constitutes evidence, which evidence we value most, and what we do with the evidence that we choose to attend to are all expressions of our values. For example, clinical psychology training and the mental health system emphasize the importance of specific treatment techniques for different psychological conditions. But there is also a wealth of empirical literature showing that the most important factor in therapeutic recovery regardless of the condition is not what the therapist does but, rather, the quality of the relationship between the therapist and client. That evidence, however, gets a back seat in mainstream psychology and psychiatry. It may be that future research will show Rogers's theory of personality development and his relational theory of therapy to be unfounded, but to date, his theories remain to be refuted.

Occam's razor says that we should look to the simplest explanation first. To my mind, the person-centered approach usually offers the most parsimonious scientific explanation for many psychological phenomena. Therefore, it should be the first choice for most researchers to rule out before turning to explore other theoretical and more prescriptive approaches.

Concluding comments

In sum, these findings from positive psychology and related social psychological fields support important elements of Rogers's personality theory. The lack of research, or at least the perceived lack of research, has held the person-centered approach back in recent decades. In the past, its critics said that humanistic theory and the person-centered approach were not research-based. I don't think it was true then, and it certainly isn't true today. There is more than sufficient evidence to justify its practice. Now, after treading water for decades, the person-centered approach is in much better health in the 21st century. Yet there are ever-increasing demands for research to address its use with different populations and disorders. Such research is important if the approach is to continue to maintain and develop in contemporary contexts. It is a rebuttal to those who would say that the approach is only for the "worried well." But there is the danger that such research, by adopting the language of disorder and illness, simultaneously undermines the approach by seemingly condoning an illness ideology. Research must be undertaken with an awareness of its purpose, in this case to help position the approach as a form of helping within contemporary systems, not because there is an agreement with those systems. Other research must continue to develop the approach in its own terms as a challenge to medicalized ways of thinking and working. Rogers's approach is ultimately about how people flourish and how to promote the good life.

Chapter 10
Looking ahead

Rogers and his colleagues offered a truly revolutionary way of applying psychology. As an academic, I have been fascinated by his approach, and it has kept me busy as a researcher and an educator for many years. Increasingly, however, I have felt like I am writing as a historian, helping to keep alive a tradition of a long-lost language of interest to a few enthusiasts, and that is increasingly at odds with the dominant language. In this final chapter I will offer some reflections on Rogers's approach today and for the future. Following a discussion of how Rogers revolutionized the helping professions by asserting that therapy was not part of medicine, I will observe how, having freed therapy from its medical straitjacket, he began the more radical journey of exploring how and where his ideas about helping people to become themselves could be applied. Rogers had a vision for the person-centered approach, but he did not live long enough to see it applied as fully and widely as he might have liked, and questions of how and where it can be applied are yet to be fully developed. The challenge for those us working within the approach is to see it afresh, to release it for ourselves from our own straitjackets of thinking.

Today, Rogers is best remembered for his approach to therapy, and for the most part, he is remembered only for a watered-down version of the therapy, one that has been broken down for its parts. Let us remember instead just how controversial his ideas were and how threatening they remain. Rogers used the term *counseling* because at the time of his initial writings, psychotherapy was seen as the province of medicine. Fortunately, times have changed since and psychotherapy is no longer seen as the sole province of medicine, although times have not changed so much that battles over the use of these terms have ended. It is still a controversial topic, and while those of us within the approach see the terms as interchangeable, others often see psychotherapy as associated with approaches and ideas derived from more psychoanalytical and medicalized views and counseling as something that is a more superficial way of helping.

It is important that those of us interested in the person-centered approach hold this position of equivalence, as others in the wider field of therapy who still adopt the more medicalized and psychoanalytical views are again pushing to see the term *psychotherapy* reserved only for those approaches and wish to recreate a hierarchical model of therapy with person-centered counseling seen

The Humanistic Psychology of Carl Rogers. Stephen A. Joseph, Oxford University Press. © Oxford University Press (2025). DOI: 10.1093/9780197790632.003.0011

as inferior to psychoanalytically and medically derived approaches. That might suit some therapists, but to me it is an agenda driven solely by self-interest and the pursuit of professional power, not by any intellectual justification. There is no reason to think of any therapy as superior to any other. They simply represent competing ideologies; there is no natural hierarchical ordering of them. Each offers a different vision for what it is to be human, what makes for the good life, and what values ought to be promoted in society. In this way, they offer mutually incompatible visions of humanity.

The terms *counseling*, *psychotherapy*, and *therapy* do not refer to a single set of practices but a range of different ideas and approaches. But this more fine-grained understanding of the field of therapy is often not well understood by its critics. It is not uncommon among sociologists to observe the oppressive functions of therapy in society and how it can be used to "strengthen the control apparatus of the society."[1] This seems a valid criticism of the therapy profession as a whole, but it does not seem a fair comment on Rogers's approach, which, as I have argued, was itself a social critique of the same coercive systems of society. This is one of its strengths and what makes it different from so many other approaches to helping.

Through the often unnecessary medicalization of human experience, many professionals have been cogs in a larger system of oppression that, thankfully, is becoming more apparent and subject to challenge. In a highly cited article in *American Psychologist* on the subject of how clinical psychology perpetuates the creation of distress, George Albee highlighted major political differences between a medical/organic/brain-deficit model to explain mental disorders and a social-learning, stress-related model. He argued that the former is supported by the ruling class because it does not require social change and major readjustments to the status quo. The social model, on the other hand, seeks to end or reduce poverty with all its associated stresses, as well as discrimination, exploitation, and prejudices as other major sources of stress leading to emotional problems. All political systems and forms of helping swing between these two positions. Albee concluded that "by aligning itself with the conservative view of causation, clinical psychology joined the forces that perpetuate social injustice."[2] Albee was writing some time ago, but the point remains valid today.

In this way, many psychologists and psychotherapists may view themselves as helping to empower people, but as I hope I have shown, the contrast of fundamental assumptions with the person-centered approach reveals that, by and large, most of these are part of a mainstream neoliberal culture of controlling and manipulating people. If people cannot be trusted, then relieving them of their personal power and creating a coercive and controlling society is the only way to create order out of the chaos that would otherwise ensue. In contrast, Rogers's view is that people can be trusted given the right conditions and that their personal power is to be respected. Rogers's approach succeeded in doing this because he theorized the nature of psychological problems as having a unitary cause in incongruence and he offered a form of therapy that was ultimately about changing the social environment such that people could flourish without impediment to their development.

Recent years have seen increased challenges to those professions that adhere to the medical model of distress and new calls for a paradigm shift away from disease models and diagnosis[3] from individuals who are seemingly unaware that such a paradigm already exists and has for more than 80 years. Person-centered therapy offers a form of helping that does not perpetuate the medicalization of distress in the same way as some other therapies. The application of psychological ideas is central to humanities future, but unless we take a person-centered approach to how we apply psychology, there is the danger that it will simply become another technology of oppression. Certainly, it would seem to me that the person-centered approach has always been on the side of social justice, at least in its scholarship, although in practice it is hard to maintain due to the pressures on therapists in a working environment immersed in a medical model. It is a continuing battle to win over the minds of those in positions of influence and power to the person-centered approach.

We must decide what sort of society we wish for and whether we ourselves are part of the problem or part of the solution. I imagine that people will always be divided on their views of human nature, and in politics as with psychotherapy, there will always be a tension maintained between those of us who adopt different ideological stances on human nature. Whether one agrees with Rogers's stance or not is unimportant; the point is that all professionals who apply psychological theory need to be aware of their own stance. All interventions are based on some understanding of human nature. The social sciences and their applications are a battle of competing ideologies about the nature of humanity, what we want it to look like, and how people might develop in more constructive ways. It is perhaps success enough if all those of us who are interested in the person-centered approach simply maintain that tension: to be the opposing voice that serves as a bulwark against what would otherwise be an overwhelming wave of the more directive, coercive, and controlling philosophies of others.

Going upstream

Many would argue that mainstream clinical practice overemphasizes the biological and psychological causes of mental health problems at the expense of social-environmental causes, thus perpetuating social injustice. The criticism is that by leading people to believe that their problems reside in their biology or their way of thinking, psychologists and psychiatrists are serving to divert people's attention from the real causes of their distress. For example, as Gillian Proctor wrote,

> The psychologisation of distress firmly places the cause for psychological ill-health within the individual . . . Thus deprivation, abuse, oppression and the social and political context of distress can largely be ignored and the practice of clinical psychology can continue to try to mop up problems caused by a sick society.[4]

The analogy is that the roof is broken, and the rain keeps flooding the house. We actually need to fix the roof, but therapists just constantly mop the floor. Such views follow in the wake of other psychologists who have been critical of many of the traditional approaches to mental health. This is how psychiatric medication is often seen: as little more than mopping the floor and, as a result, inadvertently condoning and maintaining the social injustices and oppressive forces that lead to people's difficulties. It is apparent that what research evidence tells us about the effectiveness of any intervention is not set in stone; as societies change, the role of those interventions changes. At one time the roof may be in good repair, and that will define the nature of therapy and its role in that society. Later, the roof might be badly damaged; now therapy means something different. In this way, we must be wary of therapy as a solution for what are social problems. Even person-centered therapy becomes an oppressive technology if it is used to help ignore the rain pouring in through the broken roof.

Psychotherapy is the only obvious application of the person-centered approach that is still widely practiced today, but in this context, it is about a self-righting process, helpful to people whose tendency toward actualization has already been usurped and thwarted. Psychotherapy is a limited vision for the application of the person-centered approach. Therapy is not the best answer to social problems. Another analogy is that therapy is like going downstream and helping to pull a person out of the river to save them from drowning. What we might need is for more of us to go upstream to stop people from falling into the river in the first place.

Of more importance in today's world, in my view, is that we expend energy on upstream interventions to facilitate people's psychological development in the first place such that the eventual need for psychotherapy is reduced. I discussed the application of the person-centered approach in two key areas: our working lives as part of organizations and education. While Rogers's influence has been greatest in the fields of one-to-one counseling and psychotherapy—where the person-centered approach remains widely practiced and well supported by empirical evidence—I believe his contributions to these other areas are the most significant and far reaching for the modern world.

In his 1969 book *Freedom to Learn*, Rogers asked the question of whether education could prepare people for the coming years, to deal with racial tensions, international tensions, and irrational nationalism. Would it "come to grips with the real problems of modern life? Or will it continue to be shackled by the tremendous social pressures for conformity and retrogression, added to its own traditionalism?"[5]

More than five decades later, it seems clear that the person-centered approach has not succeeded in its mission, but neither has it failed, in the sense that educational theorists and their policy makers have not put it to the test in any meaningful way. The same questions and issues with which Rogers was grappling decades ago remain topics for debate and discussion today, with the same ideas being recycled using different language. One must conclude that, ultimately, those with the power to implement change do not want change and that the agenda of education throughout the world is not the liberation and freedom of people to live more authentically, peacefully, and in harmony with each other and the natural world, but is actually the control and coercion of people to conform to the values of a society that have been predetermined for them.

I strongly believe in the power of person-centered education to be transformational, but in my experience it is hard to implement. In an education system that is teacher-centered, students come expecting more of the same, and when they are greeted with student-centered classes, they can feel discombobulated. My experience is in running student-centered classes for students learning to be person-centered therapists so the pedagogy of the class matches the pedagogy of the therapy. Because of this, it is easier for students to see that we have a rationale for what we do, but some nonetheless find it hard to adjust to this new style of learning after years in traditional education. Most take some time to settle into the different way of learning. They are learning to learn. Student-centered learning in a teacher-centered society is challenging. The problems found in offering student-centered learning aren't necessarily inherent in the approach, but in the fact that the approach is consistently undermined by the competing messages that students receive from the wider education system.

Realistically, attempts to develop more person-centered systems within traditional existing systems may be well intentioned but, by definition, are always a case of doing the best one can to be person-centered, given the freedom to do so granted by the institution of which one is part. This was the realization that Lisbeth Sommerbeck had, which I discussed in Chapter 5. As educators, psychologists, and other professionals, we are all cogs in much larger systems, and we each have a responsibility to decide whether we condone or oppose the system that we are maintaining.

I would ask you to think back to the reflection in Box 1 in the introduction, where I invited you to take the opportunity to reflect on why you have come to be interested in the person-centered approach, the events and experiences in your life that may have led you to this point, and your expectations for yourself and for your learning. Looking back at your answers, would you now say anything different? Do you feel you met your expectations? Are there things you have learned about yourself or the approach that were unexpected?

Seeing the person-centered approach afresh

As we have seen, part of the problem that the person-centered approach has had in more recent years is its association with the wider profession of therapy, which has become increasingly medicalized such that people often misunderstand what therapy is and can only conceive of it in terms of the medical model, making it an uncomfortable home for the person-centered practitioner. Of the existing structures, the one that seems to provide the most theoretically coherent fit is that of social psychology. Perhaps seeing ourselves as applied social psychologists is a way forward. Another is to think of ourselves as educational theorists.

While revisiting how to situate the person-centered approach within contemporary structures seems helpful, the question is whether existing structures are all just too embedded, either explicitly or implicitly, within an illness ideology. Can we step outside these existing structures altogether as, for example, suggested by O'Hara who, as mentioned in Chapter 1, suggested that we think of ourselves as social innovators? More recently, another possibility discussed by Murphy and Joseph in the *Cambridge Journal of Education* is to try instead to align the person-centered approach with that of the social pedagogy movement, with its emphasis on the development of individuals, groups, and communities through learning community actions and the central role of relational approaches.[6] Social pedagogy is a form of education but one that carries the notion of community at its core. The implications of this redefine what has been typically considered mental health practice as pedagogical practice. This step moves the field toward a new conceptualization of supporting the development of psychological well-being and opens debate about how this can be best achieved. This also raises questions as to who and which professions might be best placed to support the progress of such human development and how professions might best be structured and defined to facilitate optimal human development.

Whatever the way forward, the point is to shake off the associations with medicine and healthcare and see the person-centered approach afresh for what it is. Imagine what a more genuine, empathic, and accepting world would look like. Imagine also a society that takes personal growth seriously, makes it central to education, sees it as ongoing throughout the life span, and takes steps to promote it at every turn, in workplaces, in healthcare settings, and as part of social policy, and sees its benefits for parenting, management, and leadership.

Rogers's approach is ultimately about promoting authenticity in people and in our relationships with each other. In that respect, his approach is always going to be a challenge to more authoritarian societies that demand conformity. Some might say that we ought to keep politics out of psychology, but my understanding is that the two are intertwined; the application of psychological ideas is inevitably an expression of an ideology about the nature of people and how society should be arranged.[7]

The title of this chapter, "Looking Ahead," was taken from Rogers's 1980 book, *A Way of Being*, in which he used it as heading for the last section, where he speculated tentatively and optimistically on the future. He wrote about how "The winds of scientific, social, and cultural change are blowing strongly. They will envelop us in this new world."[8] Out of this, he believed, could arise a more humane world and the emergence of the "person of tomorrow"—the phrase Rogers used to describe a person who would be more authentic, open, whole, caring, ecologically minded, and less materialistic.

Overall, I am not sure Rogers would look at the world today and see the person of tomorrow whom he envisaged as overwhelmingly present. But in this I don't think he would be surprised, given that one page after describing the person of tomorrow, he discussed the opposing forces that they would inevitably face—from governing elites, traditional institutions, and the use of technology—to maintain the status quo. He recognized how threatening his person-centered scenario was: "as these persons of tomorrow continue to emerge into the light, they will find increasing resistance and hostility . . . they may very well be overwhelmed by such forces."[9]

The social and technological winds of change over the last few decades have probably been far stronger than Rogers could have expected. They have created new freedoms for people in many ways but also led to new and insidious means of creating conditions of worth, especially for younger people. Evidence suggests that the well-being of young people has declined over the past decade along with the increase in electronic screentime.[10] Younger people today are likely to feel more powerless, alienated, and apathetic than those of a similar age several decades ago.[11] The person of tomorrow now seems like a more distant vision.

Decades before the modern age of social media and disinformation, Rogers talked about how people needed the right information, the facts, to be able to make the best choices for themselves and each other, but there were many in positions of power over others who deliberately concealed the facts for their own purposes. Increasingly, we seem to live in a world characterized by disinformation. The opposing forces that Rogers described seem just as present as, if not more so than, when he was writing. And, it could be argued, psychology as a profession has turned more toward the maintenance of neoliberal ideologies at the expense of humanistic philosophies, itself becoming one of the oppressive technologies.

In looking ahead, there are concerns for the many existential crises that confront us, especially climate change and other tragedies of the commons, as well as mental health challenges and cultural zeitgeists such as artificial intelligence and social media, and the dangers of political polarization, nationalism, immigration, and armed conflict. These are crises with human causes. Managing and overcoming them requires the application of psychology, although this is not straightforward. Psychology can be applied to oppress or to free people, to escalate or to lessen challenges, and this can be done either knowingly or unknowingly. Given the scale of the crises now confronting us, applying psychological ideas wisely seems ever more important.

Throughout this book I have discussed how important theory is, but I understand that theory can appear removed from the everyday reality of practice and policy and that people often just want to know "What works, and what are the facts?" I hope my discussion has shown that such questions are never actually neutral in the way that might be supposed, but always have some inherent ideology. Understanding this is the first step to what it means to apply psychological ideas wisely.

The person-centered approach can be used to alternatively conceptualize a wide variety of areas of study and practice. Jeffrey Cornelius-White, Renate Motschnig-Pitrik, and Michael Lux, in their 2013 edited book *Interdisciplinary Handbook of the Person-Centered Approach*, write that the person-centered approach

> can be seen as providing one meta-model that can help connect many fields of study. It provides a parsimonious explanation and as astonishingly straightforward and elegant theory on how to move forward to address those dimensions of the unique challenges of the present and the future that concern interaction within and between people.[12]

In this book, and its companion volume, *Interdisciplinary Applications of the Person-Centered Approach*, Cornelius-White, Motschnig-Pitrik, and Lux bring together a collection of authors who discuss how the person-centered approach relates, or can be applied, to a variety of fields including the social sciences, educational science, management science, conflict resolution, coaching, health and intensive care, natural science and medicine, systems theory, and the expressive arts.

The message is that in policy and practice related to education, mental health, or any social change, there is always a theory at the root, whether it is made explicit or not. Theory gives direction and meaning. Whatever the context of policy, there is always a tension between using social structures to shape and control human behavior or to promote personal agency and freedom. The person-centered approach gives us a framework to distinguish between organizations, policies, and laws that create freedom and those that are oppressive. It does this because it tells us what human needs are in relationships and how they must be satisfied for human flourishing to occur.[13]

It is helpful to reiterate that the person-centered approach is an approach to all human relationships and that there is no prescribed way of doing it. All that it means is that whatever is done, is done in a way that is consistent with the ideas of the approach, which, in short, is characterized by its growth paradigm—its fundamental philosophical assumptions about human nature: the tendency toward actualization; how, under certain social environmental conditions, this tendency will operate in such a way as to release creativity; and other constructive social and interpersonal interactions.

The most pressing problems for humanity involve conflict between different groups. Human conflict is often about one person's vision for the future and another's story about the past. The former says that we must start from where we are and accept what has happened, and the latter says that the past should not be forgotten and reparations must be made. For one to succeed, the other must be defeated. Such is the nature of much of the conflict around the world. As Rogers recognized, the only truly peaceful way forward is through listening to each other with empathy, acceptance, and a genuine desire to seek solutions in which everyone is valued.

I grew up during the 1960s and 1970s in Northern Ireland. It was a time of great political conflict and violence. Because of this, one of Rogers's projects that interests me most is an encounter group of people from Northern Ireland that Rogers facilitated with his colleague Pat Rice in 1972. The group included those from the Catholic nationalist and Protestant unionist communities affected by and involved in the political violence that was then taking place. The protagonists were brought over to America, and the encounter was held in Pittsburgh. A year later, a film about the encounter groups, called *Steel Shutter*, was released. How radical, and even dangerous, this project was for those involved might be hard to imagine from today's vantage point, and this work continues to resonate with those of us living in Northern Ireland, even to this day.[14] It was a controversial project that was not always welcome, and those involved had some fears for their safety, but it showed that when the willingness was there, people from different conflicting traditions could meet in ways that were accepting of each other and that this could lead to deeper and meaningful relating. Sadly, the work is not as well known today as it deserves to be and is one of the many aspects of Rogers's work, and that of his colleagues of the time, that deserves much greater acknowledgment. Rogers provided the theoretical and practical foundations for conflict resolution and peace-building processes.

The theme of conflict resolution was always present in Rogers's early work, and he had spoken about how communication could be improved between groups and even nations as far back as 1951, but as his biographer, Howard Kirschenbaum, notes, this *Steel Shutter* project and his involvement with Pat Rice was a turning point in Rogers's career at which he began to more clearly relate his ideas to broader social and political issues. Indeed, in the latter part of his life and career, after he joined Western Behavioral Sciences Institute, he dedicated himself to the task of helping people listen to each other across divisions, and famously, he was nominated for the Nobel Peace Prize in 1987 in recognition of his work.

Throughout the 1980s, Rogers was most active in the development of the Carl Rogers Peace Project, and he and his colleagues facilitated large encounter groups, most notably in Europe, South Africa, and the Soviet Union, where protagonists of different groups came together to meet in a person-centered environment. The Rust workshop was one such meeting, held in 1985 in Austria, at which those with leading roles in the contemporary Central American conflict were present, including ex-presidents of Central American countries, ambassadors, government officials, academics, and activists. Rogers's work showed that it was possible to bring people who are divided and in conflict together and create meaningful dialogue.[15]

As mentioned, Rogers was nominated for the Nobel Peace Prize, but sadly the nomination letter arrived the day after he died, and so his nomination was never actually considered. Although conflict resolution continued to be important for many in the person-centered community, and the understanding of how to create the right social environments for people to come together across divisions is well established, this work has never been built upon and developed to the extent that I am sure Rogers would have liked to see happen. Today, the same issues confront humanity, and politicians, scholars, and activists are again asking the same questions, often unaware that this is well-trodden territory. Most of the newer ideas and research simply echoes Rogers's earlier work, sometimes acknowledged and sometimes not, and while some of the terminology might be different, the ideas are often the same.

Rogers was optimistic about the future and for people to resolve their own problems, but not when the social environment was suboptimal. Ultimately that is the issue that, in the longer term, humanity must aim to correct, to build societies in which people's innate tendencies toward growth and full functioning are respected. Only then is the capacity for people to truly enter into dialogue with each other possible. Most of us are so powerless in our own lives, struggling to survive, and caught in webs of conditions of worth shaped by materialistic ideas of value and success that we are unable to see our way toward being part of more optimal social environments. People's abilities to be empathic, to be unconditionally accepting, and to want to step into others' frame of reference are diminished by the fact that these qualities have not been nurtured in them in the first place. The more cynical person might say that surely this must all be by design, and indeed evidence that this is the case is clear when one looks, for example, at the role of social media today in fostering divisions between people.

Rogers's theory showed how to create better societies, but it also showed how to control people through social systems of conditional regard. Aware that such psychological knowledge could be used to manipulate public behavior, Rogers discussed how it could either prop up a dictatorship or contribute to a viable democracy.[16] That psychology could be used for political ends was clear in his later writings, as was his view on how the ideas of humanistic psychology were threatening to some:

> A governmental-military-police-industrial complex would be more than happy to use scientific technology . . . for the control of human behavior . . . humanistic psychologists, emphasizing the essential freedom and dignity of the unique human person and his capacity for self-determination, would be among the first to be incarcerated by such a government.[17]

The person-centered psychology of Rogers in which people genuinely listen to each other with empathy and acceptance is as radical an idea today as it ever was, and it seems more needed than ever if we are to heal tensions between different peoples, develop and grow from the adversities and challenges ahead, and eventually move toward creating the just and humane societies that he envisaged.

Concluding comments

We live in times of unprecedented challenge for the human race, where there are threats not only to democracy but to civilization itself, and even the continued survival of our species. I am hopeful that Rogers's ideas might gain in popularity again and become a new force for social change, but during the two years that I have been working on this book, my hope has ebbed and flowed. At times the need for a more person-centered approach to human problems has seemed greater than ever and also further away from being acted on. Maybe, however, it is only when the challenges we face are at their greatest that humanity will realize that we need to learn to live together more harmoniously. I discussed how events in a person's life can lead to a breakdown and disorganization of their self-structure, which, in time, can be the catalyst for great change for that person as they rebuild themselves in ways that are more fully functioning. Important to the context of this discussion is the recognition that it is a process that operates not only at the individual level but also at the societal level. On the one hand, people may double down on established ways of thinking, often inadvertently fueling the fire of the very problems themselves that they seek to solve, but on the other, they may recognize the need to abandon older patterns in search of new ways of acting. We can hope that in facing the current challenges, the latter wins out. The person-centered approach promises a revolution and a rehumanizing of society.

Afterword

I have found it humbling to read Rogers's works and those of the many other scholars writing about the person-centered approach. I wrote in the introduction that as I was writing this book, I came to think that the world did not need another book about Carl Rogers's theory and therapy. So much has already been written. If I had not been committed to this project, I may have abandoned it there and then, but now that I am at the end, I am glad I did not because I have learned so much for myself in writing it, and I feel that I have accomplished my goal to present the information in a helpful way for others.

Reflecting on what this book is about, I would say it is that Rogers's approach is about authenticity, how it arises and what thwarts it, how it can be promoted, and how authenticity is at the core of much human happiness and misery. What I hope readers get from this book is a more joined up story than is typical in most textbooks, one that has more engagement with contemporary ideas, more clearly communicates the way that Rogers's approach was distinctive, and shows how we can still learn from it today. Not everyone will agree with how I have presented the material but my wish is that readers come away from this book more ready and motivated to read the other books, to go deeper for themselves. In the next section I have listed some of those books.

Every book comes to an end, and I have heard it said that no book is ever finished; the writer just stops writing. That is certainly how the writing of this book feels. I feel that I have done sufficient justice to each of the topics I have covered and that the reader will come away with fresh insights and a new understanding, but each chapter in this book could be a full book in itself. I have only just opened the door for the reader to enter. I hope that those embarking on research projects see the potential for new research to, reconceptualize other constructs in person-centered terms, explore the psychological processes described by Rogers, or evaluate the outcomes of applications of the approach. I especially hope that readers who only knew Rogers as a counselor will be inspired to learn about his latter years of work on education, conflict resolution, and the application of the person-centered approach to wider social issues. But while I have addressed these topics more so than many textbook authors have, there is so much more to say. There are many more articles and books by Rogers and other scholars and practitioners than I have cited that would have been included if I had kept writing. My hope is that readers will continue the journey for themselves and continue to explore the influences, the turning points, and the different points of view; to be able to see contemporary scholarship through the lens of what has gone before; and to understand the scope of what could be.

Further reading

Biography

Kirschenbaum, H. (2007). *The life and work of Carl Rogers.* PCCS Books.

This is the definitive biography of Rogers. At over 700 pages, it provides depth of detail about each step in his life and career, the influences on him, his influence on others, and an exploration of the contributions that he made.

Rogers's own works

Rogers, C. R. (1989). *The Carl Rogers reader.* (H. Kirschenbaum & V. L. Henderson, Eds.). Houghton Mifflin.

An indispensable book containing copies of Rogers's major scientific and technical works, including both his 1957 paper on the six necessary and sufficient therapeutic conditions and a shortened version of his most important 1959 chapter.

Rogers, C. R. (1957). The necessary and sufficient conditions of therapeutic personality change, *Journal of Consulting Psychology, 21*, 95–103.

This is Rogers's classic 1957 paper on his theory of therapy. It is perhaps the best known of all his scholarly writings. It was Rogers's attempt to provide an integrative statement of why therapy is helpful, in which he proposes the six relationship conditions.

Rogers, C. R. (1959). A theory of therapy, personality, and interpersonal relationships: As developed in the client-centered framework. In S. Koch (Ed.), *Psychology: A study of a science, Vol. 3: Formulations of the person and the social context* (pp. 184–256). McGraw-Hill.

This is Rogers's most important and comprehensive theoretical work. It covers his theory of personality development and his theory of therapy, as well as his thinking about the wider applications of his person-centered approach. This chapter is fundamental to understanding the approach. Importantly, Rogers describes the key person-centered concepts and theoretical mechanisms, such as the actualizing tendency, the need for positive regard, conditions of worth, self-actualization, self-structure, incongruence of self and experience, breakdown and disorganization, and fully functioning. He explains how these concepts relate to each other to clarify the process of child development and personality formation. Note, however, that the version of the chapter later published in *The Carl Rogers Reader* does not contain the extensive section that defines the theoretical concepts.

Rogers, C. R. (1961). *On becoming a person.* Houghton Mifflin.

The first of several of Rogers's more popular books aimed at the general reader. Unlike the previous articles, it does not contain detailed descriptions of theory, but it offers his ideas in a more accessible way, and for many, brings his work to life in a way that his other more technical writings do not.

Psychopathology

Joseph, S. (2017). (Ed.). *The handbook of person-centred therapy and mental health: Theory, research and practice.* PCCS Books.

Containing chapters by many of the leading writers in the approach, this book is about how the person-centered approach tackles serious psychological problems and the various issues and challenges faced by practitioners.

Murphy, D. (2019). *Person-centred experiential counselling for depression: A manual for training and practice.* Sage.

Applying the person-centered approach to working with depression, this book is a necessary guide to theory and practice.

Clinical case studies

Farber, B. A. E., Brink, D. C., & Raskin, P. M. (1996). *The psychotherapy of Carl Rogers: Cases and commentary.* Guilford Press.

This book contains transcripts of Rogers's own therapy sessions that were recorded at different points in his career, along with commentary by leading scholars in the approach.

Worsley, R., & Joseph, S. (2007). (Eds.). *Person-centred practice: Case studies in positive psychology.* PCCS Books.

This is an engaging collection of case study material showing the different ways in which person-centered practitioners work.

Historical context

Barrett-Lennard, G. T. (1998). *Carl Rogers' helping system: Journey and substance.* Sage.

Godfrey Barrett-Lennard worked with Rogers in Chicago in the early days of the approach and has himself been one of the foremost writers in the field. In this book he provides a detailed deep dive into the history of the approach. Although more than 20 years old, this book remains a valuable resource from one of the leading proponents in the field.

Levitt, B. E. (2008). (Ed.). *Reflections on human potential: Bridging the person-centered approach and positive psychology.* PCCS Books.

Containing chapters by many of the pioneering and most important authors in the approach, including Jerold Bozarth, Barbara Temaner Brodley, Tony Merry, Peter Schmid, Alberto Zucconi, Keith Tudor, Author Bohart, Elizabeth Freire, Kathryn Moon, Garry Prouty, Carol Wolter-Gustafson, and even Carl Rogers himself, this book examines the concept of the actualizing tendency. A book that aspires to build bridges beyond the person-centered community; anyone seeking to deepen their knowledge of the approach and broaden their understanding of its applicability will find this book valuable.

Research and applications

Cain, D. J., Keenan, K., & Rubin, S. (2016). (Eds.). *Humanistic psychotherapies: Handbook of research and practice.* American Psychological Association.

This is an edited book containing 15 chapters on research evidence for humanistic and relationally based therapies. There are chapters on the main therapeutic approaches, including the person-centered approach, focusing-oriented–experiential psychotherapy, and emotional focused therapy, as well as chapters on process and outcomes in psychotherapy and evidence regarding therapist and client factors.

Cornelius-White, J. H. D., Motschnig-Pitrik, R., & Lux, M. (Eds.). (2013). *Interdisciplinary handbook of the person-centered approach: Research and theory.* Springer.

Cornelius-White, J. H., Motschnig-Pitrik, R., & Lux, M. (2013). *Interdisciplinary applications of the person-centered approach*. Springer.

These two books examine the different ways in which experiencing and communicating the qualities of empathy, acceptance, and genuineness brings out the inherent and constructive talents of people and discuss the idea that applying these social environmental conditions is the key to finding solutions for real-world problems and crises. The editors show how Rogers's approach is a meta-model that connects many fields of study and application. Contributors to the first volume explore transdisciplinary topics including cognitive science, systems theory, developmental relating, and positive psychology. Contributors to the second volume examine the applications, including in psychotherapy, peace and conflict resolution work, encounter groups, non-violent communication, parent effectiveness training, person-centered planning for people with disabilities, relationship enhancement methods, learner-centered education, technology-enhanced learning environments, and human relations leadership training.

Personal development

Joseph, S. (2019). *Authentic. How to be yourself and why it matters*. Piatkus / Little, Brown.

Based on Rogers's concept of congruence, this book explores the topic of authenticity, exploring research in positive psychology and offering self-help and personal development exercises.

Notes

Introduction

1. Rogers, 1969, p. 131.
2. Rogers, 1969, p. 280.
3. Seligman & Csikszentmihalyi, 2000.
4. Shlien, 1956/2003, p. 17.
5. Seeman, 1984, p. 132. Seeman also went on to pioneer new ideas about positive mental health long before the positive psychology movement became established. See, for example, Seeman, J. (1989).
6. Gendlin, 2002.
7. Sanders, 2004, p. 25.
8. Joseph, 2003a.
9. See Joseph, 2011; Joseph & Williams, 2005; and also Joseph, 2003b, 2004, Joseph, 2015c Joseph & Linley, 2005a.
10. See M. Cooper, 2024. *Tribes* is a term often used to describe all the different approaches that have their origin in Rogers's writings. It originally came from Warner, 2000a, who described person-centered psychotherapy as "one nation, many tribes." For example, classical, emotion-focused, process-experiential, and focusing are commonly seen as different tribes of the approach. Personally, *tribes* is a term I do not favor, not least because we don't talk about practitioner-centered approaches in this way. There are not said to be tribes within cognitive therapy, for example, with all the attendant and, in my view, unhelpful meanings that come attached to such language.
11. Brodley, 1997.

Chapter 1

1. Rogers, 1977a, p. 3).
2. Sutich & Vich, 1969, p. 1.
3. Bugental, 1964.
4. Moss, 2001.
5. See, for example, Bentall, 2004, p. 160, where he discusses how there are always biological correlates of behavior but cautions against inferring causation from such findings or that the simple fact of biological correlation does not mean that the behavior is a disorder.
6. Cosgrove et al., 2020.
7. Rockwell, 2012.
8. Rogers, 1961, p. 5.
9. Rogers, 1961, p. 7.
10. Rogers, 1975b, p. 129.
11. See Bozarth, 2012.
12. As reported by Patterson, 2003, p. 81.
13. As stated by Rogers in his interview with Evans (1975, p. 24). See also, Rogers, 1939.
14. Rogers, 1942; Rogers & Wallen, 1946.
15. Ellingham, 2011, discusses how Rogers initially used the term *non-directive* to position himself against the "older" forms of medical and diagnostic-based therapy, although it became used not only as a description of what he was against but also, increasingly, to describe what his therapy was. Criticized for *non-directive*'s simplicity and for the confusion it caused, Rogers began to use the term *client-centered* instead.
16. Rogers, 1951, p. 63.
17. Rogers, 1957a.
18. Rogers, 1959.

19. It is interesting that the 1959 chapter was actually written prior to his 1957 article, around 1953/54, and it took several years for the book to be printed, such that the 1957 article is seen as the more authoritative of the two when it comes to describing the six conditions, although there is only slight difference in the wording between the two formulations for clarity, not thought to be of any theoretical significance. The main difference is that in the description of the first of the six conditions that are necessary and sufficient for constructive therapeutic change, Rogers talks about "psychological contact" in 1957 as opposed to "contact" in 1959.
20. See, Sommerbeck, 2017a, for a discussion of the Wisconsin project.
21. The Western Behavioral Sciences Institute is a non-profit organization devoted to research, education, and study in human relations, human potential and includes research communication, international negotiation, self-directed therapeutic groups, race relations, and education. The Centre for the Study of Persons is an organization dedicated to exploring the application of the person-centered approach (https://centerfortheperson.org/).
22. Rogers, 1971. See also Rogers, 1970.
23. Proctor, 2019.
24. Rogers & Holdstock, 1977
25. *Freedom to Learn* (Rogers, 1969); *Carl Rogers On Personal Power* (Rogers, 1977a); *A Way of Being* (Rogers, 1980).
26. O'Hara, 2007, p. 54.
27. See Rogers, 1975a.
28. Interview in Evans, 1975, p. 33.
29. Elkins, 2009, p. 267.
30. Krippner, 2001.
31. Rennie, 2012, refutes the claim that humanistic psychology failed to produce research, arguing that it played a role in the development of qualitative methods and that its research went unnoticed by critics because it is more often published in more mainstream journals that are not explicitly about humanistic psychology.
32. See, for example, Hefferon et al., 2017.
33. See, O'Hara, 2007, p. 57.
34. Patient-centered medicine is an example, but early writings on the topic were often within the framework of the Rogerian person-centered approach. See, for example, Barnard, 1984.
35. E.g., Fielding, 2006.
36. For example, M. Cooper, 2024.
37. Bozarth, 2012.
38. Lietaer, 1984, p. 42.
39. Raskin, 1947/2005, p. 346.
40. Non-directivity is what separates Rogers's approach from other, more intentionally high-process guiding therapies such as Gendlin's focusing-oriented therapy and Greenberg, Elliott, and Rice's emotion-focused therapy. The practitioner is non-directive because they are following the client's direction, and because they are following the client's direction they are said to be client-centered. But see also Frankel & Sommerbeck (2005) and Schmid (2005), who see Rogers as offering a more directive approach than my argument would imply.
41. Rogers, 1977a, p. 14.
42. Adapted from Guerney, 1984.
43. Orlinsky, 1989, p. 413.
44. See, Joseph, 2010, for an overview of the different approaches to therapy.
45. See Cain, Keenan & Rubin, 2016
46. See Joseph, 2008; Joseph, 2017a; Wood & Joseph, 2007.
47. As noted in Rogers & Sanford, 1985. See also Kirschenbaum, 2007, p. 47.
48. Standal, 1954.
49. Ellingham, 2011.
50. For example, in Evans, 1975, p. 29.
51. Kramer, 1995.
52. Gendlin, 2002.

Chapter 2

1. Lewin, 1951.
2. Rogers, 1951.
3. Rogers, 1951, p. 485.

4. The 19 Propositions were Rogers's description of his personality development theory as presented in his 1951 book. I don't go into detail of it here as his 1959 chapter presents much the same material but in a more organized and developed way, in which he clarifies the role of empathy and unconditional positive regard as well as expanding the application of his theory. See Tyler, 1999, for a discussion on the difference between these two works.
5. Joseph & Patterson, 2008.
6. Rogers, 1959, p. 196.
7. See DeCarvalho, 1991.
8. Goldstein, 1939. *The Organism* was actually written several years earlier, in 1934, while Goldstein was living in Amsterdam and before he left Nazi Germany for America prior to the outbreak of World War II.
9. For example, Rogers, 1980, p. 119. Others who developed their ideas around a self-organizing principle included Maslow, who built on these earlier ideas to further understanding of self-actualization and who also acknowledged Goldstein as a profound influence on his own thinking (e.g., Maslow, 1954). See DeCarvalho, 1991, for a full discussion.
10. Rogers, 1961, p. 35. See also Rogers's 1957 article "A Note on the Nature of Man" in the *Journal of Consulting Psychology*, in which he states that humans are intrinsically motivated toward "development, differentiation, cooperative relationships; whose life tends to move from dependence to independence; whose impulses tend naturally to harmonize into a complex and changing pattern of self-regulation; whose total character is such as to tend to preserve himself and his species, and perhaps to move towards its further evolution" (Rogers, 1957b, p. 201). In this he also recognizes that the motivation is not only for the individual but for the species itself.
11. Rogers, 1963a, p. 6.
12. Quoted in Kirschenbaum & Henderson, 1990, p. 58.
13. Motschnig-Pitrik & Barrett-Lennard, 2010.
14. Shlien & Levant, 1984, p. 2.
15. Rogers, 1977a, p. 8.
16. Rogers, 1977a, p. 8.
17. Rogers, 1951, p. 501.
18. Rogers, 1959, p. 196. See also Julian Ford's influential 1991 article in the *Journal of Humanistic Psychology*, which helped to clarify the meaning of self-actualization in Rogers's works. He explained: "self-actualization refers to a branching of the actualizing tendency that occurs with the development of the self, with part of that tendency now dedicated to the actualization of the self-structure (viz., self-actualization)" (p. 104).
19. Wilkins, 2017. Wilkins's chapter is a response to critics who claim that Rogers lacks a theory of child development.
20. Rogers, 1963a, p. 20. See Ford, 1991.
21. Rogers, 1959, p. 224.
22. Gendlin, 1978/2003, p. 32. While the term *felt sense* seems synonymous with *organismic valuing process*, Gendlin's work is seen as a different branch of the person-centered approach and has its own therapeutic approach, which is seen as more directive over process than the classical non-directive approach pioneered by Rogers.
23. Statements adapted from Aoki & Ikemi, 2014.
24. Berger, 1963, p. 140.
25. See Joseph & Linley, 2006a.
26. See also, Kim, 2018.
27. Brazier, 1993, pp. 7–8.
28. Chang & Page, 1991, pp. 4–5.
29. Hermsen, 1996.
30. Chang & Page, 1991, p. 9.
31. Rogers, 1980, p. 60. Also in Evans, 1975, p. 136.
32. Rogers, 1978, p. 26.
33. Rogers, 1978, p. 26.
34. Cornelius-White, 2007a, p. 134.
35. Cornelius-White, 2007a, pp. 135-137. See also, Cornelius-White & Kriz, 2008.
36. Rogers, 1980, p. 132.
37. Rogers, 1980, p. 130.
38. E.g., Sheldon, Arndt, & Houser-Marko, 2003 tested the idea that people tend to move in actualizing relevant directions over time.

Chapter 3

1. Bugental, 1963.
2. Maddux & Lopez, 2015.
3. Albee, 2000, argues that the uncritical acceptance of the medical model, medical concepts, and medical language was the fatal flaw of clinical psychology. He maintains that by "placing psychology graduate students in psychiatric settings for training and service, psychologists lost their students to the invalid, ideological tattered, often incompetent psychiatric worldview." (p. 247).
4. For example, Bugental, 1964.
5. For example, Rogers, 1959, 1961, 1963b, all contain discussions about being fully functioning.
6. Rogers, 1957a, p. 221.
7. Rogers, 1957a, p. 221.
8. For example, Bozarth, 1998.
9. Rogers, 1959, p. 231.
10. Rogers, 1987a.
11. Rogers, 1957a.
12. See, Tyler, 1999, for a discussion.
13. Rogers, 1961.
14. Raskin, 1947/2005, p. 346.
15. Adapted from Rogers, 1961.
16. Levitt, 2005.
17. Grant, 1990/2002.
18. Grant, 1990/2002, p. 375.
19. Bozarth, 1998, pp. 11–12.
20. Grant, 2005, p. 247.
21. Barrett-Lennard, 1998, p. 82.
22. Rogers, 1959, p. 235.
23. Rogers, 1963a.
24. Rogers, 1951, p. 522. This is the 19th of Rogers's 1951 propositions.
25. Rogers, 1963a, p. 23.
26. See Ottiger & Joseph, 2021.
27. Rogers, 1961, pp. 188–189.
28. Adapted from Joseph & Murphy, 2013a.
29. https://beckinstitute.org/blog/new-to-cbt-three-pieces-of-advice-from-dr-judith-beck/.
30. See Joseph, 2006, 2018.

Chapter 4

1. Rogers, 1961, pp. 132–155
2. Rogers & Sanford, 1985, p. 1374.
3. Bozarth, 2002.
4. Joseph & Worsley, 2005; Joseph, 2017b.
5. Murphy, 2019; see also Doyle & Murphy, 2024.
6. Rogers, 1959, p. 226.
7. Warner, 2006, 2017.
8. Hook & Murphy, 2016, p. 297.
9. Warner, 2000b, p. 150.
10. Warner, 2001, p. 183.
11. Warner, 2001, p. 183.
12. See Joseph, 2003b, 2004.
13. Joseph, 2004.
14. Rogers, 1959, pp. 228–229.
15. Janoff-Bulman, 1989, 1992.
16. Horowitz, 1986.
17. Holdstock & Rogers, 1977, p. 136.

Chapter 5

1. Shlien, 1989/2002, p. 402.
2. Quoted in Kirschenbaum & Henderson, 1990, p. 53.
3. See Joseph, 2022. Simms, 2011, gives examples of how person-centered theory can be used to formulate psychological problems.
4. See Sommerbeck, 2017b.
5. Sommerbeck, 2012, p. 188.
6. Murphy, Duggan, & Joseph, 2013, p. 717.
7. Brodley & Brody, 2011, p. 255.
8. See also Biermann-Ratjen, 1998.
9. See also Meichenbaum, 1994.
10. See also Kennedy-Moore & Watson, 1999, p. 253.
11. Adapted from Joseph, 2004.
12. M. Cooper & McLeod, 2011.
13. Ong et al., 2020.
14. Ackerman & Hilsenroth, 2003.
15. Watson & Geller, 2005.
16. Bohart, 2012, describes person-centered therapy as a "fuzzy set" with a variety of members that bear a family resemblance and makes an argument for integrative approaches.

Chapter 6

1. Raskin, 1947/2005, p. 346.
2. See Evans, 1975, p. 26.
3. Rogers, 1986a, p. 207.
4. For example, Rogers, 1973.
5. For useful reflective exercises on authenticity that can be used in training, see Joseph, 2016.
6. See Worsley & Joseph, 2007, for a book of case studies, and Farber et al., 1996, for a collection of transcripts and commentary based on Rogers's own psychotherapy cases.
7. Kabat-Zinn, 1994, p. 4.
8. Baer, 2003; Bishop et al., 2004; Brown et al., 2007a; Malinowski, 2008.
9. See Brown & Ryan, 2003, 2004.
10. Joseph, Murphy, & Patterson, 2016.
11. Rogers, 1987b, p. 38.
12. Studies of psychological therapists in training have shown that mindfulness practice/meditation is associated with developing the quality of therapeutic presence (McCollum & Gehart, 2010) as well as reduced discomfort with silence in therapy sessions, less preoccupation and self-recrimination with themselves as therapists, and better tolerance of difficult emotions (Christopher & Maris, 2010). Furthermore, Grepmair et al. (2007) found that promoting mindfulness in trainee psychotherapists could positively influence therapeutic course and client outcomes.
13. While this is clearly a question that merits empirical study to determine its veracity, there is evidence to suggest that a more mindful mode of conscious processing is associated with more autonomous self-regulation and acting in ways that are congruent with chosen interests and values rather than introjected values (Brown & Ryan, 2003; Brown et al, 2007b).
14. Kabat-Zinn, 1994, pp. 6–7.
15. Beitel et al., 2014.
16. See, for example, Brito et al., 2022.

Chapter 7

1. This chapter is based on previous writings: Joseph, S. (2021). How humanistic is positive psychology? Lessons in positive psychology from Carl Rogers' person-centered approach—it's the social environment that must change. *Frontiers in Psychology*, *12*, 709–789; Joseph, S. (2020). Why we need a more humanistic positive organizational scholarship: Carl Rogers' person-centered approach as a challenge to neoliberalism. *The Humanistic Psychologist*, *48*(3), 271;

Joseph, S., Murphy, D., & Holford, J. (2020). Positive education: A new look at Freedom to Learn. *Oxford Review of Education*, *46*(5), 549–562.
2. Seligman, 1999.
3. Seligman & Csikszentmihalyi, 2000.
4. Seligman, 2004, p. xi.
5. Robbins, 2008, 2015.
6. Greening, 2001.
7. Taylor, 2001.
8. Resnick et al., 2001.
9. Seligman et al., 2005. This review, published more than 10 years after the birth of positive psychology, includes acknowledgment of humanistic psychology pioneers. For an overview, see DeRobertis & Bland, 2021.
10. Ehrenreich, 2010.
11. See Grogan, 2013.
12. See, for example, DeRobertis, 2024.
13. See Joseph & Murphy, 2013b.
14. Joseph, 2015a.
15. Tedeschi et al., 2018, p. 3.
16. See Joseph, 2011; Linley & Joseph, 2004; Tedeschi et al., 1998; Tedeschi et al, 2018
17. See Joseph, 2003b, 2004, 2015c, for the original discussions of how Rogers's 1959 theory applies to trauma and posttraumatic growth, and Joseph & Linley, 2005a who developed the organismic valuing theory of posttraumatic growth.
18. Joseph & Murphy, 2015.
19. See Joseph, 2015b.
20. Cameron & Caza, 2004, p. 731.
21. See Cameron & Caza, 2004; Cameron & Spreitzer, 2012.
22. Von Kimakowitz et al., 2011.
23. Coghlan & McIlduff, 1999. For example, transforming communication (Motschnig & Ryback, 2016), developing person-centered leadership (Plas, 1996), introducing innovation management (Haasis, 2013), managing conflict transformation (Stillwell, 2013), overcoming resistance to change (Coghlan, 1993), and offering process consultation (Coghlan, 1988) and leadership coaching (Kauffman et al., 2015).
24. Massarik, 1992, p. 393.
25. Montuori & Purser, 2001.
26. Seligman et al., 2009, p. 293.
27. Gilman et al., 2009; Norrish, 2015; Parks, 2013.
28. Norrish, 2015. See also Fineburg & Monk, 2015; Kibe & Boniwell, 2015.
29. Rogers, 1957c.
30. See Rogers, 1967b.
31. Rogers, 1969.
32. Rogers, 1983.
33. Kolb, 2014, p. xvii.
34. See Heim, 2011, for a discussion on developing non-directive tutorials in a university.
35. Critics such as Ecclestone, & Hayes (2009) argue that preoccupation with emotional well-being can be at the expense of subject knowledge. In contrast, the point I am making is that the person-centered approach is a different pedagogy, such the educational system should instead be designed to support the personality developmental processes as described by Rogers.
36. Rogers, 1967a, p. 717.
37. O'Hara, 2007.
38. Similar to the description of how posttraumatic growth leads to greater resilience, Joseph, 2021a. See also Haidt & Lukianoff, 2018, for their discussion of young people and the important role of challenge in their development.
39. Rogers, 1977b.
40. For interesting examples of applications, see Heim, 2011; Nelson et al., 2014.
41. See also Levitt, 2008.
42. See Joseph & Linley, 2006b.
43. Seligman, 2004.

44. For discussion, see Joseph, 2021a; Joseph & Wood, 2010.
45. See Elkins, 2009.
46. See Elkins, 2009.

Chapter 8

1. Maddux & Lopez., 2015, pp.417-421.
2. Maddux & Lopez, 2015; see also Jansz & van Drunen, 2004.
3. Burr, 2015, p. 172.
4. Wood & Joseph, 2007; Joseph, 2017a.
5. Farson, 1975, p. xxxviii.
6. Rogers, 1951, p. 24.
7. Quoted in Kirshenbaum & Henderson, 1990, p. 48.
8. Bozarth and Motomosa, 2017, pp. 392–393.
9. See Murphy & Joseph, 2016.
10. Tufford & Newman, 2012.
11. But see Andy Rogers, 2001, 2018, Moon, 2008; and Sommerbeck, 2017a, for what seem like alternative points of view.
12. For example, Mearns & McLeod, 1984.
13. Barrineau & Bozarth, 2002, p. 321.
14. See also Wilkins & Mitchell-Williams, 2002.
15. Rogers, 1961, pp. 400–401.
16. Rogers, 1985, pp. 8–9.
17. Rogers, 1985, p. 15.
18. O'Hara, 1995.
19. Rogers, 1986b.

Chapter 9

1. Rogers, 1961, p. 25.
2. See Murphy & Joseph, 2016.
3. See Burry, 2008. This is an account by Gloria's daughter about the impact the video had on her mother and some of the aspects of the recording that have come to light since. Clips of the film itself are widely available online.
4. For example, Moon, 2007; Reilly & Jacobus, 2008; Wickman & Campbell, 2003.
5. Moreira et al., 2011.
6. See, for example, Murphy et al., 2019.
7. Murphy et al., 2019.
8. Kirschenbaum, 2007, p. 210.
9. Rogers et al., 1967.
10. See Sommerbeck, 2017b.
11. A thorough review of evidence in 1984 by Watson reached the same conclusion that "After 25 years of research on Rogers' hypotheses, there is not yet research of the rigor required for drawing conclusions about the validity of this important theory" (p. 40).
12. Elliott, 2013; Elliott & Freire, 2008; Elliott & Freire 2010; Elliott et al., 2004; see Sanders & Joseph, 2016.
13. See Murphy, 2019; Murphy & Joseph, 2016.
14. Chen et al., 2022, 2023.
15. Barrett-Lennard, 2015.
16. Chen et al., 2023.
17. See Chen et al., 2022.
18. M. Cooper & Joseph, 2016.
19. See, for example, Murphy & Joseph, 2016; Stiles et al., 2008.
20. Farber et al., 2018.
21. Kolden et al., 2018.
22. Elliott et al., 2018.
23. Bozarth & Motomasa, 2017; McAleavey & Castonguay, 2015.
24. Keenan & Rubin, 2016, p. 447.

25. M. Cooper & Joseph, 2016.
26. See M. Cooper & Joseph, 2016, for a review.
27. Csillik, 2013.
28. For example, Roth & Assor, 2010, 2012.
29. Hinze et al., 2024.
30. Cornelius-White, 2007b.
31. Deci & Ryan, 2000; Ryan & Deci, 2000. See also Joseph & Murphy, 2013a, 2013b; Patterson & Joseph, 2007a; Sheldon, 2013; Vansteenkiste & Sheldon, 2006.
32. See Patterson & Joseph, 2007a.
33. Slemp et al., 2024.
34. Bradshaw et al., 2023. This is a meta-analytic review of 105 studies.
35. Patterson & Joseph, 2007a.
36. There is also other literature that supports Rogers's theory on the damaging effects of conditional regard on developmental processes. Social psychological research has provided support for the notion of the organismic valuing process through the observation that, over time, people tend to move toward more intrinsic goals (Sheldon et al., 2003) and that as people are more intrinsically rather than extrinsically motivated, increased well-being results (see Sheldon, 2013).
37. Smith & Mackie, 2007, pp. 18-22.
38. Taylor, 2023
39. Itzchakov et al., 2024.
40. Tennant et al., 2007.
41. Holland et al., 2021; see also Longo et al., 2018, the developers of the original scale.
42. Patterson & Joseph, 2007b. See also Joseph & Linley, 2005b, 2006a.
43. See Rogers & Dymond, 1954; And specific chapters by Butler & Haigh, 1954; Dymond, 1954.
44. Shostrom, 1964.
45. Tosi & Lindamood, 1975.
46. Cartwright & Mori, 1988; Cartwright et al., 1991.
47. Patterson & Joseph, 2006.
48. Rogers, 1959, p. 209.
49. Patterson & Joseph, 2006.
50. For example, Flanagan, 2015; Kim et al., 2020; Murphy et al., 2015; Murphy et al., 2020.
51. Joseph, 2021b.
52. See Joseph, 2016.
53. Wood et al., 2008; See also Toper et al., 2022.
54. Bayliss-Conway et al., 2021.
55. Stephen, 2023. See also, Freire, Elliott, & Cooper, 2007; Stephen, & Elliott, 2022.
56. See C. Cooper, 2024.
57. Boyraz et al., 2014; Lutz et al., 2023.
58. Tohme & Joseph, 2020; Toper et al., 2024.
59. Chen & Murphy, 2019.
60. Chen et al., 2023, 2024; Kim et al., 2020.
61. Bayır-Toper et al., 2022.
62. Ottiger & Joseph, 2021; Toper et al., 2023.
63. Toper et al., 2023.
64. Joseph et al, 2012.
65. Flanagan et al., 2015; Murphy et al., 2015, Zwiercan, & Joseph, 2018.
66. See Joseph & Wood, 2010 for a detailed discussion around the issues of incorporating positive psychological measures in clinical psychology.

Chapter 10

1. Berger, 1963, p. 90.
2. Albee, 2000, p. 248.
3. Campolonghi & Orrù, 2023.
4. Proctor, 2005, p. 280.
5. Rogers, 1969, p. vii.
6. Murphy & Joseph, 2019.

7. See Proctor et al., 2006, for a series of thought-provoking discussions on the politicization of the person-centered approach.
8. Rogers, 1980, p. 356.
9. Rogers, 1980, p. 355.
10. Twenge et al., 2018.
11. For example, Twenge & Kasser, 2013; Twenge et al., 2004.
12. See Cornelius-White et al., 2013, p. viii.
13. See Lister, 2010, a useful book on social policy.
14. For example, see Montgomery, 2023.
15. See Kirschenbaum, 2007, for a detailed and in depth account of Rogers's work and life in these later years and his peace project.
16. Interview with Rogers in Evans, 1975, pp. 64–65.
17. Rogers, 1975b, pp. 134–135.

References

Ackerman, S., & Hilsenroth, M. (2003). A review of therapist characteristics and techniques positively impacting the therapeutic alliance. *Clinical Psychology Review, 23*(1), 1–33.

Albee, G. W. (2000). The Boulder model's fatal flaw. *American Psychologist, 55*, 247–248.

Aoki, T., & Ikemi, A. (2014). The Focusing Manner Scale: Its validity, research background and its potential as a measure of embodied experiencing. *Person-Centered and Experiential Psychotherapies, 13*(1), 31–46.

Baer, R. (2003). Mindfulness training as a clinical intervention: A conceptual and empirical review. *Clinical Psychology: Science and Practice, 10*, 125–143.

Barnard, D. (1984). The personal meaning of illness: Client-centered dimensions of medicine and health care. In R. F. Levant & J. M. Shlien (Eds.), *Client-centered therapy and the person-centered approach: New directions in theory, research, and practice* (pp. 337–351). Praeger Publishers / Greenwood Publishing Group.

Barrett-Lennard, G. (1998). *Carl Rogers' helping system: Journey and substance.* Sage.

Barrett-Lennard, G. T. (2015). *The relationship inventory: A complete resource and guide.* John Wiley & Sons.

Barrineau, P., & Bozarth, J. D. (2002). A person-centered research model. In D. J. Cain (Ed.), *Classics in the person-centred approach* (pp. 317–322). PCCS Books. (Original work published 1989)

Bayır-Toper, A., Sellman, E., & Joseph, S. (2022). Being yourself for the "greater good": An empirical investigation of the moderation effect of authenticity between self-compassion and compassion for others. *Current Psychology, 41*(7), 4871–4884.

Bayliss-Conway, C., Price, S., Murphy, D., & Joseph, S. (2021). Client-centred therapeutic relationship conditions and authenticity: a prospective study. *British Journal of Guidance & Counselling, 49*(5), 637–647.

Beitel, M., Bogus, S., Hutz, A., Green, D., Cecero, J. J., & Barry, D. T. (2014). Stillness and motion: An empirical investigation of mindfulness and self-actualization. *Person-Centered & Experiential Psychotherapies, 13*(3), 187–202.

Bentall, R. P. (2004). *Madness explained: Psychosis and human nature.* Penguin.

Berger, P. L. (1963). *Invitation to sociology: A humanistic perspective.* Penguin.

Biermann-Ratjen, E. M. (1998). Incongruence and psychopathology. In B. Thorne & E. Lambers (Eds.), *Person-centred therapy: A European perspective* (pp. 106–118). Sage.

Bishop, S. R., Lau, M., Shapiro, S., Carlson, L., Anderson, N. D., Carmody, J., & Devins, G. (2004). Mindfulness: A proposed operational definition. *Clinical Psychology: Science and Practice, 11*, 230–241.

Bohart, A. C. (2012). Can you be integrative and a person-centered therapist at the same time? *Person-Centered & Experiential Psychotherapies, 11*(1), 1–13.

Boyraz, G., Waits, J. B., & Felix, V. A. (2014). Authenticity, life satisfaction, and distress: A longitudinal analysis. *Journal of Counseling Psychology, 61*(3), 498–505.

Bozarth, J. (1998). *Person-centred therapy: A revolutionary paradigm.* PCCS Books.

Bozarth, J. D. (2002). Empirically supported treatment: Epitome of the "specificity myth." In J. C. Watson, R. N. Goldman, & M. S. Warner (Eds.), *Client-centred and experiential psychotherapy in the 21st century: Advances in theory, research and practice* (pp. 168–181). PCCS Books.

Bozarth, J. D. (2012). "Nondirectivity" in the theory of Carl R. Rogers: An unprecedented premise. *Person-Centered & Experiential Psychotherapies, 11*(4), 262–276.

Bozarth, J. D., & Motomasa, N. (2017). Searching for the core: The interface of client-centered principles with other therapies. In S. Joseph (Ed.), *The handbook of person-centred therapy and mental health. Theory, research and practice* (pp. 391–408). PCCS Books.

Bradshaw, E. L., Conigrave, J. H., Steward, B. A., Ferber, K. A., Parker, P. D., & Ryan, R. M. (2023). A meta-analysis of the dark side of the American dream: Evidence for the universal wellness costs of prioritizing extrinsic over intrinsic goals. *Journal of Personality and Social Psychology, 124*(4), 873–899.

Brazier, D. (1993). Introduction. In D. Brazier (Ed.), *Beyond Carl Rogers. Towards a psychotherapy for the 21st century* (pp. 7–13). Constable.

Brito, R., Joseph, S., & Sellman, E. (2022). From instrumental to integral mindfulness: Toward a more holistic and transformative approach in schools. *Studies in Philosophy and Education, 41*(1), 91–109.

Brodley, B. T. (1997). The non-directive attitude in client-centered therapy. *The Person-Centered Journal, 4*(1), 67–74.

Brodley, B. T., & Brody, A. F. (2011). Can one use techniques and still be client-centered? In K. A. Moon, M. Witty, B. Grant, & B. Rice (Eds.), *Practicing client-centered therapy: Selected writings of Barbara Temaner Brodley* (pp. 249–255). PCCS Books.

Brown, K. W., & Ryan, R. M. (2003). The benefits of being present: Mindfulness and its role in psychological well-being. *Journal of Personality and Social Psychology, 84,* 822–848.

Brown, K. W., & Ryan, R. M. (2004). Fostering healthy self-regulation from within and without: A self-determination theory perspective. In P. A. Linley & S. Joseph (Eds.), *Positive psychology in practice* (pp. 105–124). Wiley.

Brown, K. W, Ryan, R. M., & Creswell, J. D. (2007a). Mindfulness: Theoretical foundations and evidence for its salutary effects. *Psychological Inquiry, 18*(4), 211–237.

Brown, K. W, Ryan, R. M., & Creswell, J. D. (2007b). Addressing fundamental questions about mindfulness. *Psychological Inquiry, 18*(4), 272–281.

Bugental, J. F. T. (1963). Humanistic psychology: A new breakthrough. *American Psychologist, 18*(9), 563–567.

Bugental, J. F. (1964). The third force in psychology. *Journal of Humanistic Psychology, 4*(1), 19–26.

Burr, V. (2015). *Social constructionism* (3rd ed.). Routledge.

Burry, P. J. (2008). *Living with "The Gloria Films": A daughter's memory.* PCCS Books.

Butler, J. M. & Haigh, G. V. (1954). Changes in the relation between self-concepts and ideal concepts consequent upon client-centered counseling. In C. R. Rogers & R. F. Dymond (Eds.), *Psychotherapy and personality change: Coordinated research studies in the client-centered approach* (pp. 55–75). University of Chicago Press.

Cain, D. J., Keenan, K., & Rubin, S. (2016), (Eds.). *Humanistic psychotherapies: Handbook of research and practice* (2nd ed.). American Psychological Association.

Cameron, K. S., & Caza, A. (2004). Contributions to the discipline of positive organizational scholarship. *American Behavioral Scientist, 47,* 731–739.

Cameron, K. S., & Spreitzer, G. M. (2012). Introduction. What is positive about positive organizational scholarship? In K. S. Cameron & G. M. Spreitzer (Eds.), *The Oxford handbook of positive organizational scholarship* (pp. 1–14). Oxford University Press.

Campolonghi, S., & Orrù, L. (2023). Psychiatry as a medical discipline: Epistemological and theoretical issues. *Journal of Theoretical and Philosophical Psychology.* Advance online publication. https://doi.org/10.1037/teo0000256

Cartwright, D., DeBruin, J., & Berg, S. (1991). Some scales for assessing personality based on Carl Rogers' theory: Further evidence of validity. *Personality and Individual Differences, 12*(2), 151–156.

Cartwright, D., & Mori, C. (1988). Scales for assessing aspects of the person. *Person-Centered Review, 3,* 176–194.

Chang, R., & Page, R. C. (1991). Characteristics of the self-actualized person: Visions from the East and West. *Counseling and Values, 36*(1), 2–10.

Chen, S., Liao, F., Murphy, D., & Joseph, S. (2022). Measurement invariance of the English, Chinese, and Spanish versions of the Barrett-Lennard Relationship Inventory. *Measurement and Evaluation in Counseling and Development*, *55*(1), 30–47.

Chen, S., Liao, F., Murphy, D., & Joseph, S. (2023). Development and validation of a 12-item version of the Barrett-Lennard Relationship Inventory (BL RI: mini) using item response theory. *Current Psychology*, *42*(13), 10566–10580.

Chen, S., & Murphy, D. (2019). The mediating role of authenticity on mindfulness and wellbeing: A cross cultural analysis. *Asia Pacific Journal of Counselling and Psychotherapy*, *10*(1), 40–55.

Chen, S., Murphy, D., & Joseph, S. (2023). Dispositional authenticity, internalised homonegativity, and relationship quality in same-gender couples: An actor-partner interdependence moderation model. *Psychology & Sexuality*, *15*(1), 127–146.

Chen, S., Murphy, D., & Joseph, S. (2024). Dispositional authenticity, facilitativeness, femininity ideology, and dyadic relationship functioning in opposite-gender couples: Actor-partner interdependence analysis. *Asian Journal of Social Psychology*, *27*(1), 101–126.

Christopher, J. C., & Maris, J. A. (2010). Integrating mindfulness as self-care into counselling and psychotherapy training. *Counselling & Psychotherapy Research*, *10*(2), 114–125.

Coghlan, D. (1988). In defence of process consultation. *Leadership & Organization Development Journal*, *9*(2), 27–31.

Coghlan, D. (1993). A person-centred approach to dealing with resistance to change. *Leadership & Organizational Development Journal*, *14*(4), 10–14.

Coghlan, D., & McIlduff, E. (1999). Facilitating change in organizations: Toward a framework of organization development for person-centred practitioners. *Person-Centered Journal*, *6*(1), 48–58.

Cooper, C. (2024). What is wrong with individual differences research? *Personality and Individual Differences*, *221*, 112550.

Cooper, M. (2024). *Tribes of the person-centred nation.* PCCS Books.

Cooper, M., & Joseph, S. (2016). Psychological foundations for humanistic psychotherapeutic practice. In D. J. Cain, K. Keenan, & S. Rubin (Eds.), *Humanistic psychotherapies: Handbook of research and practice* (pp. 11–46). American Psychological Association.

Cooper, M., & McLeod, J. (2011). Person-centered therapy: A pluralistic perspective. *Person-Centered & Experiential Psychotherapies*, *10*(3), 210–223.

Cornelius-White, J. H. D. (2007a). The actualizing and formative tendencies: Prioritizing the motivational constructs of the person-centered approach. *Person-Centered & Experiential Psychotherapies*, *6*(2), 129–141.

Cornelius-White, J. H. D. (2007b). Learner-centered teacher-student relationships are effective: A meta-analysis. *Review of Educational Research*, *77*(1), 113–143.

Cornelius-white, J. H. D., & Kriz, J. (2008). The formative tendency: Person-centered systems theory, interdependence and human potential. In B. E. Levitt (Ed.), *Reflections on human potential: Bridging the person-centered approach and positive psychology* (pp. 116-130). PCCS Books.

Cornelius-White, J. H. D., Motschnig-Pitrik, R., & Lux, M. (Eds.). (2013). *Interdisciplinary handbook of the person-centered approach. Research and theory.* Springer.

Cosgrove, L., Troeger, R., & Karter, J. M. (2020). "Do antidepressants work?" A humanistic perspective on a long-standing and contentious debate. *The Humanistic Psychologist*, *48*(3), 221–231.

Csillik, A. S. (2013). Understanding motivational interviewing effectiveness: Contributions from Rogers' client-centered approach. *The Humanistic Psychologist*, *41*, 350–363.

DeCarvalho, R. J. (1991). *The growth hypothesis in psychology: The humanistic psychology of Abraham Maslow and Carl Rogers.* EMText.

Deci, E. L., & Ryan, R. M. (2000). The "what" and "why" of goal pursuits: Human needs and the self-determination of behavior. *Psychological Inquiry*, *4*, 227–268.

DeRobertis, E. M. (2024). Historical foundations of existential-humanistic developmental psychology. *The Humanistic Psychologist, 52*(1), 1–19.

DeRobertis, E. M., & Bland, A. M. (2021). Humanistic and positive psychologies: The continuing narrative after two decades. *Journal of Humanistic Psychology*, https://doi.org/10.1177/00221678211008353.

Doyle. R., & Murphy, D. (2024), Person-centred experiential counselling for depression. In M. Cooper (Ed.), *Tribes of the person-centred nation* (pp. 132–157). PCCS Books.

Dymond, R. F. (1954). Adjustment changes over therapy from self-sorts. In C. R. Rogers and R. F. Dymond (Ed.), *Psychotherapy and personality change* (pp. 76–84). University of Chicago Press.

Ecclestone, K., & Hayes, D. (2009). Changing the subject: The educational implications of developing emotional well-being. *Oxford Review of Education, 35*(3), 371–389.

Ehrenreich, B. (2010). *Smile or die: How positive thinking fooled America and the world.* Granta Books.

Elkins, D. N. (2009). Why humanistic psychology lost its power and influence in American psychology: Implications for advancing humanistic psychology. *Journal of Humanistic Psychology, 49*(3), 267–291.

Ellingham, I. (2011). Carl Rogers' fateful wrong move in the development of Rogerian relational therapy: Retitling "relationship therapy" "non-directive therapy." *Person-Centered & Experiential Psychotherapies, 10*(3), 181–197.

Elliott, R. (2013). *Big data and little data.* Presentation to the British Association for the Person-Centred Approach Research Group. Edge Hill University, June 29, 2013.

Elliott, R., Bohart, A. C., Watson, J. C., & Murphy, D. (2018). Therapist empathy and client outcome: An updated meta-analysis. *Psychotherapy, 55*, 399–410.

Elliott, R., & Freire, B. (2008). *Person-centred experiential therapies are highly effective: Summary of the 2008 meta-analysis.* The British Association for the Person-Centred Approach. http://www.bapca.org.uk/images/files/meta-summary.bapca.pdf

Elliott, R., & Freire, E. (2010). The effectiveness of person-centred and experiential therapies: A review of the meta-analyses. In M. Cooper, J. C. Watson, & D. Hölldampf (Eds.), *Person-centered and experiential therapies work: A review of the research on counseling, psychotherapy and related practices* (pp. 1–15). PCCS Books.

Elliott, R., Greenberg, L. S. & Lietaer, G. (2004). Research on experiential psychotherapies. In M. J. Lambert (Ed.), *Bergin and Garfield's handbook of psychotherapy and behavior change* (5th ed., pp. 493–539). John Wiley & Sons.

Evans, R. I. (1975). *Carl Rogers: The man and his ideas.* E. P. Dutton.

Farber, B. A. E., Brink, D. C., & Raskin, P. M. (1996). *The psychotherapy of Carl Rogers: Cases and commentary.* Guilford Press.

Farber, B. A., Suzuki, J., & Lynch, D. (2018). Positive regard and psychotherapy outcome: A meta-analytic review. *Psychotherapy, 55*, 411–423.

Farson, R. (1975). Part B—Carl Rogers, quiet revolutionary. In R. I. Evans (1975). *Carl Rogers. The man and his ideas* (xxviii-xLiii). Dutton.

Fielding, M. (2006). Leadership, radical student engagement and the necessity of person-centred education. *International Journal of Leadership in Education, 9*(4), 299–313.

Fineburg, A. C., & Monk, A. (2015). Different approaches to teaching positive psychology. In S. Joseph (Ed.), *Positive psychology in practice: Promoting human flourishing in work, health, education, and everyday life* (pp. 267–278). John Wiley & Sons.

Flanagan, S., Patterson, T. G., Hume, I. R., & Joseph, S. (2015). A longitudinal investigation of the relationship between unconditional positive self-regard and posttraumatic growth. *Person-Centered & Experiential Psychotherapies, 14*(3), 191–200.

Ford, J. G. (1991). Rogerian self-actualization: A clarification of meaning. *Journal of Humanistic Psychology, 31*(2), 101–111.

Frankel, M., & Sommerbeck, L. (2005). Two Rogers and congruence: The emergence of therapist-centered therapy and the demise of client-centered therapy. In B. Levitt (Ed.),

Embracing non-directivity: Reassessing person-centered theory and practice in the 21st century (pp. 40–61). PCCS Books.
Freire, E., Elliott, R., & Cooper, M. (2007). The Strathclyde Inventory: Validation of a person-centred outcome measure. In *13th Annual BACP Counselling and Psychotherapy Research Conference, York, UK.*
Gendlin, E. T. (2003). *Focusing: How to gain direct access to your body's knowledge.* (25th anniversary ed.). Rider. (Original work published 1978)
Gendlin, E. T. (2002). Foreword. In C. R. Rogers & D. E. Russell, *Carl Rogers: The quiet revolutionary. An oral history* (pp. xi–xxi). Penmarin Books. https://www.focusing.org/gendlin/docs/gol_2155.html
Gilman, R., Huebner, E. S., & Furlong, M. J. (Eds.). (2009). *Handbook of positive psychology in schools.* Routledge.
Goldstein, K. (1939). *The organism.* American Book Company.
Grant, B. (2002). Principled and instrumental nondirectiveness in person-centered and client-centered therapy. In D. Cain (Ed.), *Classics in the person-centered approach* (pp. 371–377). PCCS Books. (Original work published 1990)
Grant, B. (2005). Taking only what is given: Self-determination and empathy in non-directive client centered therapy. In B. Levitt (Ed.), *Embracing non-directivity. Reassessing person-centered theory and practice in the 21 st century* (pp. 248–260). PCCS Books.
Greening, T. (2001). Commentary. *Journal of Humanistic Psychology, 41*(1), 4–7.
Grepmair, L., Mitterlehner, F., Loew, T., Bachler, E., Rother, W., & Nickel, M. (2007). Promoting mindfulness in psychotherapists in training influences the treatment results of their patients: A randomized, double-blind, controlled study. *Psychotherapy and Psychosomatics, 76*(6), 332–338.
Grogan, J. (2013). *Encountering America: Humanistic psychology, sixties culture and the shaping of the modern self.* Harper Perennial.
Guerney, B. G. (1984). Contributions of client-centered therapy to filial, marital, and family relationship enhancement therapies. In R. F. Levant & J. M. Shlien, *Client-centered therapy and the person-centered approach: New directions in theory, research, and practice* (pp. 261–277). Praeger Publishers / Greenwood Publishing Group.
Haasis, K. (2013). A person-centred approach to innovation management: Experiences and learnings. In J. H. D. Cornelius-White, R. Motschnig-Pitrik, & M. Lux (Eds.), *Interdisciplinary applications of the person-centered approach* (pp. 193–198). Springer.
Haidt, J., & Lukianoff, G. (2018). *The coddling of the American mind: How good intentions and bad ideas are setting up a generation for failure.* Penguin UK.
Hefferon, K., Ashfield, A., Waters, L., & Synards, J. (2017). Understanding optimal human functioning—the "call for qual" in exploring human flourishing and well-being. *Journal of Positive Psychology, 12,* 211–219.
Heim, C. (2011). Tutorial facilitation in the humanities based on the tenets of Carl Rogers. *Higher Education, 63*(3), 289–298.
Hermsen, E. (1996). Person-centered psychology and Taoism: The reception of Lao-tzu by Carl R. Rogers. *The International Journal for the Psychology of Religion, 6*(2), 107–125.
Hinze, V., Montero-Marin, J., Blakemore, S. J., Byford, S., Dalgleish, T., Esposti, M. D., Greenberg, M. T., Jones, B. G., Slaghekke, Y., Ukoumunne, O. C., Viner, R. M., Williams, J. M. G., Ford, T. J., & Kuyken, W. (2024). Student-and school-level factors associated with mental health and well-being in early adolescence. *Journal of the American Academy of Child & Adolescent Psychiatry, 63*(2), 266–282.
Holdstock, T. L. & Rogers, C. R. (1977). Person-centred theory. In R. J. Corsini (Ed.), *Current personality theories* (pp. 125–151). Peacock.
Holland, J., Murphy, D., & Joseph, S. (2021). Assessment of well-being in the clinic: Using the state version of the short Scale of General Well-Being as a clinical outcome measure. *Journal of Clinical Psychology, 77*(7), 1629–1643.

Hook, L., & Murphy, D. (2016). Related but not replaceable: A response to Warner's reworking of person-centered personality theory. *Person-Centered & Experiential Psychotherapies, 15*(4), 285–299.

Itzchakov, G., Weinstein, N., Leary, M., Saluk, D., & Amar, M. (2024). Listening to understand: The role of high-quality listening on speakers' attitude depolarization during disagreements. *Journal of Personality and Social Psychology, 126*(2), 213–239.

Janoff-Bulman, R. (1992). *Shattered assumptions: Toward a new psychology of trauma.* Free Press.

Jansz, J., & van Drunen, P. (Eds.). (2004). *A social history of psychology.* Blackwell.

Joseph, S. (2003a). Client-centred psychotherapy: Why the client knows best. *The Psychologist, 16*, 304–307.

Joseph, S. (2003b). Person centred approach to understanding posttraumatic stress. *Person Centred Practice, 11*, 70–75.

Joseph, S. (2004). Client-centred therapy, post-traumatic stress disorder and post-traumatic growth: Theoretical perspectives and practical implications. *Psychology and Psychotherapy: Theory, Research and Practice, 77*(1), 101–119.

Joseph, S. (2006). Person-centred coaching psychology: A meta-theoretical perspective. *International Coaching Psychology Review, 1*, 47–55.

Joseph, S. (2008). Psychotherapy's inescapable assumptions about human nature. *Counselling Psychology Review, 23*(1), 34–40.

Joseph, S. (2010). *Theories of counselling and psychotherapy: An introduction to the different approaches.* Palgrave.

Joseph, S. (2011). *What doesn't kill us: The new psychology of posttraumatic growth.* Basic Books.

Joseph, S. (2015a). *Positive therapy: Building bridges between positive psychology and person-centred psychotherapy.* Routledge.

Joseph, S. (Ed.). (2015b). *Positive psychology in practice: Promoting human flourishing in work, health, education, and everyday life.* John Wiley & Sons.

Joseph, S. (2015c). A person-centered perspective on working with people who have experienced psychological trauma and helping them move forward to posttraumatic growth. *Person-Centered & Experiential Psychotherapies, 14*, 178–190.

Joseph, S. (2016). *Authentic: How to be yourself and why it matters.* Piatkus / Little, Brown.

Joseph, S. (2017a). The problem of choosing between irreconcilable theoretical orientations: Comment on Melchert (2016). *American Psychologist, 72*(4), 397–398.

Joseph, S. (Ed.). (2017b). *The handbook of person-centred therapy and mental health: Theory, research and practice* (pp. 473–477). PCCS Books.

Joseph, S. (2018). The person-centred approach to coaching (3rd ed.). In E. Cox, T. Bachkirova, & D. Clutterbuck (Eds.), *The complete handbook of coaching* (pp. 52–65). Sage.

Joseph, S. (2020). Why we need a more humanistic positive organizational scholarship: Carl Rogers' person-centered approach as a challenge to neoliberalism. *The Humanistic Psychologist, 48*(3), 271–283.

Joseph, S. (2021a). Posttraumatic growth as a process and an outcome: Vexing problems and paradoxes seen from the perspective of humanistic psychology. *The Humanistic Psychologist, 49*(2), 219–239.

Joseph, S. (2021b). *Permutations of self-regard.* Talk given to the Human Flourishing Research Group, University of Nottingham, October 2021.

Joseph, S. (2022). Psychological formulation, a critical viewpoint: Illness ideology in disguise. *Journal of Humanistic Psychology, 62*(5), 683–693.

Joseph, S., & Linley, P. A. (2005a). Positive adjustment to threatening events: An organismic valuing theory of growth through adversity. *Review of general psychology, 9*(3), 262-280.

Joseph, S., & Linley, P. A. (2005b). Positive psychological approaches to therapy. *Counselling and Psychotherapy Research, 5*(1), 5-10.

Joseph, S., & Linley, P. A. (2006a). *Positive therapy. A meta-theory for positive psychological practice.* Routledge.

Joseph, S., & Linley, P. A. (2006b). Positive psychology versus the medical model. *American Psychologist, 61*, 332–333.

Joseph, S., Maltby, J., Wood, A. M., Stockton, H., Hunt, N., & Regel, S. (2012). The Psychological Well-Being—Post-Traumatic Changes Questionnaire (PWB-PTCQ): Reliability and validity. *Psychological Trauma: Theory, Research, Practice, and Policy, 4*(4), 420-428.

Joseph, S., & Murphy, D. (2013a). Person-centered approach, positive psychology, and relational helping: Building bridges. *Journal of Humanistic Psychology, 53*(1), 26–51.

Joseph, S., & Murphy, D. (2013b). Person-centered theory encountering mainstream psychology: Building bridges and looking to the future. In J. H. D. Cornelius-White, R. Motschnig-Pitrik, & M. Lux (Eds.), *Interdisciplinary handbook of the person-centered approach* (pp. 213–226). Springer.

Joseph, S., & Murphy, D. (2015). Special section 1: Posttraumatic growth and person-centered therapy. *Person-Centered & Experiential Psychotherapies, 14*(3), 177.

Joseph, S., Murphy, D., & Holford, J. (2020). Positive education: A new look at Freedom to Learn. *Oxford Review of Education, 46*(5), 549–562.

Joseph, S., Murphy, D., & Patterson, T. G. (2016). Mindfulness and person-centred therapy. In I. Ivtzan & T. Lomas (Eds.), *Mindfulness in positive psychology* (pp. 295–307). Routledge.

Joseph, S., & Patterson, T. G. (2008). The actualising tendency: A meta-theoretical perspective for positive psychology. In B. E. Levitt (Ed.), *Reflections on human potential: bridging the person-centred approach and positive psychology* (pp. 1–16). PCCS Books.

Joseph, S., & Williams, R. (2005). Understanding posttraumatic stress: Theory, reflections, context and future. *Behavioural and Cognitive Psychotherapy, 33*(4), 423–441.

Joseph, S., & Wood, A. (2010). Assessment of positive functioning in clinical psychology: Theoretical and practical issues. *Clinical Psychology Review, 30*(7), 830–838.

Joseph, S., & Worsley, R. (Eds.). (2005). *Person-centered psychopathology: A positive psychology of mental health.* PCCS Books.

Kabat-Zinn, J. (1994). *Wherever you go, there you are.* Hyperion.

Kauffman, C., Joseph, S., & Scoular, A. (2015). Leadership coaching and positive psychology. In S. Joseph (Ed.), *Positive psychology in practice: Promoting human flourishing in work, health, education and everyday life* (2nd ed., pp. 377–389). Wiley.

Keenan, K., & Rubin, S. (2016). The good therapist. Evidence regarding the therapist's contribution to psychotherapy. In D. J. Cain, K. Keenan, & S. Rubin (Eds.), *Humanistic psychotherapies: Handbook of research and practice* (pp. 421–454). American Psychological Association.

Kennedy-Moore, E., & Watson, J. C. (1999). *Expressing emotion: Myths, realities, and therapeutic strategies.* Guilford.

Kibe, C., & Boniwell, I. (2015). Teaching well-being nd resilience in primary and secondary school. In S. Joseph (Ed.), *Positive psychology in practice: Promoting human flourishing in work, health, education, and everyday life* (pp. 297–312). John Wiley & Sons.

Kim, J. (2018). Consideration of the applicability of person-centered therapy to culturally varying clients, focusing on the actualizing tendency and self-actualization–from East Asian perspective. *Person-Centered & Experiential Psychotherapies, 17*(3), 201–223.

Kim, J., Joseph, S., & Price, S. (2020). The positive psychology of relational depth and its association with unconditional positive self-regard and authenticity. *Person-Centered & Experiential Psychotherapies, 19*(1), 12–21.

Kirschenbaum, H. (2007). *The life and work of Carl Rogers.* PCCS Books.

Kirschenbaum, H. E., & Henderson, V. L. E. (1990). *Carl Rogers: Dialogues: Conversations with Martin Buber, Paul Tillich, B. F. Skinner, Gregory Bateson, Michael Polanyi, Rollo May, and others.* Constable and Company.

Kolb, D. A. (2014). *Experiential learning: Experience as the source of learning and development.* Pearson Education.

Kolden, G. G., Wang, C. C., Austin, S. B., Chang, Y., & Klein, M. H. (2018). Congruence/genuineness: A meta-analysis. *Psychotherapy, 55*, 424–433.

Kramer, R. (1995). The birth of client-centered therapy: Carl Rogers, Otto Rank, and "The Beyond." *Journal of Humanistic Psychology, 35*(4), 54–110.

Krippner, S. (2001). Research methodology in humanistic psychology in the light of postmodernity. In K. J. Schneider, J. F. T. Bugental, & J. F. Pierson (Ed.), *The handbook of humanistic psychology: Leading edges in theory, research, and practice* (pp. 289–304). Sage.

Levitt, B. E. (Ed.). (2005). *Embracing non-directivity: Reassessing person-centered theory and practice in the 21st century*. PCCS Books.

Levitt, B. E. (Ed.). (2008). *Reflections on human potential: Bridging the person-centered approach and positive psychology*. PCCS Books.

Lewin, K. (1951). *Field theory in social science: Selected theoretical papers* (Edited by Dorwin Cartwright.). Harper & Row.

Lietaer, G. (1984). Unconditional positive regard: A controversial basic attitude in client-centered therapy. In R. F. Levant & J. M. Shlien (Eds), *Client-centered therapy and the person-centered approach: New directions in theory, research and practice* (pp. 41–58). Praeger.

Linley, P. A., & Joseph, S. (2004). Positive change following trauma and adversity: A review. *Journal of Traumatic Stress, 17*, 11–21.

Lister, R. (2010). *Understanding theories and concepts in social policy*. The Policy Press.

Longo, Y., Coyne, I., & Joseph, S. (2018). Development of the short version of the Scales of General Well-Being: The 14-item SGWB. *Personality and Individual Differences, 124*, 31–34.

Lutz, P. K., Newman, D. B., Schlegel, R. J., & Wirtz, D. (2023). Authenticity, meaning in life, and life satisfaction: A multicomponent investigation of relationships at the trait and state levels. *Journal of Personality, 91*(3), 541–555.

Maddux, J. E., & Lopez, S. J. (2015). Deconstructing the illness ideology and constructing an ideology of human strengths and potential. In S. Joseph (Ed.), *Positive psychology in practice: Promoting human flourishing in work, health, education, and everyday life* (pp. 411–427). Wiley.

Malinowski, P. (2008). Mindfulness as psychological dimension: Concepts and applications. *The Irish Journal of Psychology, 29*(1), 155–166.

Maslow, A. H. (1954). *Motivation and personality*. Harper.

Massarik, F. (1992). The humanistic core of industrial/organizational psychology. *The Humanistic Psychologist, 20*(2–3), 389.

McAleavey, A. A., & Castonguay, L. G. (2015). The process of change in psychotherapy: Common and unique factors. In O. C. G. Gelo, A. Pritz, & B. Rieken (Eds.), *Psychotherapy research* (pp. 293–310). Springer Vienna.

McCollum, E. E., & Gehart, D. R. (2010). Using mindfulness meditation to teach beginning therapists therapeutic presence: A qualitative study. *Journal of Marital and Family Therapy, 36*(3), 347–360.

Mearns, D., & McLeod, J. (1984). A person-centered approach to research. In R. F. Levant & J. M. Shlien (Eds.), *Client-centered therapy and the person-centered approach: New directions in theory, research, and practice* (pp. 370–389). Praeger Publishers / Greenwood Publishing Group.

Meichenbaum, D. (1994). *Treating post-traumatic stress disorder. A handbook and practice manual for therapy*. Wiley.

Merry, T. (2003). The actualisation conundrum. *Person-Centred Practice, 11*(2), 83–91.

Montgomery, M. R. (2023). The steel shutter revisited: The importance of encounter. *Peace Review, 35*(3), 438–447.

Montuori, A., & Purser, R. (2001). Humanistic psychology in the workplace. In K. J. Schneider, J. F. T. Bugental, & J. F. Pierson (Eds.), *The handbook of humanistic psychology: Leading edges in theory, research, and practice* (pp. 635–644). Sage.

Moreira, P., Gonçalves, Ó. F., & Matias, C. (2011). Clients' narratives in psychotherapy and therapist's theoretical orientation: An exploratory analysis of Gloria's narratives with Rogers, Ellis and Perls. *Journal of Cognitive and Behavioral Psychotherapies, 11*(2), 173–190.

Moon, K. A. (2007). A client-centered review of Rogers with Gloria. *Journal of Counseling & Development, 85*(3), 277–285.

Moon, K. A. (2008). An essay on children, evil, and the actualizing tendency. In B. E. Levitt (Ed.), *Reflections on human potential: Bridging the person-centered approach and positive psychology* (pp. 203-214). PCCS Books.

Moss, D. (2001). The roots and genealogy of humanistic psychology. In K. J. Schneider, J. F. T. Bugental, & J. F. Pierson (Eds.), *The handbook of humanistic psychology: Leading edges in theory, research, and practice* (pp. 5–20). Sage.

Motschnig, R., & Ryback, D. (2016). *Transforming communication in leadership and teamwork.* Springer.

Motschnig-Pitrik, R., & Barrett-Lennard, G. (2010). Co-actualization: A new construct in understanding well-functioning relationships. *Journal of Humanistic Psychology, 50*(3), 374–398.

Murphy, D. (2019). *Person-centred experiential counselling for depression: A manual for training and practice.* Sage.

Murphy, D., Demetriou, E., & Joseph, S. (2015). A cross-sectional study to explore the mediating effect of intrinsic aspiration on the association between unconditional positive self-regard and posttraumatic growth. *Person-Centered & Experiential Psychotherapies, 14*(3), 201–213.

Murphy, D., Duggan, M., & Joseph, S. (2013). Relationship-based social work and its compatibility with the person-centred approach: Principled versus instrumental perspectives. *British Journal of Social Work, 43*(4), 703–719.

Murphy, D., & Joseph, S. (2016). Person-centered therapy: Past, present, and future orientations. In D. J. Cain, K. Keenan, & S. Rubin (Eds.), *Humanistic psychotherapies: Handbook of research and practice* (2nd ed., pp. 185–218). American Psychological Association.

Murphy, D., & Joseph, S. (2019). Contributions from the person-centred experiential approach to the field of social pedagogy. *Cambridge Journal of Education, 49*(2), 181–196.

Murphy, D., Joseph, S., Demetriou, E., & Karimi-Mofrad, P. (2020). Unconditional positive self-regard, intrinsic aspirations, and authenticity: Pathways to psychological well-being. *Journal of Humanistic Psychology, 60*(2), 258–279.

Murphy, D., Slovak, P., Thieme, A., Jackson, D., Olivier, P., & Fitzpatrick, G. (2019). Developing technology to enhance learning interpersonal skills in counsellor education. *British Journal of Guidance & Counselling, 47*(3), 328–341.

Nelson, L., Cushion, C. J., Potrac, P., & Groom, R. (2014). Carl Rogers, learning and educational practice: Critical considerations and applications in sports coaching. *Sport, Education and Society, 19*(5), 513–531.

Norrish, J. M. (2015). *Positive education: The Geelong Grammar School journey.* Oxford University Press.

O'Hara, M. (1995). Carl Rogers: scientist and mystic. *Journal of Humanistic Psychology, 35*(4), 40–53.

O'Hara, M. (2007). Psychological literacy for an emerging global society: Another look at Rogers' "persons of tomorrow" as a model. *Person-Centered & Experiential Psychotherapies, 6*(1), 45–60.

Ong, W. T., Murphy, D., & Joseph, S. (2020). Unnecessary and incompatible: A critical response to Cooper and McLeod's conceptualization of a pluralistic framework for person-centered therapy. *Person-Centered & Experiential Psychotherapies, 19*(2), 168–182.

Orlinsky, D. E. (1989). Researchers' images of psychotherapy: Their origins and influence on research. *Clinical Psychology Review, 9*(4), 413–441.

Ottiger, A. S., & Joseph, S. (2021). From ego-centred to eco-centred: An investigation of the association between authenticity and ecological sensitivity. *Person-Centered & Experiential Psychotherapies, 20*(2), 139–151.

Parks, A. C. (Ed.). (2013). *Positive psychology in higher education.* Routledge.

Patterson, C. H. (2003). *First hundred years are the hardest.* In D. Bower (Ed.), Person-centered/client-centered: Discovering the self that one truly is. iUniverse.

Patterson, T. G., & Joseph, S. (2006). Development of a self-report measure of unconditional positive self-regard. *Psychology and Psychotherapy: Theory, Research and Practice, 79*(4), 557–570.

Patterson, T. G., & Joseph, S. (2007a). Person-centered personality theory: Support from self-determination theory and positive psychology. *Journal of Humanistic Psychology, 47*(1), 117–139.

Patterson, T. G., & Joseph, S. (2007b). Outcome measurement in person-centred practice. In R. Worsley & S. Joseph (Eds.), *Person-centred practice: Case studies in positive psychology.* (pp. 200–215). PCCS Books.

Plas, J. M. (1996). *Person-centered leadership.* Sage.

Proctor, G. (2005). Clinical psychology and the person-centred approach: An uncomfortable fit? In S. Joseph & R. Worsley (Eds.), *Person-centred psychopathology: A positive psychology of mental health* (pp. 276–292). PCCS Books.

Proctor, G. (2019). Acknowledging inequalities and meeting the unknown other: Facilitating encounter. *Person-Centered & Experiential Psychotherapies, 18*(3), 243–254.

Proctor, G., Cooper, M., Sanders, P., & Malcolm, B. (Eds.). (2006). *Politicizing the person-centred approach: An agenda for social change.* PCCS Books.

Raskin, N. J. (2005). The non-directive attitude. In B. Levitt (Ed.), *Embracing non-directivity: Reassessing person-centered theory and practice in the 21st century* (pp. 329–347). PCCS Books. (Original work published 1947)

Reilly, J., & Jacobus, V. (2008). Students evaluate Carl Rogers and his relationship with Gloria: A brief report. *Journal of Humanistic Psychology, 48*(1), 32–41.

Rennie, D. L. (2012). Occluded humanistic qualitative research: Implications for positive psychology. *The Humanistic Psychologist, 40*(2), 166–178.

Resnick. S., Warmoth. A., & Serlin. I. A. (2001). The humanistic psychology and positive psychology connection: Implications for psychotherapy. *Journal of Humanistic Psychology, 41*(1), 73–101.

Robbins, B. D. (2008). What is the good life? Positive psychology and the renaissance of humanistic psychology. *The Humanistic Psychologist, 36,* 96–112.

Robbins, B. D. (2015). Building bridges between humanistic and positive psychology. In S. Joseph (Ed.), *Positive psychology in practice: Promoting human flourishing in work, health, education, and everyday life* (pp. 31–45). Wiley.

Rockwell, D. (2012). Humanizing mental health: Existentialism and the DSM-5: Can humanistic psychology light the way? *The Humanistic Psychologist, 40,* 207–211.

Rogers, A. (2001). Do we need "a" theory of personality? *Person-Centred Practice, 9*(1), 37–42.

Rogers, A. (2018). Carl Rogers: Absence and presence in the contemporary therapy landscape. In R. House, D. Kalisch, & J. Maidman (Eds.), *Humanistic psychology: Current trends and future prospects* (pp. 149–159). Routledge.

Rogers, C. R. (1939). *The clinical treatment of the problem child.* Houghton Mifflin.

Rogers, C. R. (1942). *Counseling and psychotherapy: Newer concepts in practice.* Houghton Mifflin.

Rogers, C. R. (1951). *Client-centred therapy: Its current practice, implications and theory.* Houghton Mifflin.

Rogers, C. R. (1957a). The necessary and sufficient conditions of therapeutic personality change, *Journal of Consulting Psychology, 21,* 95–103.

Rogers, C. R. (1957b). A note on the nature of man. *Journal of Consulting Psychology, 4*(3), 199–203.

Rogers, C. R. (1957c). Personal thoughts on teaching and learning. *Merrill-Palmer Quarterly, 3*(4), 241–243.
Rogers, C. R. (1959). A theory of therapy, personality and interpersonal relationships, as developed in the client-centered framework. In S. Koch (Ed.), *Psychology: A study of science, Vol. 3: Formulations of the person and the social context* (pp. 184–256). McGraw-Hill.
Rogers, C. R. (1961). *On becoming a person. A therapist's view of psychotherapy.* Houghton Mifflin.
Rogers, C. R. (1963a). The actualizing tendency in relation to "motives" and to consciousness. In M. R. Jones (Ed.), *Nebraska Symposium on Motivation*, Vol. 11 (pp. 1–24). University of Nebraska Press.
Rogers, C. R. (1963b). The concept of the fully functioning person. *Psychotherapy: Theory, Research & Practice, 1*(1), 17–26.
Rogers, C. R. (1967a). A plan for self-directed change in an educational system. *Educational Leadership, 24*(8), 717–731.
Rogers, C. R. (1967b). The interpersonal relationship in the facilitation of learning. In R. Leeper (Ed.), *Humanizing education* (pp. 1–18). Association for Supervision and Curriculum Development.
Rogers, C. R. (1969). *Freedom to learn.* Charles E. Merrill.
Rogers, C. R. (1970). *On encounter groups.* Harper & Row.
Rogers, C. (1971). Carl Rogers describes his way of facilitating encounter groups. *American Journal of Nursing, 71*(2), 275–279.
Rogers, C. R. (1973). My philosophy of interpersonal relationships and how it grew. *Journal of Humanistic Psychology, 13*(2), 3–15.
Rogers, C. R. (1975a). The emerging person: A new revolution. In R. I. Evans (Ed.), *Carl Rogers: The man and his ideas* (pp. 149–175). E. P. Dutton.
Rogers, C. R. (1975b). In retrospect: Forty-six years. In R. I. Evans (Ed.), *Carl Rogers: The man and his ideas* (pp. 134–135). E. P. Dutton.
Rogers, C. R. (1977a). *Carl Rogers on personal power: Inner Strength and its revolutionary impact.* Constable and Company.
Rogers, C. R. (1977b). The politics of education. *Journal of Humanistic Education, 1*(1), 6–22.
Rogers, C. R. (1978). The formative tendency. *Journal of Humanistic Psychology, 18*(1), 23–26.
Rogers, C. R. (1980). *A way of being.* Houghton Mifflin.
Rogers, C. R. (1983). *Freedom to learn for the 80's.* Charles E. Merril.
Rogers, C. R. (1985). Toward a more human science of the person. *Journal of Humanistic Psychology, 25*(4), 7–24.
Rogers, C. R. (1986a). Client-centered therapy. In I. I. Kutash & A. Wolf (Eds.), *Psychotherapist's casebook: Theory and technique in the practice of modern therapies* (pp. 197–208). Jossey-Bass.
Rogers, C. R. (1986b). Carl Rogers on the development of the person-centered approach. *Person-Centered Review, 1*, 257–259.
Rogers, C. R. (1987a). The underlying theory: Drawn from experience with individuals and groups. *Counseling and Values, 32*(1), 38–46.
Rogers, C. R. (1987b). Comments on the issue of equality in psychotherapy. *Journal of Humanistic Psychology, 27*(1), 38–40.
Rogers, C. R., & Dymond, R. F. (Eds.). (1954). Psychotherapy and personality change: Coordinated research studies in the client-centered approach. University of Chicago Press.
Rogers, C. R., Gendlin, E. T., Keisler, D. J., & Truax, C. (1967). *The therapeutic relationship with schizophrenics.* University of Wisconsin Press.
Rogers, C. R., & Holdstock, T. L. (1977). Person-centered personality theory. In R. Corsini (Ed.), *Current personality theories* (pp. 125–151). F. E. Peacock.

Rogers, C. R., & Sanford, R. C. (1985). Client-centered psychotherapy. In H. I. Kaplan & B. J. Sadock (Eds.), *Comprehensive textbook of psychiatry, Volume 2* (4th ed., pp. 1374–1388). Williams & Wilkins.

Rogers, C. R., & Wallen, J. L. (1946). *Counseling with returned servicemen*. McGraw Hill.

Roth, G., & Assor, A. (2010). Parental conditional regard as a predictor of deficiencies in young children's capacities to respond to sad feelings. *Infant and Child Development, 19*(5), 465–477.

Roth, G., & Assor, A. (2012). The costs of parental pressure to express emotions: Conditional regard and autonomy support as predictors of emotion regulation and intimacy. *Journal of Adolescence, 35*(4), 799–808.

Ryan, R. M., & Deci, E. L. (2000). Self-determination theory and the facilitation of intrinsic motivation, social development and well-being. *American Psychologist, 55*, 68–78.

Sanders, P. (2004). Radical psychology and the person-centred approach: A glimpse of a possible future. *Person-Centred Practice, 12*(1), 24–31.

Sanders, P., & Joseph, S. (2016). Person-centered psychology: An organismic positive approach to the problems of living and helping people flourish. In A. M. Wood & J. Johnson (Eds.), *The Wiley handbook of positive clinical psychology* (pp. 429–444). Wiley.

Schmid, P. F. (2005). Facilitative responsiveness: Non-directiveness from anthropological, epsitmeological and ethical perspectives. In B. Levitt (Ed.), *Embracing non-directivity: Reassessing person-centered theory and practice in the 21st century* (pp. 75–95). PCCS Books.

Seeman, J. (1984). The fully functioning person: Theory and research. In R. F. Levant & J. M. Shlien (Eds.), *Client-centered therapy and the person-centered approach: New directions in theory, research, and practice* (pp. 131–152). Praeger Publishers / Greenwood Publishing Group.

Seeman, J. (1989). Toward a model of positive health. *American Psychologist, 44*(8), 1099–1109.

Seligman, M. E. P. (1999). The president's address. *American Psychologist, 54*, 559–562.

Seligman, M. E. P. (2004). Foreword. In P. A. Linley & S. Joseph (Eds.), *Positive psychology in practice* (pp. xi–xiii). Wiley.

Seligman, M. E. P., & Csikszentmihalyi, M. (2000). Positive psychology: An introduction. *American Psychologist, 55*, 5–14.

Seligman, M. E. P., Ernst, R. M., Gillham, J., Reivich, K., & Linkins, M. (2009). Positive education: Positive psychology and classroom interventions. *Oxford Review of Education, 35*(3), 293–311.

Seligman, M. E. P., Steen, T. A., Park, N., & Peterson, C. (2005). Positive psychology progress. *American Psychologist, 60*, 410–421.

Sheldon, K. (2013). Self-determination theory, person-centered approaches, and personal goals: Exploring the links. In J. H. D. Cornelius-White, R. Motschnig-Pitrik, & M. Lux (Eds.), *Interdisciplinary handbook of the person-centered approach: Research and theory* (pp. 227–244). Springer.

Sheldon, K. M., Arndt, J., & Houser-Marko, L. (2003). In search of the organismic valuing process: The human tendency to move towards beneficial goal choices. *Journal of Personality, 71*, 835–886.

Shlien, J. M. (2002). Boy's person-centered perspective on psychodiagnosis: A response. In D. Cain (Ed.), *Classics in the person-centered approach* (pp. 400–402). PCCS Books. (Original work published 1989)

Shlien, J. M. (2003). A criterion of psychological health. In P. Sanders (Ed.), *To lead an honourable life: Invitations to think about client-centered therapy and the person-centered approach* (pp. 15–18). PCCS Books. (Original work published 1956)

Shlien, J. M., & Levant, R. F. (1984). Introduction. In R. F. Levant & J. M. Shlien (Eds.), *Client-centered therapy and the person-centered approach: New directions in theory, research, and practice* (pp. 1–16). Praeger Publishers / Greenwood Publishing Group.

Shostrom, E. L. (1964). An inventory for the measurement of self-actualization. *Educational and Psychological Measurement, 24*, 207–218.

Simms, J. (2011). Case formulation within a person-centred framework: An uncomfortable fit. *Counselling Psychology Review, 26*(2), 24–36.

Slemp, G. R., Field, J. G., Ryan, R. M., Forner, V. W., Van den Broeck, A., & Lewis, K. J. (2024). Interpersonal supports for basic psychological needs and their relations with motivation, well-being, and performance: A meta-analysis. *Journal of Personality and Social Psychology*. Advance online publication. https://dx.doi.org/10.1037/pspi0000459

Smith, E. R., & Mackie, D. M. (2007). *Social psychology* (3rd ed.). Taylor & Francis.

Sommerbeck, L. (2012). Being nondirective in directive settings. *Person-Centered & Experiential Psychotherapies, 11*(3), 173–189.

Sommerbeck, L. (2017a). An evaluation of research, concepts and experiences pertaining to the universality of client-centred therapy and its application in psychiatric settings. In S. Joseph (Ed.), *The handbook of person-centred therapy and mental health: Theory, research and practice* (pp. 416–436). PCCS Books.

Sommerbeck, L. (2017b). Complementarity between client-centred therapy and psychiatry: the theory and the practice. In S. Joseph (Ed.), *The handbook of person-centred therapy and mental health: Theory, research and practice* (pp. 116–133). PCCS Books.

Standal, S. W. (1954). *The need for positive regard: A contribution to client-centered therapy* [Doctoral dissertation, University of Chicago].

Stephen, S. (2023). Congruent functioning: The continuing resonance of Rogers' theory, *Person-Centered & Experiential Psychotherapies, 22*(4), 397–416.

Stephen, S., & Elliott, R. (2022). The Strathclyde Inventory: Development of a brief instrument for assessing outcome in counseling according to Rogers' concept of the fully functioning person. *Measurement and Evaluation in Counseling and Development, 55*(3), 187–206.

Stiles, W., Barkham, M., Mellor-Clark, J., & Connell, J. (2008). Effectiveness of cognitive-behavioural, person-centred, and psychodynamic therapies in UK primary-care routine practice: Replication in a larger sample. *Psychological Medicine, 38*(5), 677–688.

Stillwell, W. (2013). Conflict transformation. In J. H. D. Cornelius-White, R. Motschnig-Pitrik, & M. Lux (Eds.), *Interdisciplinary applications of the person-centered approach.* (pp. 213–220). Springer.

Sutich, A. J., & Vich, M. A. (1969). Introduction. In A. J. Sutich & M. A. Vich (Eds.), *Readings in humanistic psychology* (pp. 1–18). Free Press.

Taylor, E. (2001). Positive psychology and humanistic psychology: A reply to Seligman. *Journal of Humanistic Psychology, 41*(1), 13–29.

Taylor, S. (2023). *DisConnected: The roots of human cruelty and how connection can heal the world.* Iff Books.

Tedeschi, R. G., Park, C. L., & Calhoun, L. G. (Eds.) (1998). *Posttraumatic growth: Positive changes in the aftermath of crisis.* Erlbaum.

Tedeschi, R. G., Shakespeare-Finch, J., Taku, K., & Calhoun, L. G. (Eds.) (2018). *Posttraumatic growth. Theory, research, and applications.* Routledge.

Tennant, R., Hiller, L., Fishwick, R., Platt, S., Joseph, S., Weich, S., Parkinson, J., Secker, J., & Stewart-Brown, S. (2007). The Warwick-Edinburgh mental well-being scale (WEMWBS): Development and UK validation. *Health and Quality of life Outcomes, 5*(1), 1–13.

Tohme, O., & Joseph, S. (2020). Authenticity is correlated with mindfulness and emotional intelligence. *Journal of Humanistic Psychology, 65*(1), 0022167820940926.

Toper, A., Sellman, E., & Joseph, S. (2022). Examining the structure of authenticity: A Factor analytic study of the Authenticity Scale and Authenticity Inventory Subscales. *The Humanistic Psychologist, 50*(2), 304.

Toper, A., Sellman, E., & Joseph, S. (2023). The prosocial and pro-environmental aspects of authenticity and the mediating role of self-transcendence. *Person-Centered & Experiential Psychotherapies, 23*(4), 461–474.

Toper, A., Sellman, E., & Joseph, S. (2024). The confluence of authenticity and mindfulness: Principal component analysis of the Authenticity Scale and the Five-Facet Mindfulness Questionnaire. *The Humanistic Psychologist, 52*(1), 54–69.

Tosi, D. J., & Lindamood, C. A. (1975). The measurement of self-actualization: A critical review of the Personal Orientation Inventory. *Journal of Personality Assessment, 39*(3), 215–224.

Tufford, L., & Newman, P. (2012). Bracketing in qualitative research. *Qualitative Social Work: Research and Practice, 11*(1), 80–96.

Twenge, J. M., & Kasser, T. (2013). Generational changes in materialism and work centrality, 1976–2007: Associations with temporal changes in societal insecurity and materialistic role modeling. *Personality and Social Psychology Bulletin, 39*(7), 883–897.

Twenge, J. M., Martin, G. N., & Campbell, W. K. (2018). Decreases in psychological well-being among American adolescents after 2012 and links to screen time during the rise of smartphone technology. *Emotion, 18*(6), 765–780.

Twenge, J. M., Zhang, L., & Im, C. (2004). It's beyond my control: A cross-temporal meta-analysis of increasing externality in locus of control, 1960–2002. *Personality and Social Psychology Review, 8*(3), 308–319.

Tyler, K. (1999). Examining unconditional positive regard as the primary condition of therapeutic personality change. *The Person-Centred Journal, 6*(2), 100–107.

Vansteenkiste, M., & Sheldon, K. M. (2006). There's nothing more practical than a good theory: Integrating motivational interviewing and self-determination theory. *British Journal of Clinical Psychology, 45*(1), 63–82.

von Kimakowitz, E., Pirson, M., Spitzeck, H., Dierksmeier, C., & Amann, W. (Eds.). (2011). *Humanistic management in practice.* Palgrave Macmillan.

Warner, M. S. (2000a). Person-centered psychotherapy: One nation, many tribes. *Person-Centered Journal, 7*(1), 28–39.

Warner, M. S. (2000b). Person-centred therapy at the difficult edge: A developmentally-based model of fragile and dissociated process. In D. Mearns & B. Thorne (Eds.), *Person–centred therapy today: New frontiers in theory and practice* (pp. 144–171). Sage.

Warner, M. S. (2001). Empathy, relational depth and difficult client process. In S. Haugh & T. Merry (Eds.), *Rogers' therapeutic conditions: Evolution, theory and practice, Vol. 2. Empathy.* (pp. 181–191). PCCS Books.

Warner, M. S. (2006). Toward an integrated person-centered theory of wellness and psychopathology. *Person-Centered & Experiential Psychotherapies, 5*(1), 4–20.

Warner, M. S. (2017). A person-centred view of human nature, wellness and psychopathology. In S. Joseph (Ed.), *The handbook of person-centred therapy and mental health: Theory, research and practice* (pp. 92–115). PCCS Books.

Watson, J. C., & Geller, S. M. (2005). The relation among the relationship conditions, working alliance, and outcome in both process–experiential and cognitive–behavioral psychotherapy. *Psychotherapy Research, 15*(1–2), 25–33.

Watson, N. (1984). The empirical status of Rogers's hypotheses of the necessary and sufficient conditions for effective psychotherapy. In R. F. Levant & J. M. Shlien (Eds.), *Client-centered therapy and the person-centered approach: New directions in theory, research, and practice* (pp. 17–40). Praeger Publishers / Greenwood Publishing Group.

Wickman, S. A., & Campbell, C. (2003). An analysis of how Carl Rogers enacted client centered conversation with Gloria. *Journal of Counseling & Development, 81*(2), 178–184.

Wilkins, P. (2017) Person-centred theory and "mental illness" In S. Joseph (Ed.), *The handbook of person-centred therapy and mental health: Theory, research and practice* (pp. 39–56). PCCS Books.

Wilkins, P., & Mitchell-Williams, Z. (2002). The theory and experience of person-centered research. In J. C. Watson, R. N. Goldman, & M. S. Warner (Eds.), *Client-centered and experiential psychotherapy in the 21st century: Advances in theory, research and practice* (pp. 291–302). PCCS Books.

Wood, A., & Joseph, S. (2007). Grand theories of psychology can not be reconciled: A comment on McAdams and Pals. *American Psychologist, 62*, 57–58.

Wood, A. M., Linley, P. A., Maltby, J., Baliousis, M., & Joseph, S. (2008). The authentic personality: A theoretical and empirical conceptualization and the development of the Authenticity Scale. *Journal of Counseling Psychology, 55*(3), 385–399.

Worsley, R., & Joseph, S. (2007). *Person-centred practice: Case studies in positive psychology.* PCCS Books.

Zwiercan, A., & Joseph, S. (2018). Focusing manner and posttraumatic growth. *Person-Centered & Experiential Psychotherapies, 17*(3), 191-200.

Index

For the benefit of digital users, indexed terms that span two pages (e.g., 52–53) may, on occasion, appear on only one of those pages.

Tables, figures, and boxes are indicated by an italic *t*, *f*, and *b* following the paragraph number.